This Book Belongs to

Maurice Glicksman

From the Beginning

Archaeology and Art in the Israel Museum, Jerusalem

From the Beginning

Archaeology and Art in the Israel Museum, Jerusalem

Karl Katz   P.P. Kahane   Magen Broshi

Photographs by David Harris

Introduction by Philip Hendy

Reynal & Company, Inc.
in association with
William Morrow & Company, Inc., New York

Designed by Behram Kapadia for George Weidenfeld and Nicolson Limited
Phototypeset by BAS Printers Limited, Wallop, Hampshire
Printed in Italy by Amilcare Pizzi S.p.A., Milan for
REYNAL & COMPANY, INC.
in association with
William Morrow & Company, Inc., New York

Library of Congress Catalog Card Number: 68–23229

Contents

The Israel Museum, Jerusalem

Board of Directors and Chief Executives

Philip Hendy

Introduction

The Israel National Museum has been made one with the storied Jerusalem landscape. Far from distorting the rough and beautiful hill which it crowns, it gives it human purpose. Designed not to impress but to welcome, it is one of very few museums which can be seen from outside to be performing its function; indeed on one side, in the Sculpture Garden, this is integrated with the olives and the rock. Among national museums this one is perhaps unique in the combination of reticence and distinction with which it states its intentions.

The most famous of its exhibits, the manuscript scrolls, symbol of a national unity which has endured longer than any of the crown jewels of Europe, is preserved in a building of its own, perfectly distinct in style. With its shimmering dome, the Shrine of the Book seems to belong no more to the hill than to the sky; inviting reverence rather than pride of ownership, it is on the way up to the main block of the Museum: an introduction to the first of its purposes.

The greater part of the Museum's Permanent Collection is the fruit of scientific excavation in Israel; for the Ministry of Education and Culture has an exceedingly active Archaeological Section, and under its guidance the uncovering of the ancient roots of Palestinian culture has become the disinterested pastime of the nation – as it could do only in this country of eager intelligence. Thus in this first and largest Section the sadness of history is transformed into the joy of rediscovery, as beauty is recognised in the man-made things which have survived. There is no visual equivalent of the great Book of Isaiah; but in the artifacts of many millennia one may read not only the prose of social history and of technical excellence and fitness, but the poetry of a sense of beauty constantly engaged.

While all these contributions of a diverse, remote and shattered ancestry come from the soil of Palestine, the latterday objects of ritual and costume of the next Section, belonging mostly to the last few centuries, have been brought from all over the Diaspora; and this means almost from the whole of the cultured world. Thus does the National Museum epitomise the history of the Jews, while holding up to every inhabitant of Israel a mirror in which he may see himself and far beyond. Even more appropriate in Jerusalem would be the famous motto with which Princess Czartoryski, nearly two centuries ago, dedicated her museum in Cracow: *the past for the future.* It must have a special poignancy here.

The future is made no less clear than the past. If what is still the larger part of the Collection represents the ancient heritage of a nation newly come together from all parts of the world, the remainder, of which much belongs to the immediate present, is proof of an equally determined internationalism. Where else in the whole of the

Near East and beyond is there a museum – or a group of museums – of art which is deliberately setting out to compass the world? From halls in which western painting of the last four centuries is represented – not to mention the well stocked and world-wide Graphic Section – one may step out into a Sculpture Garden which is not the first, or perhaps as yet quite the best of its kind but certainly, if only because of its site, that which has the best potential; or one may pass on to the Youth Wing, where the artists and the critics of the future have their training.

These are some of the creative functions of a great museum, enlarging the mind of everyone who enters, showing him both his own birthright and the stake which he holds in a civilisation which was once divisible but is scarcely so any longer. The Israel National Museum is one of the great achievements of modern Israel, conceived and planned and brought to a high pitch of efficiency with perceptive dynamism. Perhaps I may say these things who am not an Israeli and have only recently been honoured by membership of the Museum staff. But then I must state also the corollary: that even this achievement must be only a beginning; that museums can be creative only so long as they are alive; that they are subject to the laws of nature and can live only by growing with the times, not necessarily in physique but in quality and character. A great ambition has been proclaimed and partly fulfilled. Its fulfilment can be completed only by an effort which must be continuously sustained.

Karl Katz

Background to a Museum

Life in Israel is intensely three-dimensional. There is, certainly, the immediacy and urgency of daily life, but this is flanked by a reliance on the past, both recent and remote, and by a constant awareness of the near and more distant future. This is life in Israel, and this, too, is the scope of its National Museum. For a museum reflects our own day's respect for the past and its faith in the future; in it is housed the tangible evidence of our many yesterdays together with works of art of the present time. It is here that they are collected and exhibited for the education and enjoyment of people, now and tomorrow.

The Israel Museum (plate 1), straddles the crest of a rocky ridge – Neveh Shaanan. It is a hill in Judea where no one has left a permanent mark, though through the ages this spot, as so many others in these parts, must undoubtedly have witnessed passing Canaanites and Israelites, Assyrians and Judaeans, Romans and Hebrews, pagans and the early Christians, Muslims and Crusaders, as well as pilgrims of every persuasion on their way to Jerusalem. Ringing this hill of Neveh Shaanan are not only monuments of the past, such as a Byzantine-Crusader monastery (the Monastery of the Cross), but institutions dedicated both to today's pressing problems and to Israel's future – the Parliament (Knesset), and the Hebrew University. And set in the centre of this complex is the Israel Museum, holding together, as it were, these diversities of time and space.

1 The Israel Museum seen on the hill above the beautiful Byzantine-Crusader Monastery of the Cross in the valley.

The Israel Museum is still young, but already it is known throughout the world. It was dedicated in May 1965. People came from all parts of the world to attend the ceremony and to honour this new museum which time, energy and so much devotion had created. Conceived in a spirit of daring – almost, one might say, presumptuousness – the Museum has succeeded far beyond the imaginings of those who first planned it.

In 1958, the staff of the Art and Archaeological Museum requested UNESCO ICOM to send the architect Dr Franco Minissi of Rome to help draw up the programme and specifications for the Israel Museum

2 The Billy Rose Art Garden was designed by Isamu Noguchi within the Museum's grounds. Without the confines of a conventional gallery, the sculptures assert their three-dimensionality.

architectural competition. Two museums were to unite, and together they would form the Israel Museum. An elaborate programme was prepared bringing together all the needs of the museums, their separate and common problems, and the directions of growth envisaged for them. In 1958 it was hardly possible to anticipate what in fact came about – the unification of five different museums. The result, by 1966, was an institution very much larger than the sum of its original component parts. The various units which now make up the Israel Museum are: 1. The Bezalel National Art Museum; 2. The Samuel Bronfman Biblical and Archaeological Museum; 3. The

Youth Wing (Children's Museum); 4. The Shrine of the Book – The D. Samuel and Jeane H. Gottesman Centre for Biblical Manuscripts; 5. The Billy Rose Art Garden. The first three are situated in the central structure, the Shrine of the Book and the Billy Rose Art Garden within the twenty-acre complex.

Professor Alfred Mansfield and Mrs Dora Gad submitted the winning architectural plan. The Museum was to be built to accommodate Neveh Shaanan which, on a north-south axis, slopes sharply to the west and gently to the east. It was planned so that the Monastery of the Cross could be seen from every vantage point, while the steep western slopes were to be used as a garden. The architects had also taken into account one major problem, and used it as the point of departure for the basic architectural concept: there was no way of telling what excavations would bring to light in Israel over the years, and what kinds of collections the Museum would acquire in the future, but to accommodate all possibilities the architects conceived of a modular system, so that the future growth of the museum would be determined by this basic module. In this way, however many new buildings had to be added, architectural harmony would be retained.

The basic module measures 1 metre 40 centimetres square. Both

3, 4 & 5 Sculpture in the open air: Picasso (*above left*) cuts shapes in sandblasted concrete creating, in 'Profile', forms observed through forms; while Henry Moore's 'Reclining Woman' (*above right*) uses spaces and simplified forms to create volumes reminiscent of the earliest mother-goddess figures. In contrast Menashe Kadishman's 'Suspense' (*above centre*) uses strong simple shapes, painted a brilliant primary yellow to create an effect in its way as timeless as its landscape background.

6 (*opposite*) 'Adam', a particularly fine, over life-size example of Rodin's work that the Museum is fortunate to own, benefits from its outside display.

RODIN

8 The dramatic juggled off-centre arched passage leading to the heart of the Shrine, where the Isaiah scroll is exhibited, forms an approach so different that the brilliance, fluidity and simplicity of the dome's interior is thrown into even sharper emphasis.

7 (*opposite*) Designed by the architects F. Kiesler and A. Bartos, the white dome of the Shrine of the Book juxtaposed with the black stone wall, are striking and prominent landmarks, both within the Museum grounds and from the surrounding hills.

the floor and the pitched ceilings are covered by a functional grid system which follows this module. The light points are spaced at intervals of 1.40 metres and the standard gallery unit is a square, equal to eight by eight basic modules measuring 11 m 20 cm square. The central post supporting the pitched ceiling of each gallery contains all the machinery necessary for the air-conditioning, heating, humidifying and dehumidifying. There is clerestory lighting in all these galleries.

The many innovations, both in the design of the Museum and in display, permit maximum flexibility and smooth working operations. For instance, the public has direct access to temporary exhibitions, without having to pass through the permanent galleries. There is also direct access to the Children's Museum (plate 15), and to the library and auditorium which are at present under construction. Since the Museum is built on a hill and follows its contours, there are, of course, small changes of level in the building. To facilitate movement, either for transporting heavy and precious objects or for raising and lowering people in wheelchairs, at each flight of stairs there is a small platform lift operated by an hydraulic jack.

Because of the many additions to the Museum's permanent collection and the frequent exhibitions, the whole interior has been designed with the accommodation of new displays in mind. All the floor surfaces have a grid system of sockets for inserting free standing walls and electric connections. Free standing vitrines can be placed in almost any spot and cases can be cantilevered into the wall. It is

also possible to hang a wall from the ceiling rather than to lift it from the floor, an exciting way of creating visually interesting divisions of space (plate 12).

9 A collection of Channukah lamps displayed on one wall makes an eye-catching exhibit in the section devoted to Jewish ceremonial art.

Lighting techniques vary with the objects displayed. Each cantilevered wall case has its own special connections and lighting panel, and the interior lights in every vitrine are both cold and hot so that the light patterns can be varied within each case, depending on the arrangement of the objects inside the vitrine. In many cases, however, because of the nature of the material being displayed, cold lighting is the only type that can be used. Some of the exhibition spaces, as in the painting galleries, dispense with clerestory lighting and have top lighting only, or, like the Graphics Gallery, have no natural light.

Both the Art Museum and the Archaeological Museum are equally accessible to the administrative section and the technical services, ensuring the greatest possible smoothness of administration. In fact very close attention has been given to the relationship between the 'museum behind the scenes' and the 'museum for visitors'. There is almost as much storage as exhibition space. Vertical relationships exist between exhibited and stored objects, and there is an elevator to carry the work to be exhibited from the store-room into a closed preparation room adjoining the gallery. The professional members of the staff usually have their offices adjoining the store-rooms for which they are responsible and this horizontal propinquity, combined with the vertical relationship of the stored object to the gallery in which it will be exhibited, make the layout extremely functional.

10 In the Museum the emphasis is on the attractive presentation of exhibits.

11 (*left*) The Bezalel National Art Museum founded in 1906 by Professor Boris Schatz, was the precursor of the Israel Museum. A far cry from the present concept of the Museum, nevertheless it is due to these early efforts that the Museum exists today.

THE BEZALEL NATIONAL ART MUSEUM: The Bezalel National Art Museum (plate 11), now entering its sixty-second year, was an anomaly in Ottoman-Turkish Palestine. Professor Boris Schatz named it 'Bezalel' after Bezalel ben Uri ben Chur, whom Moses had commissioned with the construction and adornment of the Tabernacle and the Ark of the Covenant (Exodus, 31:2–11).

Schatz sought to create a museum similar in spirit to those he had admired in his native Europe. He also founded an art school, in which he hoped the occidental and oriental Jews would again take up the handicrafts and artforms of their ancestors. Although a prominent place was given to Jewish art, the Museum's aim was to pursue a general art policy. Art of all periods, including recent works, from both east and west was the official collecting policy. The first step towards the fulfilment of this ambitious project was the purchase in 1906 of an old Turkish building – which had originally been used as a harem – and in the same year Professor Schatz' art school was inaugurated, in a building adjoining the Museum. The purchase of local antiquities, relying on gifts from individuals in Palestine and abroad, exhibiting the works of promising young artists working in the neighbouring school, and often exhibiting his own works and the

12 Free standing walls are a means of adding extra exhibition space and of creating visually interesting spatial divisions.

works of European painters and sculptors he knew, gave the Museum its initial character and direction. The heterogeneous display of Palestinian archaeology, Jewish ritual objects, stuffed birds, handicrafts and contemporary art must have made a visit to the old Bezalel quite an extraordinary experience.

The distinguished scholar, Mordechai Narkiss, succeeded Professor Schatz as director in 1932. By then, after the First World War, the country was under the British mandate. Jerusalem was acquiring a cosmopolitan air and this diversity was soon to be reflected in the Museum's acquisitions and the variety of its exhibitions. Narkiss, a great scholar and enthusiast, pioneered numerous activities in the field of art education, at a community and at a national level. By the end of Israel's War of Liberation (1948), the Bezalel had outgrown its Turkish building, finding itself able to exhibit only a very small fraction of its Judaica, some fine paintings and pieces of sculpture, drawings and prints, representative examples of near, middle and far eastern art, a library, and a growing ethnological and primitive art collection. Its huge archives of reproductions supplying material for travelling exhibitions were inaccessible. By 1958 the Museum was ready for a dramatic change.

13 The way in which the visitor is helped to understand the exhibits is shown by this reconstruction of the gate from the ancient Biblical city of Hazor, displayed against a large scale photograph of part of the excavations of one of the houses found there.

THE SAMUEL BRONFMAN BIBLICAL AND ARCHAEOLOGICAL MUSEUM: The history of the Archaeological Museum is a reflection of the dynamics of change in a country which has always had a turbulent history. In 1927, John D. Rockefeller Jr financed the construction in Jerusalem of the Palestine Archaeological Museum.

In 1948, however, when the armistice lines dividing Jerusalem were decided upon, the Palestine Archaeological Museum was situated in the Hashemite Kingdom of Jordan; Israel, with its capital in Jerusalem, was left without a central archaeological museum. The Ministry of Education and Culture immediately established a Department of Antiquities, and a small museum was opened adjoining the Department. Intensive development in Israel's early years meant that many ancient sites throughout the country were being incidentally uncovered. These were professionally excavated and most of the antiquities were sent to the Department in Jerusalem; some of the finds were displayed in the Department's museum, but because of lack of space a large number had to be kept in the store-rooms, inaccessible to the public. Naturally, with more and more material arriving, the need for suitable exhibition space became increasingly pressing. The Samuel Bronfman Biblical and Archaeological Museum, made possible by a grant from the Bronfman family, in honour of Samuel Bronfman, was opened to the public in 1965 solving, to a large extent, this urgent problem.

The new Museum is devoted to the archaeology of the Land of the Bible, from prehistory to the threshold of modern times. Situated in Jerusalem, the spiritual centre of Israel and its people, the Museum was in the fortunate position of being able to build up its permanent exhibition on the rich archaeological finds from excavations carried out by local and foreign expeditions, and mainly from the excavations of the Department of Antiquities, which had put its treasures at the disposal of the new Museum. About ninety-five per cent of the objects exhibited are from scientific excavations; thus the provenance, dating and original function of the great majority of objects displayed are known. This fact defines the character of the Museum – the presentation of antiquities in their historical sequence. For a fuller understanding of local archaeology, due consideration is given to the archaeology of neighbouring cultures.

A number of reconstructions, models, maps, plans, photographs and explanations serve to illustrate the cultural environment of the antiquities exhibited in their period halls (plate 13). A balance has been carefully maintained between the explanatory material and an attractive visual presentation of the antiquities. The aim is to give the visitor a general impression of the character of each period.

THE YOUTH WING: One of the sharpest impressions Israel gives is the great emphasis it places on youth. Our country has brought together people from such widely different backgrounds as western Europe and the Yemen, and it is inevitable that there is some disparity in the level of culture and sophistication between these groups. But it is hoped that through their children, who will go through the same educational machinery and face the same influences and challenges, the new, vital culture of Israel will be born. In an effort to raise the cultural level as much as possible and to confront children of whatever origin with the same creative stimuli, the Youth Wing of the Israel Museum was inaugurated on the Museum's first birthday. In a magnificent setting, it has introduced a new dimension into education in Israel. The essential creative integrity of children of varying backgrounds is respected – they are given the freedom to express themselves as individuals – yet the result is that each child, through this diversity of expression, learns to respect the other. The daily activities of the Youth Wing make it a microcosm of a democracy in evolution.

This Children's Museum is immediately accessible from the main entrance of the Israel Museum, but it is also autonomous; it has its own galleries, auditorium, studio and workshops. On the other hand, there is a complete interrelationship between the Museum's programme and the Youth Wing's activities. Other youth wings in other museums in Israel are now under way as a result of this successful venture in Jerusalem. Eventually, this activity of the Museum may well be one of the key solutions to the integration of peoples from east and west.

THE SHRINE OF THE BOOK: *The D. Samuel and Jeane H. Gottesman Centre for Biblical Manuscripts.* The discovery in 1947 of ancient Hebrew scrolls which had been buried in caves by a monastic Jewish sect living near the Dead Sea, was to be seen by many people as an omen, presaging an extraordinary event. Within months of their

14 (*above*) One of the aims of the Museum is that it should be used as a place of recreation as well as study. Here students admire the Museum's superb Italian eighteenth-century synagogue.

15 In the Youth Wing, children are encouraged to participate in creative and study programmes. There are also special exhibitions of the art and culture of other peoples.

16 (*opposite*) The Shrine of the Book provides an almost unique opportunity for studying the writings of the Prophets in their earliest extant form.

17 In the ethnological section, an elderly Bokharan couple examine the magnificent ceremonial costumes similar to those worn by their ancestors. The Bokharans are among the oldest and most colourful Jewish communities.

discovery the State of Israel had come into being. This historical coincidence of the unearthing of the scrolls and the foundation of the State jolted the imagination of people throughout the world. The Scrolls pre-dated by one thousand years any previously known Hebrew manuscripts of the Torah and the Prophets. Many of them, together with additional related material, eventually found their way to Israel and an appropriate repository became increasingly necessary. Eventually a Shrine was designed to house the Dead Sea Scrolls, together with the manuscripts and material later found at Masada and Nachal Hever (plates 7 and 8). Central to this building was its unique function, and the building, given by the Gottesman Foundation and designed by F. Kiesler and A. Bartos, was created around the objects it housed. It is a sculptured, fluid, three-dimensional space, an edifice which is also a symbol. At the heart of this sanctuary, fully opened around a drum, is the scroll of Isaiah, an impressive parchment eight metres long, written probably around 100 BC.

THE BILLY ROSE ART GARDEN: The name of the Museum hill – Neveh Shaanan – means 'tranquil place'. Five acres of this peaceful Judaean hill were used to create a garden in which sculptures could be exhibited, and entering it is like walking into the timeless world of antiquity. However, its designer, Isamu Noguchi, was asked, by Billy Rose, to create a setting not for ancient marbles and classic figures, but for modern sculpture. In a sense, the garden is the homage of one age to another. The artistic ideas of the age of the machine and atom are given a high place in this city which Crusader cartographers called 'the navel of the earth'. Here, in an art garden carved into the Judaean landscape, contemporary sculptures from all over the world reflect every influence of time and place (plate 2).

Great stones, excavated on the spot, were used to build gigantic terraces and retaining walls, and by shaping the paths between these terraces and setting up subtly spaced labyrinthine walls, the Garden has that indigenous rhythm of walls and terraces so typical of the Middle East. Two pavilions have also been designed by Noguchi to permit the exhibition of small and more delicate sculptures.

SOME VISITORS: A family of Yemenites whose recent meteoric journey through time from their medieval life in San'a, capital of their native south Arabian country, to their present lives in a small cooperative village in the Judaean hills, visited the Museum, asking to see the gifts King Solomon had received from the Queen of Sheba. Unfortunately, this was one request which was impossible to grant, but we decided to show them what was actually in the Museum. There were enough treasures to satisfy them and their question was forgotten.

Cautiously, a venerable member of the Bokharan Jewish community approached the Museum's entrance, automatically kissing the mezuzah on the doorpost. With his wife walking quietly behind him he ventured into this institution which his grandchildren had told him about; both were overwhelmed. They could not help feeling that it was somewhat alien until, that is, they reached the Ethnological Section where, displayed in one of the large vitrines, was a brocade coat from Samarkand similar to one that this aged Bokharan's grandfather had left him (plate 17).

18 One of the many free standing showcases in which precious small exhibits, such as this Havdalah group, are displayed.

North Africans, Persians, Yemenites and many others have had similar experiences and have all reacted in much the same way. The fact that the Museum exhibits their cultures' costumes, jewelry and Judaica, objects which they immediately understand, brings them added self-respect, equates their cultures with others, and in an intangible way helps to make them better citizens in a country where there is such a variety of traditions. Eventually even the more remote exhibits become acceptable and meaningful, and the Museum becomes a place of pleasure in their leisure time.

A school class came one day with their teacher to visit the Museum and found they had walked into the eighteenth century. These Israeli children have strange conceptions of time. 'Very old' for them is either the birth of the State (which is but twenty now) or the time of the destruction of the Second Temple. They often neglect the intervening two thousand years and find it hard to visualise European cultures. In a fine eighteenth-century synagogue from a small village north of Venice (plate 14), or in the French room of the same period (plate 192) with boiserie, gobelins and paintings of the highest quality, they were able to see European cultural history. Leaving the Museum, the children walked back into the Jerusalem sun, undoubtedly richer for their eighteenth-century experience.

Joshua with his ram's horn or David with his sling must have been rather pastoral compared to the young soldier who came in on leave. He was looking for the tangible might that had made it possible for the Israelites to settle the twelve tribes in the land of Canaan, or that gave the Maccabees strength to withstand Antiochus' armies. We were not entirely successful in fulfilling his needs, but this young farmer-fighter discovered while walking through the galleries that close to the spot where he had made his home an ancient Israelite settlement had been excavated. The agrarian life of these early monotheists could be seen in the plain pots and pans of their culture and the soldier felt at home.

Shortly after the frontiers were obliterated and Jerusalem was reunited, a young Arab and his wife visited the Museum. It was noticed that they kept returning to a small exhibition of children's work from a painting competition which had been run by one of the kibbutz movements. They looked incredulously at some of the drawings, and after a while we discovered the reason. They thought their own children had submitted the drawings. We told them that their own children's drawings and those of the young kibbutz children were alike because children everywhere, at certain age levels, paint in the same way. They were amazed that their children and the young Israelis had so much in common.

19 Visitors from abroad study the Ketubot or marriage contracts.

These people were on a world tour, they had experienced the richest and best, they were blasé. Another capital city, another foreign currency, and yet another museum. But then, in front of a provincial Torah scroll binder from a small village in Germany, they read the label and found a connection with their own past. Their grandparents had emigrated from the same place and the name on the binder and the traveller's were the same. A thread of history had enmeshed them and brought them back dramatically to a village whose Jews were no more, and whose only synagogue lay in ashes.

It is difficult to say whether the Israel Museum has an answer for each of the half million people or more who visit it annually, but then most people ask nothing more difficult than 'What have you there?' It is a general art museum, which strives to maintain international standards, keep people aware of what is happening, accumulate the best of the treasures of the past, be the national repository for the art and archaeology of the country, and promote the creative arts. This is the function of most museums, and here it is just like any other museum with its normal national idiosyncrasies. But the Israel Museum is much more than this, and in a way which makes it different from any other museum in the world. It represents the sum total of Jewish experience, it is a cross-section of four thousand years of Hebrew history, a spectrum of people who have survived against all adversity with greater tenacity over a longer time period and geographic span than any other people. In this Museum the tangible remains of a people finds its repository, and through it the visitor can literally see the patriarchs, kings and prophets, and its people of antiquity, its sages, rabbis, and devout Jews. It is this continuity which makes the Israel Museum unique. For what could be more different than a country that has been host to more than half a million years of people? For five thousand centuries man has patiently progressed in this country's fertile valleys and on its coastal plain and the Museum pieces together the fragments of this incredible span of years.

A general art museum in the centre of the Middle East is unique, and yet this is not enough. Set in this part of the world, it not only has the broad function of collecting and exhibiting the best of every period and every culture, it also has a responsibility to its region; the Museum constantly strives, and will continue to strive, to relate the lengthy history of the ancient and glorious lands that surround it.

5,000 Centuries of Art

P. P. Kahane

Archaeology from Caves to the Crusades

PREHISTORY – BEFORE 500,000–4000 BC: In the course of hundreds of thousands of years man developed from a creature similar to the anthropoid ape – already a tool-maker, hunter and food-gatherer – into a human being capable of food production and the domestication of animals. Five to ten thousand years ago, the primary elements of human civilisation and culture, such as religion, art and craftsmanship, social organisation, urbanisation, agriculture, animal domestication and trade, appear or become intensified. At this stage of growth the conditions existed for the creation of tribal myths and man was on the threshold of historical times.

The general interest in the prehistory of man increases from decade to decade. Adolescents are usually more fascinated than adults by this period. The explanation may be that for young people the elementary patterns of human behaviour are more interesting than the details of historical happenings. Prehistory is the time of the first primitive arms and the first tools for work, implements intended to defend the individual and society from the harshness of nature, wild beasts, sickness and hunger. The young feel comfortable in this realm of invention and action. Adults view prehistory from a more detached viewpoint; for them it is only the beginning of human civilisation and culture, the basis for what came afterwards. However, the study of the beginnings of civilised mankind has an even deeper significance; it is one of the most important scientific paths available for finding an answer to that eternal question – the origins of humanity.

20

PEBBLE-TOOLS

(*top*) CHOPPER

(*bottom*) SPHEROID

Both: Lower Palaeolithic, Ubeidiya excavations

Palestine and Tanganyika are the only places in the world where examples of these earliest types of stone tools have been discovered.

The prehistoric exhibition takes up a comparatively large part of the archaeological wing of the Israel Museum. One important reason for this arrangement is time itself. If we assume that the Stone Age ended about 4000 BC, then the proportion of historic to prehistoric time is only six thousand to roughly six hundred thousand years, if not more. In such a time span the fact that so great a quantity of prehistoric material has come down to us is easily understandable, especially since the surviving objects are mainly of stone.

The earliest traces of man in the region of Israel were found in Ubeidiya in the Jordan Valley, south of Lake Tiberias. It was here that the oldest skull fragments of Pithecanthropus in the Near East were found in the same layer with some primitive pebble-tools (plate 20), belonging to the time of the Great Pluvial (*c.* 500,000–300,000 BC). In plate 20 we see representations of the earliest types of tools made by human hands: spheroid pebbles, weapons for throwing in battle and for hunting; and choppers, tools shaped like potatoes but with a distinct cutting edge. At first glance these pebbles look like chance freaks of nature but they were actually standard types of primitive stone tools. The chopper was used for cutting and scraping

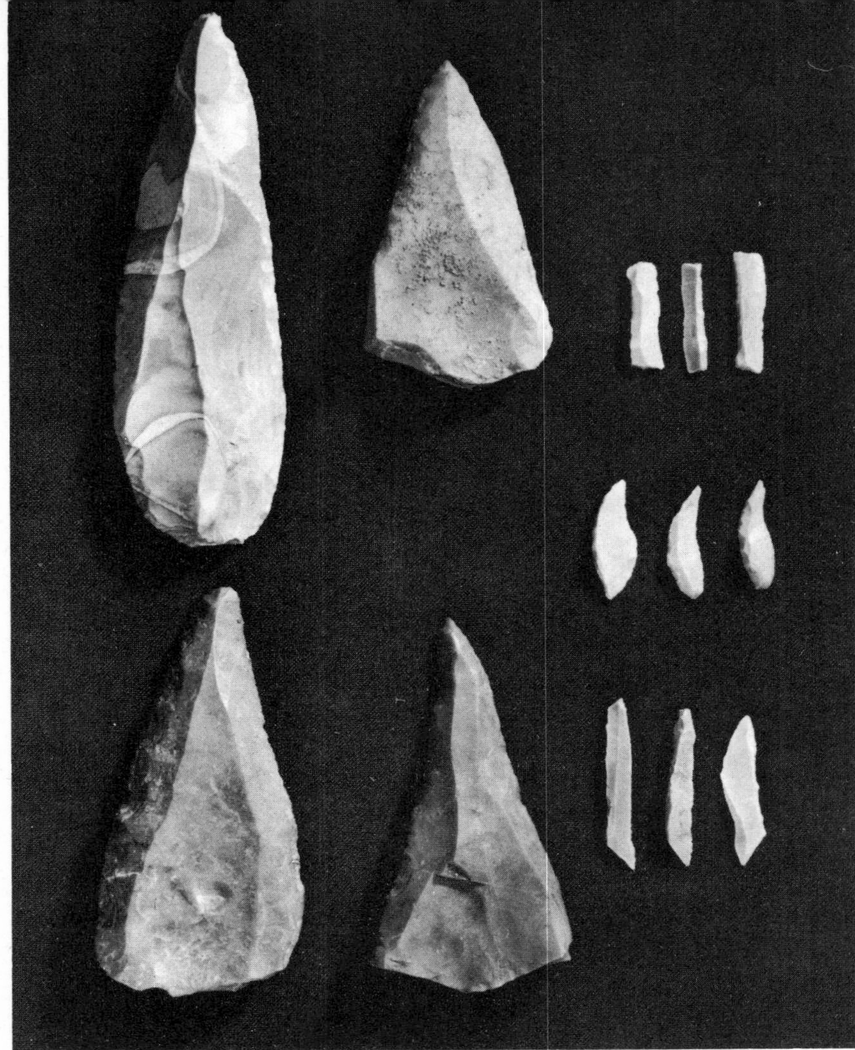

21 (*left*)

POINTS AND MICROLITHS

FOUR POINTS

All: Lower Palaeolithic, Abu Zif

MICROLITHS

All: Upper Palaeolithic, Kefar Vitkin

'Flake-tools', made by splintering a large stone, were attached to handles of bone or wood and used as spears, knives and similar implements.

22 (*right*)

HAND-AXES

(*top left to right*)

Stone, Ubeidiya excavations

Flint, Holon

Basalt, Gesher Benot Ya'aqov

Flint, Ma'ayan Barukh

All: Lower Palaeolithic

Early men, from western Europe to Africa and southern Asia, used axes similar to the one at the top left. The two below are later developments, while that at the top right shows a sophistication that can hardly be thought of as 'primitive'.

animal hides, and for taking meat from the bones of the slaughtered animal. It is considered the precursor of the hand-axe because of its functions. Such pebble-tools have so far been found only in Israel and Tanganyika. A developed variety of the hand-axe (plate 22 left) from the Ubeidiya site is also represented. It is an early and crude form of the triangular, pointed, bifacial hand-axe, a type which was the chief stone implement of the Lower Palaeolithic Age (before 70,000 BC). Its continuity and geographical range are extraordinary; it is found in western Europe, Africa and southern Asia as well as in the Near East, including Canaan, throughout a period of about three hundred thousand years. The axes shown in plate 22 (bottom) are later representations of the type in basalt and flint. At the pinnacle of this development is the stone tool (far right), conspicuous for its earthy brown patina and technical perfection.

The pebble-tools and hand-axes of the Lower Palaeolithic were called 'core-tools', so named because they were made by trimming round a core. However, the majority of tools belonging to the Middle (70,000–35,000 BC) and Upper Palaeolithic (35,000–15,000 BC) were

manufactured by splintering the core. The resulting flake-tools were converted into tiny tools called microliths; they were used for various purposes which we often cannot determine. The four points and nine microliths in plate 21 show quite clearly the development of stone implements in the Middle and Upper Palaeolithic. The same basic types of small-sized stone tools were made throughout hundreds of thousands of years, but with increasing formal differentiation and technical skill. The points, probably spear points, and the various blade varieties and microliths can be understood only when one imagines them with their wooden or bone shafts. The microliths and other composite tools opened up new possibilities for hunting and working the land. They are most often found in the Upper Palaeolithic and the Mesolithic (15,000–7500 BC), usually on shores and in river beds, and must have been used for fishing and hunting birds.

23 (*left*)
'CAVE OF THE TREASURE' – 'CROWN'
Copper, Chalcolithic Period, from a cave near the Dead Sea
Among the ten crowns found with the other treasures, this one has details that also appear on some of the Azor ossuaries.

24 (*right*)
MORTARS AND PESTLE
(*right*) MORTAR AND PESTLE
Upper Palaeolithic, En Gev
(*left*) MORTAR
Basalt, Late Mesolithic (Natufian Culture), Eynan excavations
Although both these mortars were probably used for the preparation of food, the contrast of style and quality shows how far man's technical skills had developed in the thousands of years between their manufacture.

25 (*left*)

SCHEMATIC HUMAN FIGURE

Basalt, Mesolithic (Natufian Culture), Eynan excavations

On the floor of one of the Eynan houses two pestles and five pebbles were found arranged like this, but whether there was any significance in this remains in doubt.

26 (*right*)

SCHEMATIC FACES

Stone, Mesolithic (Natufian Culture), Eynan excavations

If the scratchings on these stones were intended to depict the human face, it suggests that the Natufian Culture was the earliest in the area to attempt representation in art.

Even if man did not progress beyond the limits of a hunting and food-gathering economy, an expansion of the standard of living in these periods can be proved. For instance, basalt mortars and pestles (plate 24, right) point to more sophisticated ways of preparing food and could even indicate the making of flour from corn.

Among the most astonishing finds belonging to the later Mesolithic Period (*c.* 10,000–7500 BC) are the discoveries made in Wadi el Natuf in the Carmel region; the culture is usually called 'Natufian', after this site. A good part of the Museum's Natufian objects come from the circular dwellings found in Eynan in the Jordan valley (plate 24, left). Eynan enjoyed such a high standard of living that it seems possible that food production and animal domestication existed there. The Eynan objects incorporate certain decorative elements which go beyond any practical necessity. The large mortar shown in plate 24 (left) for instance, excels in technical execution and formal design, with the elegant foot emphasising its profile; a simple form, such as the earlier example next to it, would have fulfilled the same function. The seven small pestles and pebbles in plate 25 were found on the floor of a circular house, arranged according to a simple pattern recalling the human figure. Again, this arrangement is non-functional and represents an early example of the urge to play, a basic element in

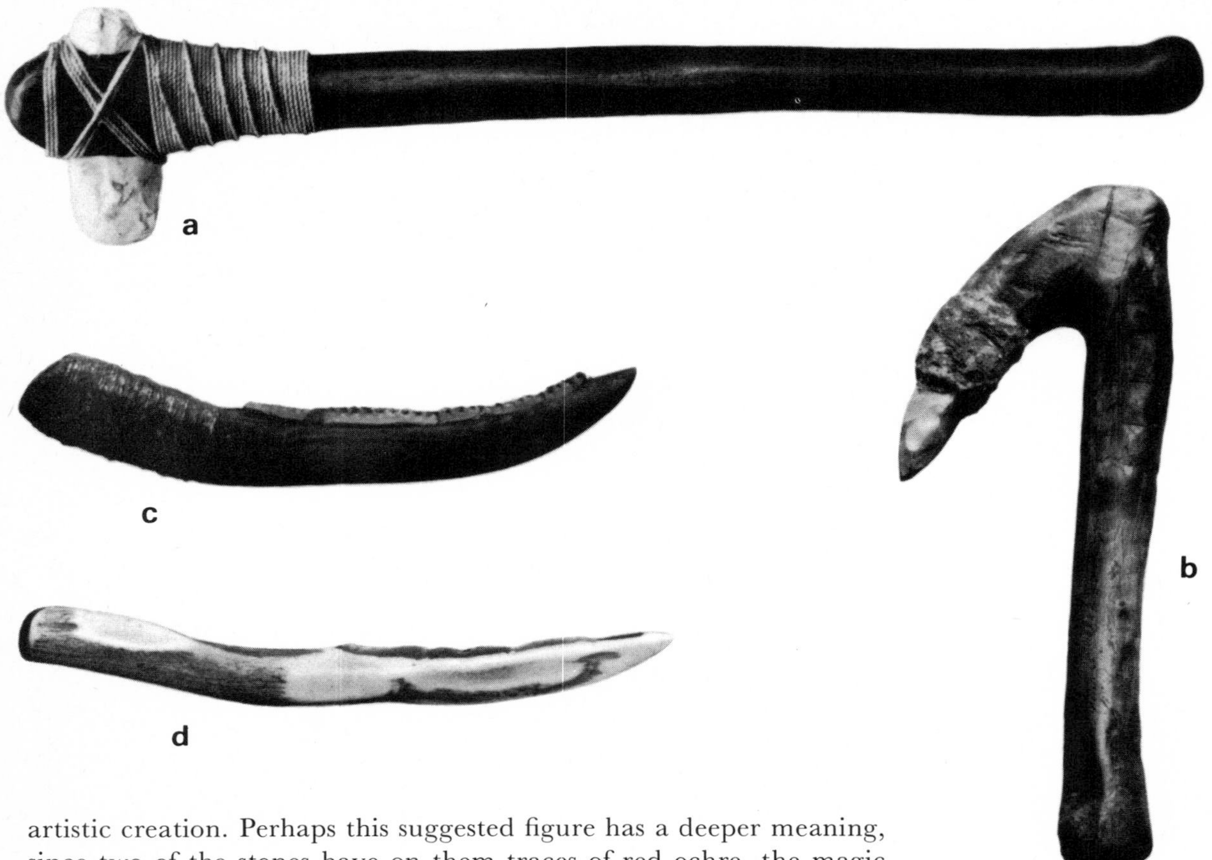

artistic creation. Perhaps this suggested figure has a deeper meaning, since two of the stones have on them traces of red ochre, the magic colour. The two pebbles in plate 26 have almost identical scratched ornamentations, and again seem to be simplified references to human features, this time the face. These examples are sufficient to support the fact that in the Middle East the Natufian Culture made the decisive step towards art and representation. These highly stylised pieces contrast with the naturalistic carved depictions of animals and humans found in the region.

The next phase in man's development occurred during the Neolithic Period. The Neolithic civilisation was once thought of as revolutionary but today it has come to be interpreted in an evolutionary way though not, however, in any way negating its radical achievements. This evolution is based on man's striving for independence from the adverse forces of nature. A rapid progress to this end is evident from the eighth to the fifth millennium BC, hastened by gradual climatic changes from a pluvial to a dry period resulting in a climate similar to our own by the end of the Neolithic Age.

In this period advances in food production were made but we are not sure to what extent agriculture was practised. In a continuation of the Natufian tradition, stone mortars, querns and pestles served for making flour from corn grains. Flint blades, deeply serrated and originally set in bone or wooden handles, were used as sickles for

27

AGRICULTURAL IMPLEMENTS WITH RECONSTRUCTED HANDLES

(a) AXE
Stone, Neolithic Period, pre-Ceramic Phase

(b) ADZE
Stone, Neolithic Period, pre-Ceramic Phase

(c) SICKLE
Stone, Late Mesolithic (Natufian Culture)

(d) SICKLE
Stone, Neolithic Period

The flint blades of implements like these are usually all that remain of them, as the less durable wood or bone handles have decayed with the passing of time.

mowing barley and wheat. Plate 27 shows two reconstructed sickles with original flint blades of Natufian and Neolithic origin. The top part of the plate shows a Neolithic stone axe used for felling trees and a Neolithic hoe for tilling the soil.

The production of clay vessels, mixed with straw to give extra strength, is another of the epoch-making inventions of the period. Plate 28 shows four clay vessels which were covered with a reddish-brown coat of slip, ornamented with scratched-in herring-bone patterns and burnished even at this early phase. It is assumed that these ceramics were introduced by farmers, newcomers from the Syrian-Lebanese coast during the late Neolithic. With the introduction of food production, together with the related tools of stone and clay, the conditions of sedentary life were possible. The best known and largest site of the period in this region is Neolithic Jericho.

28

DOMESTIC POTTERY

(*left to right*) TWO JARS AND TWO BOWLS

All: Neolithic Period, Ceramic Phase, Shaar Hagolan excavations

Some of these earliest ceramic vessels, though modelled by hand, are already decorated with a red slip and incised patterns.

29 (*top left*)

ANIMAL FIGURINES

Pottery, Neolithic Period, pre-Ceramic Phase except for boar, Neolithic Period, Ceramic Phase. Boar, Horvat Minha; others, Nahal Oren

Although perhaps not immediately recognisable, these animals have a spontaneity and vividness that was often lost in more advanced cultures.

30 (*below left*)

HUMAN FIGURINES

Pottery, Neolithic Period, pre-Ceramic Phase, Horvat Minha excavations

The rather stolid air of these human figures, suggests that they served as offerings or amulets.

31 (*below*)

MOTHER GODDESS

Pottery, Neolithic Period, Ceramic Phase, Horvat Minha

A seated fertility goddess of the 'dea nutrix' type, in the nursing attitude.

It is not known for sure whether animals were domesticated in the early Neolithic periods; the bones of goats, oxen, sheep and dogs do not tell us whether these animals were domesticated or wild. This uncertainty also exists when we come to the animal figurines of the age. Among the most charming creations of the pre-Ceramic and Ceramic phases of the Neolithic (*c.* 7500–4000 BC) are some small unburnt clay animal figurines, reproduced in plate 29. As far as any identification is possible, it seems that wild animals, such as the boar (here the second from the left), were depicted. The form and movement of the animals are boldly conceived in a basically naturalistic style. The figurines may have functioned as magical symbols for success in the hunt or for the proliferation of the animal kingdom; certainly, for prehistoric man, the continuation of human life itself depended on the continued existence of these animals to provide food and clothing.

The depiction of man in this period is more complex. The style of the three very small male and female clay figurines in plate 30 cannot be characterised as naturalistic or even as conventional. They are symbols which may have served as offerings or amulets and which are among the earliest known figurines made of unburnt clay. A different type of female is represented by a stone figurine found at Shaar Hagolan, an important late Neolithic community near Lake Tiberias. These 'pebble-idols' seek to obtain a maximum of magical effect with a minimum of detail; the head is summarised and the lower parts of the body are defined with simple clarity. A precursor of later mother goddess figures, the idol was probably a fertility symbol. Plate 31 shows a 'dea nutrix' figurine at the summit of its development in the late Neolithic civilisation. The sitting goddess is made of clay; her face is powerfully expressive, with a large nose, ears, and slanting eyes in appliqué. The mouth may have been painted. This is evidently the prototype of the dea nutrix of later periods: her left arm supports her breasts, and the missing right arm must have rested on her right thigh; the legs are only suggested. The figure belongs to the steatopygous type of prehistoric fertility goddesses. The style may be described as symbolic-realistic – if not 'surrealistic' – because the female forms are heavily stressed, probably for some magical emphasis on their function. The style of this dea nutrix is in contrast to the style of the simple, local pebble-idols, and may have been influenced by a similar type found in Anatolian Hacilar, an important community of the sixth millennium BC. An object like this shows us how closely intertwined were religion, cult and art in the early periods of mankind.

32 (*left*)
BEERSHEBA IVORY
FEMALE FIGURINE
Chalcolithic Period, Beersheba excavations
The craftsmanship of the Beersheba ivory 'guilds' was of a very high standard, and the execution of this figure, probably a fertility goddess, is in marked contrast with earlier ones.

33 (*far left*)
BEERSHEBA IVORY (*detail*)
MALE FIGURE
Chalcolithic Period, Beersheba excavations
Figures of this brachycephalic type, with long noses and short skulls, are thought to represent a distinct ethnic group, possibly the people of Chalcolithic Beersheba who may have introduced the use of metal to the region.

THE CHALCOLITHIC PERIOD – 4000–3200 BC: The Chalcolithic Period which followed has many characteristics of a transition period. Compared to the preceding prehistoric ages it is brief, covering less than a thousand years (*c.* 4000–3200 BC). Working tools and arms were still being made of stone but were increasingly replaced by copper utensils made by a complicated process using moulds. The transition from stone to copper is expressed in the name of this age – chalco-lithic – that is, copper-stone. The development from food gathering to food production, by no means completed during the Neolithic, and the change from a hunting to a farming civilisation, reach their final developments during the Chalcolithic. At the same time, the development of settled communities which became what we can call villages or small towns steadily continued, so that by this time one can already speak of proto-urbanisation.

Three large groups in the Archaeological Museum show the importance and complexity of this period: the finds from Beersheba, Azor (south of Tel-Aviv), and from the 'Cave of the Treasure' (in the Judaean Desert near the Dead Sea). The ivory figurines in plates 32 and 33 are representatives of the famous group from Beersheba. Plate 32 shows a pregnant woman, whose head and feet are missing, carved according to a naturalistic concept with the exception of the navel and the sexual parts, which may again have been stressed for magical purposes relating to fertility. In addition to ivory pieces, the Beersheba excavation revealed other objects of high quality produced by the 'guilds' of Chalcolithic times: ceramics, polished basalt bowls with incised patterns, flint tools and various metal objects. Chalcolithic Beersheba seems to have been a centre for metal casting. The ethnic group which possibly introduced the use of metals from Anatolia may be depicted in the ivory figurine reproduced in plate 33. Their distinctive features – the short skull and unusually long nose – may reflect the Armenian-Anatolian ethnic group with which the Beersheba people are supposedly identified.

The group of ossuaries from Azor shown in plate 34 is not a reconstruction of a Chalcolithic village: they are containers, in the form of clay houses, used for what is known as secondary burial, the transfer of the bones of the deceased into an ossuary. These ossuaries and others like them were found along the coast of Israel buried in artificially dug sandstone caves, veritable 'proto-catacombs'. The practice points to complex ideas concerning the afterlife. Questions have arisen concerning the significance of these burial rites in view of the absence of nearby settlements. According to some archaeologists, the Chalcolithic shepherds and husbandmen may have left Beersheba during the hot season or in drought years and moved on to the more fertile coastal plain, where they buried the bones of their dead. No cemeteries have been found in Chalcolithic Beersheba to

contradict this theory. Today, nomadic Bedouins often bury their dead far from their camping sites.

Remains of about one hundred ossuaries were found; most of the clay houses are square with an entrance high up on one of the narrower sides; some have high doors and four legs reminiscent of houses on stilts (Pfahlbauten); a few are in the shape of large oval jars with an entrance and gable, probably based on round dwellings. Roofs vary from flat, to vaulted or gabled. The fronts and backs of the houses are often crowned with high gables decorated with (as yet undeciphered) carved or painted symbols, often in the form of a nose, occasionally a human face.

The third important group of the Chalcolithic Period was found in a cave at Nahal Mishmar, in a steep cliff wall three hundred metres high. The archaeologist, when he set out in March 1960, was determined to find more Dead Sea Scrolls in the Judaean Desert, but returned instead with a treasure consisting of 429 pieces, mostly copper arms and tools, from the Chalcolithic Age (plates 35, 36). Objects of the Second Temple and the Bar-Kochba periods (37 BC–AD 135) were indeed found, but only in the upper strata of the cave, while the ancient copper treasure was found in the lower strata in a closed hollow of the cave's inner wall. It was wrapped in a straw mat and contained two hundred and forty mace-heads (plate 36), eighty tubular handles for 'standards' (plate 35), ten 'crowns' (plate 23), and twenty copper axes and adzes. They are technically and

34
AZOR OSSUARIES
Clay, Chalcolithic Period, Azor excavations
Bone containers, like these little houses, were used for 'secondary burial', when the bones of the dead were removed from their original graves and placed in such ossuaries for reburial.

35 (*above*)

'CAVE OF THE TREASURE' – 'SCEPTRES'

Copper, Chalcolithic Period, from a cave near the Dead Sea

Among the finds in the Nahal Mishmar cave were eighty tubular 'standard' handles. Like the mace-heads their exceptional quality suggests that they were more than mere weapons.

36 (*right*)

'CAVE OF THE TREASURE' – MACE-HEADS

Copper, Chalcolithic Period, from a cave near the Dead Sea

Some of the 240 mace-heads, of extremely high quality workmanship, found by archaeologists while searching for more scrolls in the Nahal Mishmar area near the Dead Sea.

aesthetically of a very high quality, and the number of variations within the categories of 'standards' and 'crowns' is considered to be astounding. One exceptional standard is adorned with moulded ibex heads (plate 38), and details of the finest 'crown' (see plate 23) recall the gable-crowned façade of the Azor ossuaries. Technically no less perfect are the mace-heads (plate 36); basically these mace-heads and 'standards' were arms, but judging from their artistic rendering and perfect state of preservation, they may have served as cult implements.

A sacred precinct discovered in the same Dead Sea region near the source of En Gedi, situated high on a mountain terrace, has been interpreted as a central sanctuary of the Chalcolithic Period. Plate 37 (a model) shows its irregular fortress walls, a propylon, and two buildings of the broad-house type, the larger one with an altar, the smaller with typical Chalcolithic pottery. In the middle of the courtyard there is a round structure, probably an altar. One hypothesis suggests that the copper implements from the Nahal Mishmar Cave were brought from the sanctuary to the cave for safe-keeping.

37 (*below*)
EN GEDI SANCTUARY
(*Plaster model*)
Thought to have been an important religious site in Chalcolithic times, this enclosure is 150 metres north of the En Gedi spring.

38 (*right*)
'CAVE OF THE TREASURE' – 'SCEPTRE'
Copper, Chalcolithic Period, from a cave near the Dead Sea
Of the Nahal Mishmar 'sceptres', this is probably the finest. The superb workmanship attests the high technical standards reached by Chalcolithic craftsmen.

EARLY CANAANITE PERIOD (EARLY BRONZE AGE) – 3200–2200 BC: The beginning of the Canaanite Period is approximately contemporary with the First Dynasty in Egypt and the Early Dynastic Period in Sumer. These two great river civilisations advanced to their high levels of culture due to a complex of factors, among them the rise in general well-being, urbanisation, socio-economic structures managed by systems of public service, elaborate military organisations, and city-states governed by kings and priests. Before the Bronze Age, the prerequisites for high culture, chiefly farming and the elements of settled life, originated not in Egypt or Mesopotamia but in the neighbouring areas, including the Land of Canaan. In spite of this, in the Bronze Age that followed all the lands of the Near East were under the influence of these two powers, Egypt and Mesopotamia.

The 'mosaic' of the Early Bronze Age excavations and discoveries is not complete enough to give a general history of the age. As R. de Vaux put it, 'the history of Palestine during this period cannot be written'. However, archaeology has progressed far enough today for us to be able to answer general questions about this period. After the Chalcolithic Beersheba civilisation had disappeared, leaving no palpable traces, an ethnic group from the north became its successor. They brought with them a tradition of architecture and town-planning, which explains the sudden growth of towns in the region. Relying on the Biblical tradition and Egyptian sources with early Semitic place names, we can assume that the dominant inhabitants of the Early Bronze Age in Palestine were the Canaanites.

In plate 39 are reproduced two handmade terracotta houses. The one at the back is in the form of a tower with two windows, which ends in a jar-neck for a plate with incense; it has no floor or entrance and must have served as an incense-stand in a sanctuary. The house in front is a red-painted model of a broad-house with a flat roof and an entrance in the centre of the longer side. Both types of dwellings can be found in excavations of this time. Although precursors exist from Natufian Eynan, Neolithic Jericho and Chalcolithic Beersheba, we can speak of an age of urbanisation only when we get to the Early Bronze Age. The well-known sites of the period, Tel el-Farah, Bet Yerah, Bet Shean, Megiddo, Gezer, Ai, Jericho, Ophel (Jerusalem) and Arad, must have been centres of Canaanite city states.

39
HOUSE MODELS

TOWER-SHAPED INCENSE STAND
Early Canaanite Period, Ai excavations

RED-PAINTED BROAD-HOUSE
Early Canaanite Period, Arad excavations

These models, in terracotta, have been identified as two distinct types of Canaanite house. A bowl of incense probably rested on the taller one, the purpose of the other is uncertain.

In each one of these city states we have to assume at least one temple. Ritual figurines and utensils are scarce in this country but they suffice to prove a progressive elaboration in the fertility cult and the cult of the dead. The small, artless 'madonna' of terracotta (plate 40) was probably a votive figurine placed in a temple, a house or a grave. The figure is related to the ancient mother goddess type.

It is from the more practical objects like pottery that the archaeologist can get a better understanding of the daily life of the period.

40 (*left*)

MOTHER AND CHILD FIGURINE

Pottery, Early Canaanite Period, Bet Yerah excavations

Figurines, like this mother goddess and child, were probably used as votive offerings or amulets.

41 (*right*)

CULT MASK

Pottery, Late Canaanite Period, Hazor excavations

This impressive mask, probably used for ritual purposes, was found in the potter's workshop at the Hazor sanctuary, together with the potter's wheel.

42 (*left*)
IMPORTED POTTERY
(*left*) TWO PAINTED MYCENAEAN VASES – *Hazor excavations*
(*centre*) SYRIAN ELONGATED FLASK
(*right*) CYPRIOT JUGLET AND BOWL
All: Late Canaanite Period
The trade links between Canaanite cities and eastern Mediterranean islands are attested by many finds.

43 (*below*)
'BET YERAH WARE'
(*left*) TWO HOUR-GLASS SHAPED STANDS
(*right*) LARGE BOWL
(*above*) DISH
Early Bronze Period
Although by this time the potter's wheel was being used, much of the very fine pottery Bet Yerah Ware was still handmade.

44
COPPER TOOLS AND WEAPON
(*left*) SAW
(*centre*) CURVED KNIFE
(*right*) SPEARHEAD
Early Canaanite Period, Kefar Monash
These weapons were part of a copper hoard which contained weapons, tools and some 800 small plaques, possibly armour scales.

Since its invention in the late Neolithic, pottery was handmade. In the Chalcolithic the 'tournette', a simple form of the potter's wheel, existed. But, surprisingly enough, the vessels shown in plate 43, conspicuous for their form and colour, particularly the huge double cone-shaped stand topped by a large platter, and the crater with stylised relief decoration, are still handmade. The red and black colours were not painted, but caused by various degrees of heat in the potter's kiln. The pottery is named after the site where most of them were found, Khirbet Kerak (now Bet Yerah), in the vicinity of Lake Tiberias. It is not of local origin and was produced by an ethnic group which emigrated, it seems, to northern Canaan before the middle of the third millennium BC. Similar pottery has been found in the Caucasus region, in Anatolia, Syria and Cyprus. After several centuries (*c.* 2650–2350 BC) the type disappeared, probably with those who made it, and local ceramic varieties dominated the market. Although of inferior aesthetic quality they were exported to Egypt, together with the new inventions of the potter's craft – the potter's wheel, polychromy and ledge handles on jars. Canaan served in many respects as a bridge for Mesopotamia, Anatolia, and Egypt, but it gave as well as it received.

The tools shown in plate 44 clearly reveal the influences from the neighbouring cultures in the Early Bronze Age. The tools are from a group of copper finds used for construction, like the saw (left) or the curved knife (centre), or for hunting and battle, like the spear (right). On the saw, five and a half centimetres away from the shoulder we find, in shallow pointillé technique, a design of Hathor, the Egyptian goddess, in the shape of a horned cow's head. The tool is probably Egyptian in origin but examples of this type have also been found in Ur and Kish, both important Sumerian centres. Parallels to this spearhead, seen here without its wooden shaft, have been found in Egypt, Mesopotamia and Anatolia; as a type, it was to have an important future in the later phases of the Bronze Age.

MIDDLE CANAANITE PERIOD (MIDDLE BRONZE AGE) – 2200–1550 BC: By the Middle Canaanite Period, we are entering the domain of the Patriarchs and Biblical archaeology in general. There are no tangible objects pertaining to the Patriarchs in the Museum, nor can there be any. For generations they were semi-nomads who wandered with their large herds from one region to another, they often camped in the area of the Canaanite cities but never permanently settled anywhere. For instance, the Book of Genesis describes in detail the journey of Abraham 'the Hebrew' (Genesis, 14:13) from Ur in southern Mesopotamia to the Land of Canaan. Genesis also records the story of the relations of the Patriarchs with Egypt and Mesopotamia. However,

45 (*left*)
DOMESTIC POTTERY
(*left to right*) 'TEAPOT', JAR, BEAKER
Beginning of the Middle Canaanite Period
Pots like these household wares were used for nearly three hundred years.

46 (*above*)
CANAANITE POTTERY OF THE PATRIARCHAL AGE
(*2nd and 3rd from left*) 'YAHUDIYEH' JUGLET, *Afula* GOBLET, *Barqai*
(*2nd from right*) DISH, *Gibeon*
(*right*) QUATREFOIL BOWL, *Hazor. All: Latter part of Middle Canaanite Period*
This pottery, made with a potter's wheel, shows the range of the craftsmen of the Canaanite city cultures.

their connection with Canaan is always dominant because it is the Land promised in the Covenant between Abraham and the God of Abraham (Gen., 17:8).

With this background in mind, we have a special interest in the period. However, because of the invasions by the nomadic Amorites at the end of the Early Bronze Age, and the destruction of cities by this Semitic desert people, the ceramic finds from this period are few in type, poor in shape and decoration, and meagre in development. If we compare the three vessels typical of the early Middle Canaanite Period (*c.* 2200–1950 BC) reproduced in plate 45 to the Early Canaanite Period, they are uninspiring. Each of the three vessels represents a standard type: a storage jar, a 'teapot' and a chalice. They are solid, functional wares that continue for about two to three hundred years in the ceramic repertory of the period and then disappear.

By the latter half of the Middle Canaanite Period (1750–1550 BC), the pottery types have become completely different both in style and quality. Each piece pictured here in plate 46 has been masterfully turned on the potter's wheel. The quality of this workmanship was known and appreciated by contemporaries, and pots, the second from the left for example, were exported to Egypt. This type is called 'Yahudiyeh' ware, after the main site in Egypt where it was found. The quality of the workmanship is testimony to a highly developed urban civilisation.

During the later Middle Canaanite Period, parts of the destroyed cities were rebuilt and new ones were constructed – Hazor, Megiddo, Shechem, Gezer, Jericho, Tel Bet Mirsim, and Lachish. Most of the major cities had a new type of defence wall, a rampart of 'terre pisée', probably invented in response to a new weapon, the battering ram. In the seventeenth century BC this rampart defence is found from Carchemish in northern Syria to Tel el-Yahudiyeh, north of Cairo. Kathleen Kenyon states that '. . . the defences are evidence of an alien aristocracy superimposed on the pre-existing population'. In all probability these aliens were the Hyksos, called 'Asians' or 'Bedouins' by the Egyptians. In the seventeenth century BC they reigned over Syria, Palestine and Egypt, and in many respects connected Asia Minor to Egypt, with Canaan acting as a link.

Evidence of the relations between this region and Egypt and Mesopotamia can be found in the scarab and cylinder seals, two forms of seal stones found locally in great quantities. Plate 47 shows a group of Egyptian or Egyptian-influenced local scarabs. On the left we can see the head of the goddess Hathor, flanked by two Uraeus serpents in an heraldic arrangement reminiscent of hieroglyphic writing and on the lower left the scroll designs characteristic of Hyksos seal stones. The carved upper-side of the scarab discloses the deeper significance of this typically Egyptian creation. To them the scarab beetle (rolling balls of dung into its nest) was symbolic of a celestial scarab beetle (Khepera), which rolled the sun, the source of all life, across the sky. The seal was worn around the neck as a protection for the living and the dead.

The Mesopotamian cylinder seal existed before Dynastic times. Among the exhibited specimens (plate 48) are some examples from Hazor, all imported from Mesopotamia and used both as seals and amulets. They were decorated with engraved mythological scenes, symbols and patterns, sometimes with cuneiform signs. The impressions were made by rolling the cylinder over soft clay.

A group of objects which tells us about the Canaanite civilisation is from an isolated sanctuary located on the sea-shore at Nahariya, north of Haifa. The isolation of the sanctuary is explained by the discovery of a well of fresh water which at that time existed near the temple but which is now covered by the Mediterranean Sea. The temple consists of a small rectangular building and a large altar with steps (bamah) adjoining it. Inside the holy place, and especially on the bamah, remnants of burnt offerings were found together with animal bones, fragments of cooking-pots, incense stands and miniature pottery vessels (plate 49). Among the objects was a small jug with a neck shaped to look like a squatting monkey, an Egyptian motif

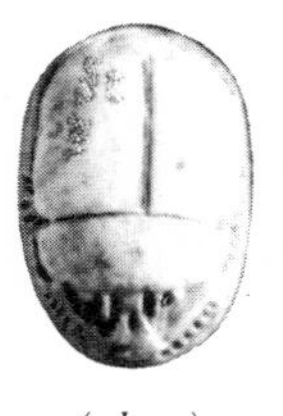

47 (*above*)

SCARABS

Mostly steatite, Middle Canaanite Period, from a tomb at Tel Nagila

These scarabs show the links with Egypt; although found in Canaan, they are often of foreign workmanship and show foreign motifs.

48 (*right*)

CYLINDER SEALS

(*top to bottom*)

1, 2. Haematite, Old Babylonian Period, 1830–1600 BC

3. Agate, Kassite Period, fifteenth century BC

4. Steatite, Second Syrian Group, 1600–1350 BC

5. Haematite, Mitannian Period, 1500–1400 BC

(*Gift of the Hahn-Voss family to the Department of Antiquities*)

Only 3 cm. long these seals are fine examples of skilled craftsmanship.

(plate 49). Another type of small vessel with seven model cups, also plate 49, was placed on the bamah and may have been filled with offerings, the first fruits of the year for instance. The excavation's most spectacular find was about a dozen silver figurines, chiefly female divinities, found on the bamah as offerings (plate 50). A stone mould for casting a similar figurine (plate 51) has also been found; a cast made after the excavation gave the front part of a long-legged goddess with horns. Silver horns have been discovered nearby which fit exactly into the form and we now have definite proof that casting was used to make silver figurines of the goddess for worshippers in the sanctuary. The divinity was probably the Canaanite sea and fishing goddess, Asherat Ha-Yam. Votives in the Nahariya sanctuary are related to the finds in other centres of the Canaanite cultural sphere: Phoenicia, Tyre, Sidon, Byblos and Ugarit (Ras Shamra). Elaborate tablets from Ugarit tell us about these Canaanite divinities and myths. As C. H. Gordon summarised it, the myths attempt to explain nature, 'to satisfy man's craving to understand the universe, and to guarantee the regularity of the process that results in fertility: the fertility of mankind, animals and plants'.

49
OFFERINGS FROM A CANAANITE HIGH PLACE
(left to right)
SEVEN-CUP OFFERING VESSEL
BIRD FIGURINE
MINIATURE JUGLET
JUGLET WITH NECK IN SHAPE OF A MONKEY
MINIATURE BOWL
Pottery
Middle Canaanite Period, Nahariya excavations
These miniature vessels were among offerings found in the sanctuary compound at Nahariya. Most of them were found on the altar adjoining the temple.

50 (*above and top right*)

OFFERINGS FROM A CANAANITE HIGH PLACE

Figurines, silver

Middle Canaanite Period, Nahariya excavations

These deities, three of a dozen found during the excavations, belong to the Canaanite-Phoenician pantheon, known to us from cuneiform Ugaritic tablets, excavated at Ras Shamra, the site of ancient Ugarit.

51 (*right*)

STONE MOULD FOR CASTING FIGURINE OF HORNED GODDESS (*with modern bronze cast*)

Middle Canaanite Period, Nahariya excavations

This figurine is probably to be identified with the Canaanite sea and fishing goddess.

LATE CANAANITE PERIOD (LATE BRONZE AGE) – 1550–1250 BC: The objects in the Museum pertaining to the Late Canaanite Period must also be understood in their relation to the great powers. In the sixteenth century BC the Hyksos rule in Egypt ended, and the XVIII Dynasty began its long rule over Canaan and Syria. The power of the Hittites from Anatolia also becomes prominent at this time, as well as the influences of the Cypriot and Mycenaean civilisations, the rising sea powers in the Mediterranean.

The so-called 'Orthostat Temple' at Hazor dates from the fourteenth century BC. One of the monuments from this Canaanite sanctuary is the huge lion statue (plate 52) made from a single basalt block. The body of the beast is rendered in flat relief, while the head is in the round. Two drilled holes and a cursory treatment of the back are clues to the architectural function of the lion. Together with a

52
LION ORTHOSTAT
Basalt, Late Canaanite Period, Hazor excavations
Two colossal lions, of which only this has survived, served as guardians at the entrance of one of the Canaanite temples. Each was carved from a single block of basalt, the body in relief and the head in the round.

companion statue (not preserved), the lion formed an entrance jamb to the sanctuary. The synthesis of relief and sculpture in the round, in an orthostat, was a characteristic element of Hittite and northern Syrian-Canaanite temple and palace sculpture.

In the 'Shrine of the Stelae', also from Hazor (plate 53), were discovered a series of basalt stelae with rounded tops in a ritual niche well above the temple floor. One relief stele shows two hands raised in prayer towards a divine moon crescent above. A basalt statuette of a man, presumably a priest or a king, was also found (plate 53, left), as well as a roughly hewn basalt slab, probably a table for offertory vessels. Another lion orthostat was discovered, similar to the one in plate 52 but of smaller dimensions and poorer quality. It has been suggested that this is a cult-site of the moon-god Sin of Harran, originally a Sumerian-Babylonian divinity. In the temple vicinity

53
'SHRINE OF THE STELAE'
(far left) STATUETTE OF SEATED MAN
(centre) STELE INCISED WITH RAISED HANDS
(far right) LION ORTHOSTAT
All: Basalt, Late Canaanite Period, Hazor excavations
Because of the hands reaching up to a moon crescent, carved on one of the stelae, archaeologists think this Canaanite shrine was dedicated to the moon-god.

54
POTTER'S WHEEL
Basalt, Late Canaanite Period, Hazor excavations
The wheel was found in a potter's workshop close to the sanctuary. Possibly the workshop near the shrine was used for the manufacture of ritual objects.

store-rooms and potter's workshops have been excavated, probably connected with the sanctuary. In one an impressive, ritual male mask (plate 41) was discovered next to a basalt potter's wheel (plate 54).

A remarkable chance discovery, illuminating the cultural influence of Mesopotamia on Canaan in the Bronze Age, is represented by a tablet from Megiddo (plate 55, top) with cuneiform characters on both sides. It contains a chapter of the celebrated Babylonian Gilgamesh epic poem. Gilgamesh, king of Uruk, mourns at the deathbed of his friend, the hero Enkidu. Together with Enkidu, Gilgamesh had killed the celestial bull Humbaba, and the gods had willed that Enkidu must pay with his life for the deed. The story was well known in the Near East, and the Babylonian epic has been transmitted in an Akkadian version dating from the third millennium BC and later in

55 (*top*)

GILGAMESH EPIC FRAGMENT

Clay tablet, Late Canaanite Period, Megiddo

This tablet, engraved with cuneiform characters, tells part of the Gilgamesh Epic, showing that this famous story was known in the region.

(*bottom*)

LIVER MODEL FOR TEMPLE DIVINERS

Clay, two fragments
Late Canaanite Period, Hazor excavations

Clay or metal models of animal livers inscribed with formulas written in cuneiform, were used in the Canaanite temples in divination ceremonies.

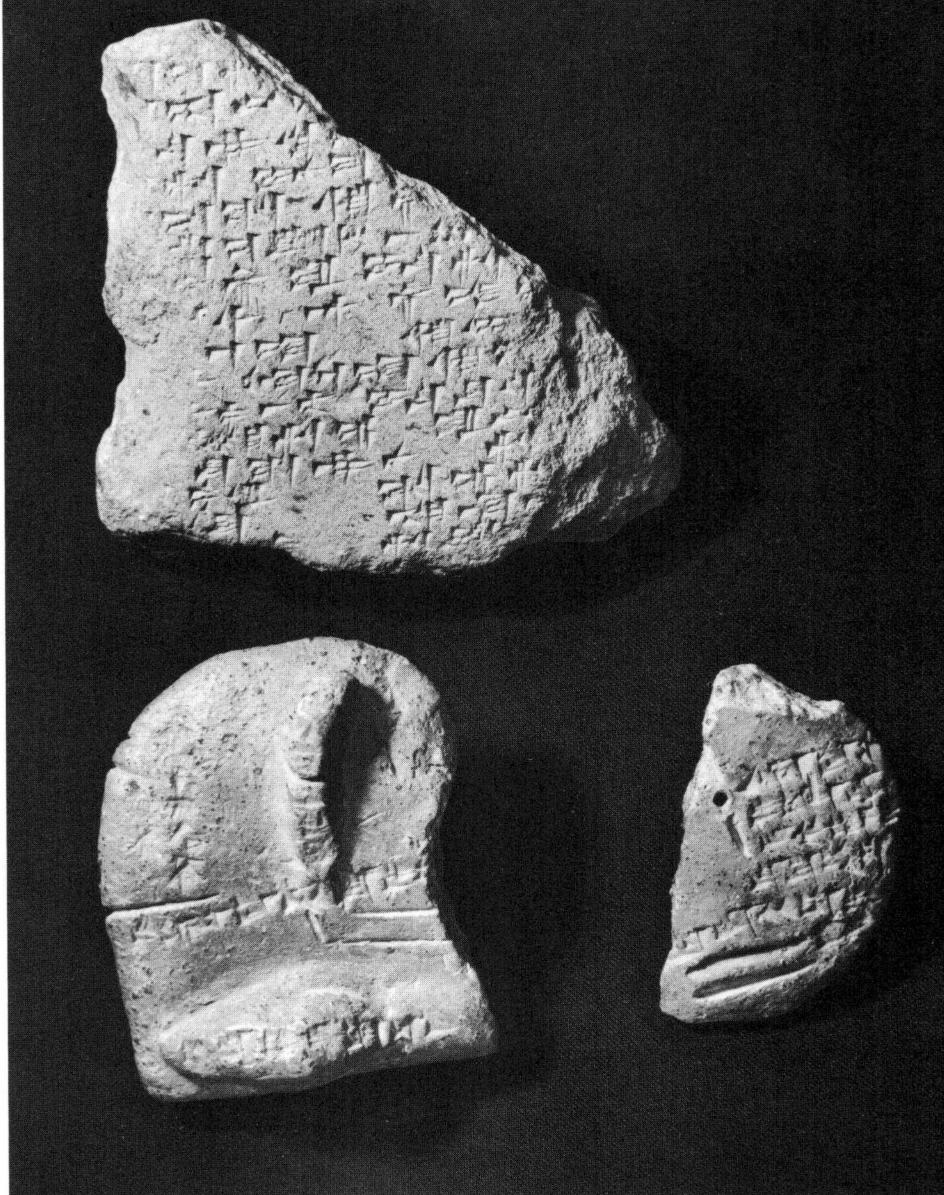

Hurrian and Hittite versions. The Megiddo fragment was inscribed in the fourteenth century BC.

In a late fifteenth-century temple at Hazor has been found a clay model of the liver of an animal (plate 55); specimens of this strange class can be traced back to Babylon in the late third millennium BC. They were used by temple diviners to predict the future. Liver models were made in clay and metal; some, like the Museum's, were covered with cuneiform omens. Liver models have been found in contemporary Mesopotamia, the Hittite lands, Phoenicia, Crete and Etruria.

A survey of the cults in this period would not be complete without mentioning the fertility goddess. She can be traced back to the Neolithic Age at least, but by the time of the Canaanite Period the various concepts of the goddess have crystallised into standard types. The three small terracotta figurines shown in plate 56 are primarily votive objects or amulets for magical purposes, and can be understood as representations of the great Canaanite goddesses of the Middle and Late Bronze Age, such as Asherah, Astarte and Anat. The figurine in the middle, crowned with a fluted tiara, supports her breasts with both hands, embodying the concept of a nourishing mother goddess. Another female aspect is evidenced by the plaque at the right. The nude frontal figure with arms hanging down emphasises fertility in a more provocative way; some experts were even led into identifying this type with divine courtesans or sacred harlots. The figurine on the left is similar in principle to this type but is highly stylised: the head is distinguished by exaggerated ears and pierced earrings; the nose is pinched up into a beak-like projection; the arms are in the form of simplified appendages. This type, created in northern Mesopotamia in the third millennium, was brought to Syria, Canaan, Cyprus, and Egypt in the second millennium BC.

56
'ASTARTE' FIGURINES
Pottery, Late Canaanite Period
(Central figurine from the Reifenberg Collection, Jerusalem)
One of the many cults that flourished in the Canaanite period was that of Astarte, or the mother goddess. These little idols or amulets show three different aspects of this theme.

In the realm of the material prosperity and culture of this age, several pottery vessels (plate 42) further illustrate the trade relations of Canaanite cities with neighbouring civilisations. The two richly painted vases from Mycenae on the left of the plate were imported, as well as the polished 'Syrian flask' (centre) and the two Cypriot vessels (right). The bowl translates a metal model into pottery, while the small jug converts the model of a leather bag into ceramic. These types as well as others were imported and copied locally. Mycenaean types and their local imitations played an important role in the Canaanite ceramic repertory of this and the early Israelite Period.

The Museum also has a clay krater from Nagila in the Negev decorated in red and black. The shoulder is painted on one side with a humped bull bound for sacrifice, on the other with an ibex and a bird. This krater represents a type of ceramic called 'bichrome ware' due to the use of the two colours. This pottery was found in considerable quantities and was probably produced between *c.* 1550 and 1450 BC in the region around southern Canaan, Syria and Cyprus.

The Canaanite civilisation of the Late Bronze Age mirrors an intense exchange of spiritual and material values from region to region. The entire age has been defined as the 'first manifestation of internationalism' (J.H. Breasted). To emphasise even more the cultural picture of the age, we should recall the 'Tell el-Amarna Letters', documents in cuneiform script dispatched by the city princes of Canaan and Syria and by the kings of Babylon, Mitanni and the Hittite Kingdom, to Pharaoh Amenhotep III (1417–1379 BC) and to his son, Amenhotep IV – Akhenaten (1379–1362 BC). These letters were kept in the royal archives of the palace in Tell el-Amarna.

ISRAELITE PERIOD (IRON AGE) – 1250–587 BC: On first perusal, the Amarna Letters give the impression of an overwhelming concentration of power in the Egyptian empire. A closer study almost reverses this impression; visions of corruption, internal strife and court rivalries disclose the true fragility of Egyptian rule and the beginning of a period of political instability. It is probable that the Exodus of the Israelites from Egypt occurred not much later, probably during the reign of Ramses II (1304–1237 BC).

This pharaoh built two treasure cities, at Pithom and at Raamses, and according to the Book of Exodus (1:11), to build these two cities the Children of Israel were enslaved. To bring an end to this unhappy period, Moses freed the Israelites and led them out of Egypt. Acting under the command and promise of God he journeyed with his people towards the Land of the Covenant, and while in the desert received the Ten Commandments on Mount Sinai. The profound influence and significance of these events on the history of Israel and the Jewish people cannot be overemphasised.

Although the literary and archaeological documentation of this period is much richer than that of any previous time, we have to bear in mind that pictorial representations cannot be expected from the Children of Israel in the post-Mosaic periods in view of the prohibition against graven images in the Ten Commandments.

Under the leadership of Joshua, the Israelites conquered Canaan. For the first time, the term 'People of Israel' appeared on an Egyptian stele, *c.* 1230 BC, the time of Pharaoh Merenptah. The establishment of the first Hebrew settlement probably took place at that time and the settlement of the Twelve Tribes followed shortly after 1200 BC. During the ensuing Period of the Judges (*c.* 1200–1020 BC), the Israelites encountered the Philistines in battles for the political and cultural power in Canaan.

Plate 57 shows vases with geometric ornamentation and highly stylised birds and plants. This type of pottery was found mainly in the coastal plain of southern Palestine. It has been classified as Philistine pottery because of the literary evidence from the Books of Judges and Samuel I and II that the Philistines conquered the southern part of the country and settled in cities such as Ascalon, Ashdod and Gaza. In addition, excavations prove that the pottery is always found in strata dating from the twelfth and eleventh centuries BC. Experts have also convincingly related the style of the vases in shape and decoration to the late Mycenaean vases of Greece, Cyprus and Rhodes, and it is generally assumed that the Philistines were originally a late Mycenaean people driven out of the Greek lands by the Dorian invasions. Defeated in a naval battle by the Egyptians under Ramses III (as depicted on a relief from Medinet Habu), the Philistines settled on the shores of Canaan, probably as Egyptian mercenaries. The pottery

57
PHILISTINE POTTERY
JUG
Azor excavations
KRATER
Tel Zippor excavations
Both: Beginning of the Israelite Period
The decoration of this pottery represents a late and degenerate development of Mycenaean vase-painting, similar to that in Aegean areas, although the shape of the jug and the lotus decoration show a distinct Egyptian influence.

58 (*overleaf left*)
HIGH-STEMMED BOWL AND INCENSE STAND
Pottery, painted and burnished
(*right*) *Israelite Period* (*eleventh-tenth centuries BC*), *Tel Zafit excavations*
(*left*) *Israelite Period* (*tenth-ninth centuries BC*), *Tel Amal excavations*
The bold strong forms of these two pieces convey an idea of the character of Judaean pottery during the period of the Judges and the early kings.

59 (*overleaf right*)
PHOENICIAN POTTERY
PAINTED MASK
RED-BURNISHED JUGS
Late Israelite Period, Akhziv excavations
The elegant forms of this urban Phoenician craftsmanship contrast strongly with the functional, sturdy ware characteristic of contemporary common Palestinian pottery.

motifs reflect these Philistine connections. On the jug shown in plate 57, (right), we see a stylised lotus flower in full bloom and flanked by water birds, and geometrical patterns. The jug's shape and the lotus pattern are Egyptian, while the geometrical patterns and birds are Mycenaean. The deep crater represents the major type of vessel in the Philistine repertory, derived from a standard Mycenaean type. As frequently occurs with a transfer of styles, the spirals are the Philistine geometrical representation of what was once, on Mycenaean vases, organic flora or marine fauna. Contrary to Greek vase-painting, the Philistine style did not develop beyond a degenerate stylisation of Mycenaean patterns. A parallel development from naturalism to stylisation appears in the face masks of the anthropoid clay sarcophagi found in Philistine graves in Bet Shean. Plate 61 shows a mask while plate 62 depicts a sarcophagus complete with the conventionalised face and a suggestion of the Philistine feather helmet. After a flourishing period in the twelfth century BC, by the eleventh century the art of the Philistines had degenerated and ossified, its identity becoming submerged in the general regional developments.

In contrast to the colourful sub-Mycenaean ceramics, typical of a high but disintegrating culture, the local pottery of the Early Israelite Period is typical of a farming civilisation. This period includes the time of the Judges, and the rule of Saul (1020–1000 BC) and David (1000–960 BC). Plate 58 shows two cult implements, a stemmed bowl with a carved petal decoration, and a fenestrated incense stand with a bowl. In plate 63 we see several ceramic types dating from the twelfth to the ninth centuries BC. The 'pilgrim's bottle' in the right foreground is a local imitation of late Mycenaean-Philistine pottery. The oil lamp (bottom centre) and the other vessels date from the tenth and ninth centuries BC, while the highly polished, elegant spouted jug (to the right) already bears witness to the urban civilisation of Solomon's time and after.

During Solomon's reign (960–930 BC) and in the post-Solomonic era (the time of the two kingdoms of Judah and Israel), another power grew influential in the life and culture of the Land. A glance at the fine red polished ceramics (plate 59) from the necropolis at Akhziv will prove that they differ markedly from the functional and rustic Israelite wares. Note, for instance, the 'mushroom' lip of the jugs on the right and the powerful build of the jug on the left. This vessel, with a globular body, conical neck and trefoil mouth, is a Phoenician type, also to be found in metal and glass. It is known that from the tenth to the sixth centuries BC Akhziv was an important Phoenician settlement. The painted model mask (plate 59), also from an Akhziv grave, and a rare Phoenician ivory fan handle inscribed with the name Abdubaal (plate 60) are testimony of the highly developed urban civilisation of the Phoenicians at this period.

60
PHOENICIAN FAN HANDLE
Ivory, Phoenician, c. 800 BC (Permanent loan from E. Borowski, Basel)
Man with attendant in front of priest. Phoenician inscription: 'belonging to Abdubaal'.
Perhaps the man standing with his attendant in front of the priest is the Abdubaal to whom, according to the inscription, the fan handle belonged.

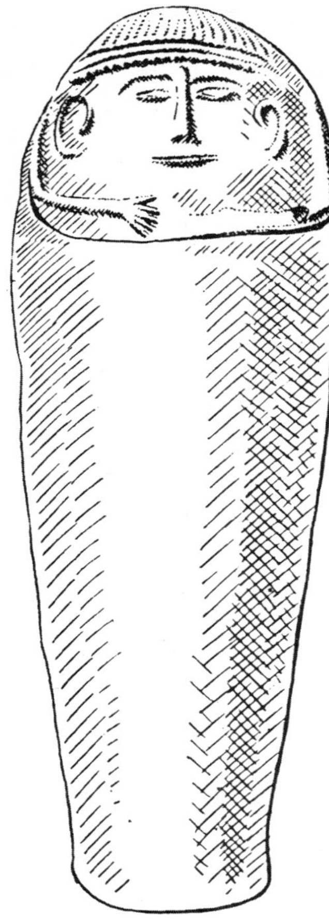

The influence of the Phoenicians on the Israelites was inestimable. During the Bronze Age, Phoenicians were identical with Canaanites, representing the northern portion of the Canaanite population that had not been engulfed by the Israelite conquest. Through them the polytheistic heritage of Canaanite civilisation continued in the form of an urban culture in commercial centres such as Tyre and Sidon. Phoenician civilisation was at the same time a permanent danger to Israelite monotheism and a challenge that promoted progress in the various fields of material culture. These two aspects of Phoenician influence were often inseparable as expressed by the constant struggle of the Prophets in the eighth and seventh centuries BC against the godless, Phoenician-inspired luxury of the House of Omri in Samaria, the residence of the kings of Israel. 'And it came to pass . . . that he [i.e. Ahab, the son of Omri] took to wife Jezebel the daughter of Ethbaal, king of the Zidonians, and went and served Baal, and worshipped him' (1 Kings, 16:31).

Plates 60, 66–69 show Phoenician objects which must have earned the disapproval of the Prophets: human masks, figuratively decorated fan handles, cosmetic implements, jewelry, amulets and richly

61 (*left*)

FACE FROM ANTHROPOID SARCOPHAGUS

Clay, beginning of the Israelite Period, Tel Rehov

A carved face, such as this one, probably formed part of the lid of a Philistine anthropoid sarcophagus.

62 (*above*)

PHILISTINE ANTHROPOID SARCOPHAGUS

Pottery

Sketch showing the type of sarcophagus on which the face in plate 61 would have been carved.

63
ISRAELITE POTTERY
(left to right)
JAR
JUG WITH SPOUT
'PILGRIM BOTTLE'
Tel Amal excavations
OIL LAMP
En Gev excavations
All: Israelite Period
Pottery of various types; the ninth-century spouted jug, in particular, requires a high degree of technical skill.

carved ivories. However, the struggle of the Prophets was not only directed against the polytheistic cults and luxury of the Phoenicians and their influences on the House of Omri in the kingdom of Israel. Small idols, mainly of the dea nutrix type (plate 65) and 'horned altars' (plate 64) were also used to satisfy superstition and to conquer fear and danger through magical means. The idea of the limestone altar from Megiddo originated from the altar in the Tent of the Covenant (Leviticus, 4:7, 19–20); in Solomon's time 'the horns of the altar' in the Temple were a refuge for persecuted persons (1 Kings, 2:28). However, by the time of the Divided Monarchy this function can no longer have been valid since all the horned altars extant have been discovered in private homes.

Although their spiritual influence on the Israelites caused internal strife, the Phoenicians contributed considerably to the art and civilisation of the Mediterranean peoples and even as far afield as Africa. Renowned as seafarers, merchants and craftsmen, they were the cultural intermediaries of the ancient world. Both artists and businessmen, they adapted themselves to their clientele, as numerous artifacts in varying styles prove. Documents attest to their trade relationships;

64

'HORNED ALTAR'

Limestone, tenth-ninth centuries BC, Megiddo excavations

This altar illustrates the Biblical passage: 'and Joab fled unto the tabernacle of the Lord, and caught hold of the horns of the altar.' (1 Kings 2:28)

66 (*right*)

ARSLAN TASH IVORY

Cow suckling calf

Phoenician workmanship, second half of the ninth century BC

(*Collection E. Borowski, Basel*)

The ivory plaques from Arslan Tash are thought to have been decorative furniture inlays which were looted from the palace at Aram-Damascus during an attack on it by the Assyrians.

65

'ASTARTE' OR DEA NUTRIX FIGURINES

Pillar-shaped, with human head (right)

'bird-headed' (left)

Pottery, Judaean types, seventh century BC (Reifenberg Collection, Jerusalem)

The use, for magical purposes, of 'graven images' like these little household amulets, was inveighed against by the Prophets in their efforts to check the growth of idolatry.

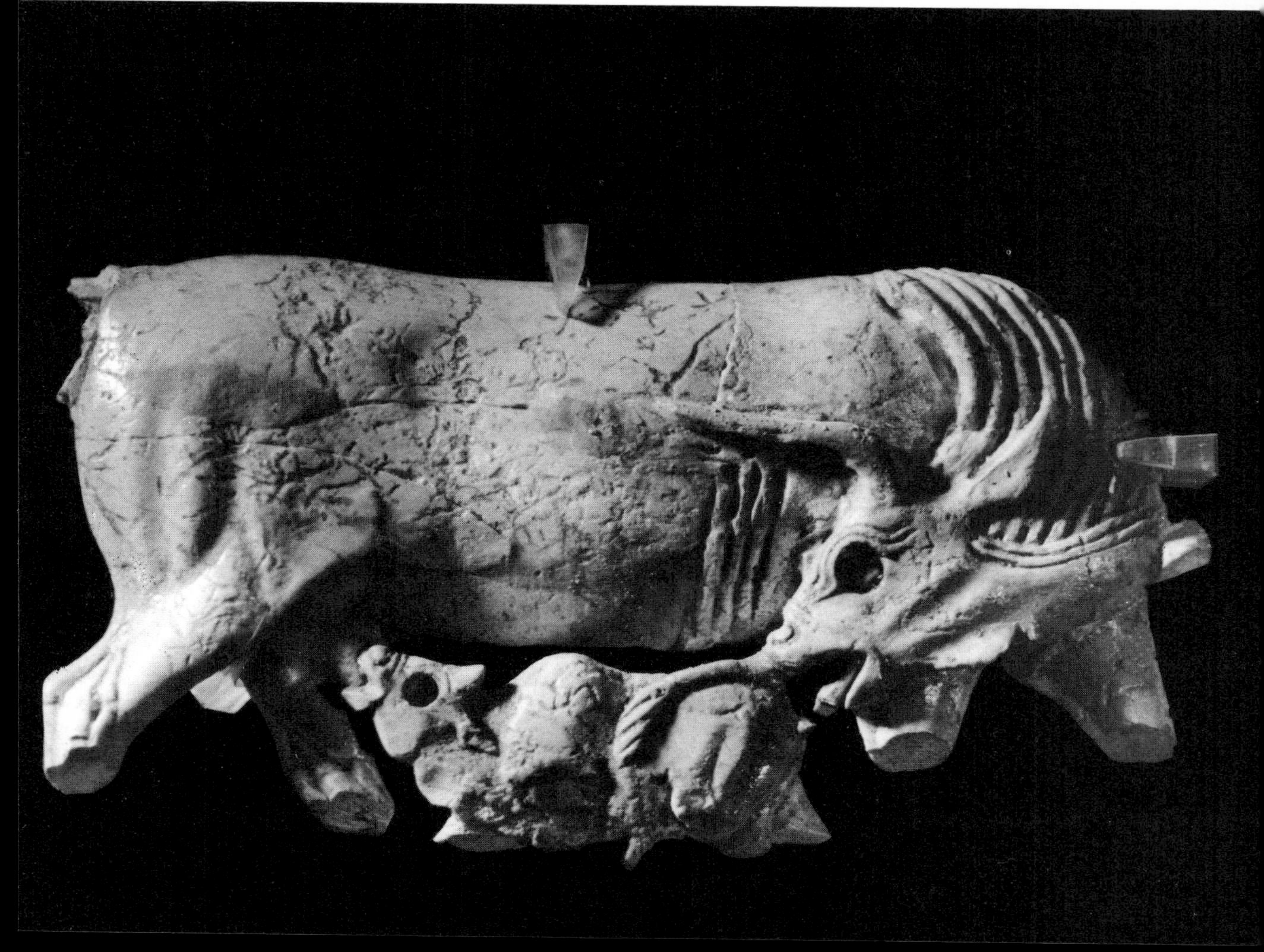

for example, an ancient Hebrew ostracon of the eighth century BC (plate 72, top) from Tel Qasile, an Israelite port north of Tel-Aviv, reads: '. . . gold of Ophir to Bet Horon – 30 shekels'. Several verses in I Kings and II Chronicles mention gold shipments from Ophir, generally thought to be in eastern Africa or southern Arabia.

Homer also comments on Phoenician goods, the polychrome robes of the Sidonians for instance, or metalwork in copper and bronze. They excelled likewise in the manufacture of gold and silver jewelry, and some of today's experts think that it was the Phoenicians from Sidon who invented the sand-core technique for the production of small glass flacons (plate 73). Glass made by the sand-core technique has been found wherever Phoenician trade existed, that is, all over the Mediterranean, and they specialised in making glass beads, such as the necklace of eye-beads shown in plate 73.

In addition to these accomplishments, the Phoenicians were also expert ivory carvers. The pieces from Arslan Tash shown in plates 66 to 68 originally adorned the royal furniture in the palace of Hazael, king of Aram-Damascus (848–805 BC). The palace was ransacked during an Assyrian campaign against Damascus and the pieces taken to the Assyrian Hadatu (modern Arslan Tash). The most powerful piece in the group is the head of a lion with his mouth open (plate 68). It was carved in the round and may have served as a terminal throne support. Plate 67 shows the torso and head of the most important piece of this group – a king or a priest, depicted in what is an Assyrian-influenced style, stiffly performs a ritual before a stylised tree of life.

68 (*right*)

ARSLAN TASH IVORY

Lion's head

Phoenician workmanship, second half of the ninth century BC

(*Collection E.Borowski, Basel*)

As well as the relief plaques, the hoard contained some ivories carved in the round, the finest being this lion's head which was probably a decoration to the royal throne.

67 (*left*)

ARSLAN TASH IVORY

King or Priest (*detail*)

Phoenician workmanship, second half of the ninth century BC

(*Collection E.Borowski, Basel*)

Originally, the stylised tree of life was flanked by two men making an offering. The heraldic stiffness in this style indicates Assyrian influence.

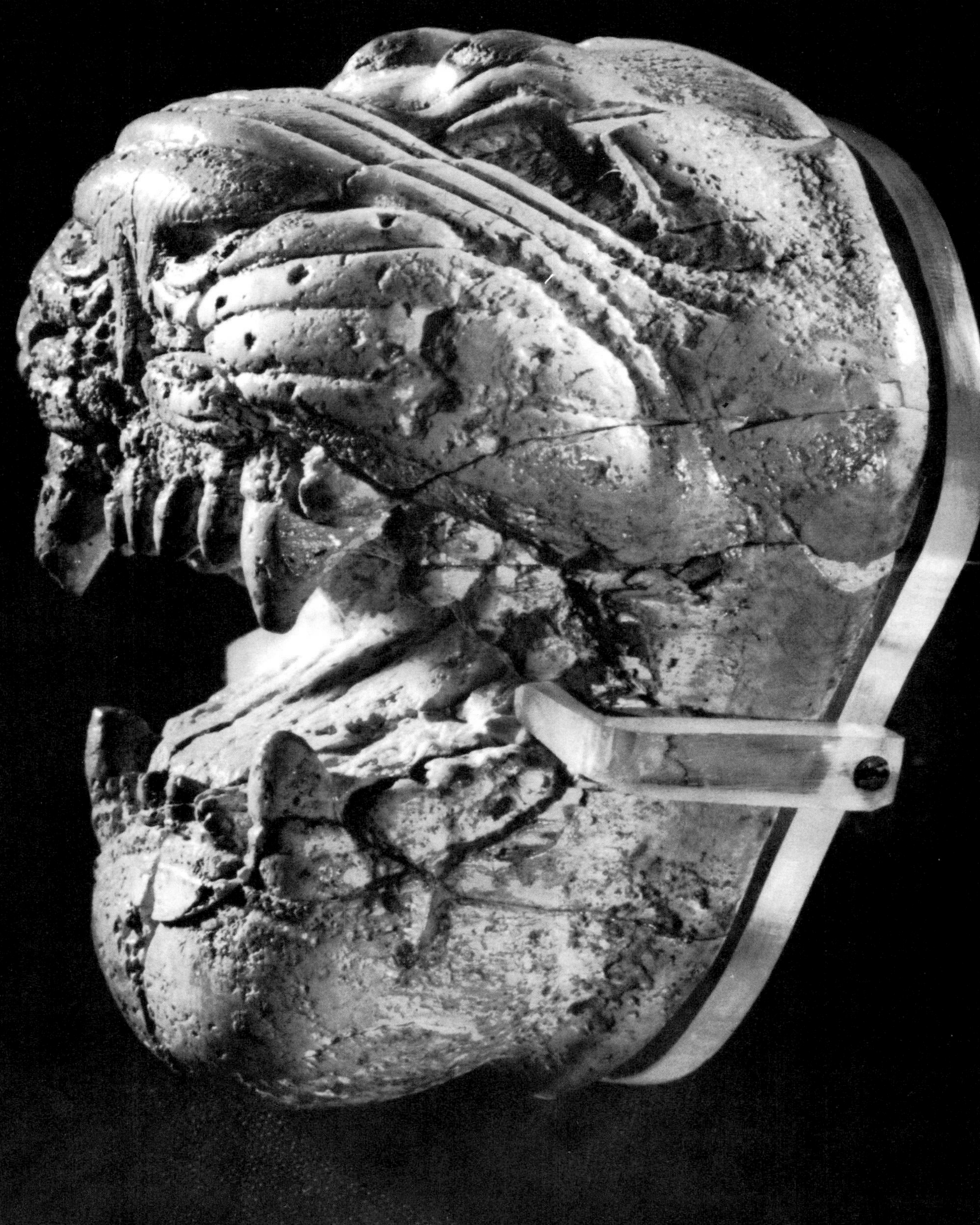

Two griffons wearing the regal uraeus and the crowns of Upper and Lower Egypt, would normally have stood heraldically at each side of the sacred tree.

In plate 69 we see the head of a woman with an elaborate head-dress peering from a window which has four column capitals as a balustrade. This may be a depiction of the goddess Astarte as she solicits the passer-by, in the manner of her sacred harlots. The window on the ivory plaque is not fanciful but is derived from contemporary architecture. A stone window balustrade from the royal palace in the citadel of Ramat Rahel near Jerusalem strikingly proves this point. The reconstruction (plate 70) is exhibited beside an enlarged photograph of the 'Woman at the Window' ivory.

71 (*above*)

HEBREW OSTRACON

Clay, c. 700 BC, Arad excavations
The Phrase 'the House of Yhwh' on this list of supplies for temple servants is probably one of the earliest references to the Temple in Jerusalem.

69 (*left*)

ARSLAN TASH IVORY

'Woman at the window'
Phoenician workmanship, second half of the ninth century BC
(Collection E. Borowski, Basel)
The plaque is thought to be a representation of the Phoenician goddess Astarte in the guise of one of her sacred harlots.

70 (*below left*)

STONE BALUSTRADE

Phoenician style, seventh century BC, Ramat Rahel excavations
That the balustrade originally formed part of an actual window, is shown by a Nimrud ivory, which is very similar to that from Arslan Tash in plate 69.

72 (*right*)

HEBREW OSTRACA

Clay, c. 700 BC, Arad excavations
In antiquity potsherds were often used as a writing material. The upper ostracon lists domestic supplies and the lower records a deal in gold.

73 (*left*)
PHOENICIAN MINOR ARTS
GLASS AMPHORISKOS
GLASS EYE-BEADS
COSMETIC PALETTE AND BONE
SPATULA, SEALS, AMULETS
WEAVING IMPLEMENTS
All: Israelite Period, eighth-sixth centuries BC
These articles reflect a high degree of material wealth.

74 (*above*)
PROTO-IONIC CAPITAL
Seventh century BC, Ramat Rahel excavations
Pillar heads of this type were found in administrative centres like Megiddo, Hazor, Samaria and Jerusalem.

The pillar head (plate 74), also from Ramat Rahel, can stand by itself as one of the most important objects in the museum. Its capital is generally called proto-Aeolic or proto-Ionic, a type which travelled from Canaan to Cyprus, Asia Minor and the eastern Greek islands, then into Greece where it developed into the classic Ionic capital. The derivation of the symbolism of the capital in general is clearly seen in the Ramat Rahel example. The design on the capital is actually a stylised old Mesopotamian symbol, the 'Tree of Life' (see plate 67). Below the double volute on our capital (and, originally, also above), we can see the fruit of the date palm, a motif which makes the meaning of the 'tree' more literal. Here again, the Phoenician middlemen were responsible for linking the eastern world of Mesopotamia and Judah with the western world of Greece.

The most influential and lasting achievement of the Phoenicians, however, was the transmission of the Hebrew-Phoenician alphabetic script to the Greeks in the early eighth century BC. The form of the letters of the Hebrew-Phoenician alphabet and the Greek alphabet of the Archaic Period are almost identical. Some letters are in different

positions, and vowels – not represented in the Hebrew alphabet – are included in the Greek alphabet. In plates 71 and 72 (top) examples of the Hebrew script of the period are shown.

Perhaps it is ironic that in the Land of the Bible, the Phoenician influence can be seen on the Temple in Jerusalem, the major spiritual centre of ancient Israel. King Solomon had called for Hiram, from the Phoenician town of Tyre, to decorate the Temple (I Kings, 7:14). We can gain an idea of the decoration by reading descriptions in I Kings, 5–8; II Chronicles, 2–5 and Ezekiel, 40ff., and comparing them with known Phoenician work. The type of 'cherubim and palm trees and open flowers' that is described was a popular decorative motif. Plate 67 shows such a palm tree. Images in the Temple were not only decorative, they were also symbolic. For example, cherubim may have been placed in the Holy of Holies of the Temple as lateral arms guarding the 'empty throne' of the invisible God, just as God placed the Cherubim in the Garden 'to keep the way of the tree of life' (Gen., 3:24). Solomon's Temple was also famous for a huge cleansing basin, the so-called 'Bronze Sea', as well as other metal implements and considerable decoration in gold.

Objects with a direct or indirect relation to the House of God in Jerusalem are extremely rare. For this reason the Museum spared no efforts to transfer a small royal temple from the citadel at Arad to its permanent exhibition hall. Plate 75 shows in the background a photograph of this site while the ritual niche, reconstructed from its original stones, is in the foreground. This part is from the Holy of Holies, with two altars crowning three steps and remnants of animal sacrifices still visible. Like the Temple in Jerusalem, the temple in Arad had a court with an altar for burnt offerings, a porch (ulam), a main hall (hekhal), and the Holy of Holies (debir). Two flat stones before the Main Hall were probably bases for columns, a parallel to the pair of columns called Yachin and Boaz in Solomon's Temple. It seems that the temple at Arad was built in Solomon's time as a 'king's chapel' (cf. Amos, 7:13) but with the increasing religious reforms, aimed at centralising the divine service in Jerusalem, it was probably destroyed under Josiah, king of Judah (640–609 BC). About one hundred Hebrew clay tablets from the time of the late Divided Monarchy were found in the Arad citadel. Almost all of them pertain to distribution of bread, wine and oil (plate 72, top). One ostracon, however, refers to supplies for a family of temple servants who are mentioned in the Bible (see plate 71). The last line includes the phrase 'the House of Yhwh'. Almost certainly this reference is to the Temple in Jerusalem during a period when the Arad temple no longer existed.

Three other Hebrew inscriptions have been found which relate to the Temple in Jerusalem and its God (see plate 76). They were incised

75

'HOLY OF HOLIES' – *From the Temple at Arad*

TWO STONE ALTARS

Ninth century BC, Arad excavations

The inner part of a Judaean sanctuary discovered in the Negev. The layout of this temple resembles that of Solomon's Temple in Jerusalem with which it was contemporary.

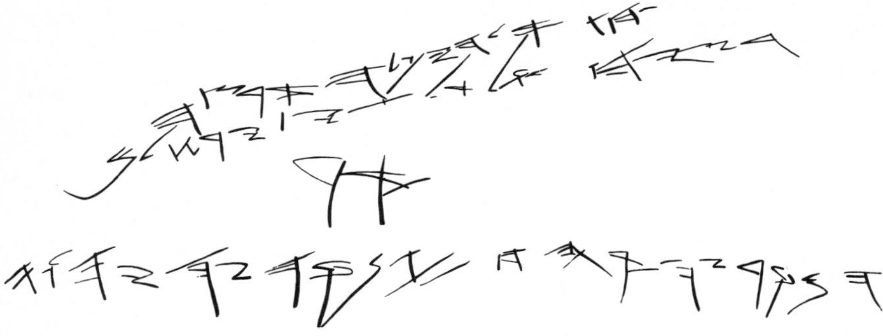

76 (*left*)

HEBREW GRAFFITI FROM TOMB-CAVE NEAR AMAZIA

c. 700 BC

These are the first two inscriptions in the tomb, and were perhaps a prayer to 'Yhwh . . . . God of Jerusalem.'

on the walls of a burial-cave in the Judaean hills not far from Lachish; they too have been transferred to the Museum. The three inscriptions are graffiti and may be part of a significant whole. They read:

> 'Yhwh is the God of the whole earth; the mountains of Judah belong to Him, to the God of Jerusalem.'
> 'The (Mount of) Moriah Thou hast favoured, the dwelling of Yah, Yhwh.'
> '(Ya)hwh deliver (us)!'

The excavator suggests dating these inscriptions to the time of King Sennacherib of Assyria (704–681 BC). By about 701 BC this king had taken forty-six Judaean cities, and Lachish (one of the cities conquered), near the burial-cave, served as his headquarters (cf. his famous relief from Nineveh, now in the British Museum). It is possible that these graffiti are the prayers of refugees or rebels; and indeed Jerusalem was not taken by the Assyrians.

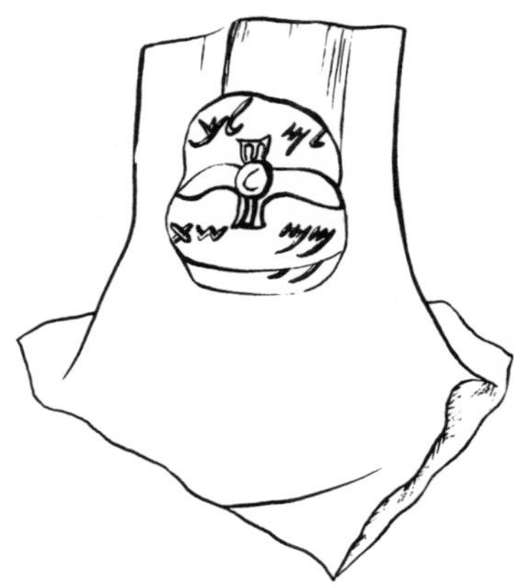

77

STAMPED ROYAL JAR HANDLE

Pottery, seventh century BC, Ramat Rahel excavations

Stamped jar handles like this came from the royal administration centres of the Kingdom of Judah, and may have been used as standard measures.

From this late Israelite Period, two objects may illustrate how administration, industry and trade were conducted. A jar handle (plate 77) comes from the royal citadel in Ramat Rahel and bears a stamped impression with a winged solar disk, inscribed with the words '[belonging to] the King – Mamshat'. Stamped jars of this type from the eighth to sixth centuries BC may have come from royal administration centres of the kingdom of Judah such as Mamshat, Hebron, Zyph and Socoh, all of which produced jars for wine, oil or grain. Some experts maintain that the stamp was an approved standard measure; others believe it served for tax collection. Raw silver pieces from the end of the period (plate 78) were possibly used as currency. If this explanation is correct, then silver pieces are one of the earliest forms of money. They were discovered in En Gedi, a centre for balm production and perfume, used both for curative and cult purposes. Probably a royal estate existed at this desert site and the importance of this estate would explain the existence of the precious ingots there.

The end of the Israelite Period was predicted by the Prophets: Samaria, the capital of the kingdom of Israel, was destroyed by the Assyrians in 721 BC. In 587 BC, the Babylonians conquered Jerusalem, and the period of Babylonian capitivity followed. It was earlier than the Jews expected that they were able to return to reconstruct their Temple in the Holy City.

78 (*right*)

SILVER INGOTS AND POT

End of Judaean monarchy, c. 600 BC, En Gedi excavations

En Gedi was an important centre for balm production at this time, so perhaps the ingots found there in this pot, were payment for the precious commodity.

PERIOD OF THE SECOND TEMPLE I: THE PHASE OF PERSIAN RULE (538–332 BC): After the prophecy of disaster, the prophecies of national rebirth were fulfilled. 'Thus saith Cyrus King of Persia, the Lord God of heaven . . . hath charged me to build Him an house at Jerusalem, which is in Judah' (Ezra, 1:2). A century passed before the walls and gates of Jerusalem could be rebuilt, but as early as 520 BC Jews returning from the Babylonian captivity began to rebuild the Temple (Ezra, 4:24). Until the conquest of Alexander the Great this region was considered a part of the Persian empire called Yehud in Aramaic. The official name appears on silver coins of the period (plate 79). The obverse shows the name and the imperial eagle, and the reverse an open flower, probably a lily. The designer of the coin masterfully solved the problem of creating clear and distinct designs on a surface of only eight and a half millimetres. In all probability the minting was local. A charming small gold earring in the form of a ram's head (plate 89), characteristic of the developed technique and the sophisticated style of the Achaemenian culture, was almost certainly executed in Persia.

Throughout this time Phoenician art and industry continued to flourish. The terracotta figurine of a pregnant woman (plate 80), found in a grave at Akhziv, shows an expectant mother, absorbed in meditation, of a type known from graves and sanctuaries along the length of the Syrian-Phoenician coast. Figurines of this and other types were mass-produced: they may have had (*inter alia*) a magical function, in this case divine help during childbirth.

From the middle of the eighth century BC a young and energetic power, the Greeks, were competing with the Phoenicians for the

80 (*right*)

FIGURINE OF PREGNANT WOMAN

Terracotta, Syrian-Phoenician type, fifth-fourth centuries BC, Akhziv excavations

One of several mass-produced mould-made terracotta types common throughout the period. Its expressiveness is testimony to the high artistic standard of the local potter.

79 (*below*)

'YEHUD' COIN

Silver, Persian Period, sixth-fourth centuries BC

(*From the collection of Hyman Bessin, Ottawa, Canada*)

Coin used in the Jerusalem area during the Persian domination; 'Yehud' is the Aramaic name for the administrative district.

Mediterranean trade. Gradually, they dominated the sea trade, their influence culminating in the cultural Hellenization of the Near East in the Hellenistic Period. Plate 81 shows an imported Attic oil bottle (lekythos), dating from the early fifth century BC, the time of the Persian Wars. At that time, the lekythos was a mass-produced cheap bottle used for the export of the famous Athenian oil throughout the Mediterranean. From left to right the rolled-out scene depicts the goddess Athena guarding Herakles, her favourite, dressed in his lion's skin, as he attacks two warriors; the first warrior is turning to his comrade for aid in his futile battle.

Some oil lamps made of clay (plate 82) complete the survey of objects used in the day-to-day life at this time. The small folded lamp in the foreground, a simple local development of the Iron Age standard type, was apparently never 'popular', but was nevertheless useful enough to endure from the late Israelite to the Herodian Period. The simple Greek type (middle left), was very common in the eastern Mediterranean throughout Persian and Hellenistic times; in Greece it was coated and polished, in Palestine it was usually left clay-coloured. Towards the right of the plate are two local lamps imitating Hellenistic prototypes; they were often grey or sometimes their natural clay-colour. The only unusual piece of the group is the Hellenistic lamp-filler in the shape of a boar's head.

81 (*above*)

ATTIC BLACK-FIGURE LEKYTHOS

Battle scene (rolled-out) from a pottery oil-bottle
Early fifth century BC, Bat Yam
A battle scene showing Athena aiding her favourite, Herakles, against two warriors, decorating one of the many mass-produced Attic vases used as containers for the export of Athenian oil.

82 (*right*)

OIL LAMPS AND LAMP-FILLER

Various local types of pottery
Persian-Hellenistic Periods, from various sites
With the exception of the lamp-filler, all these lamps were common household utensils of the time. The Greek influence on their style is obvious.

PERIOD OF THE SECOND TEMPLE II: THE HELLENISTIC PHASE (332–37 BC) – RULE OF PTOLEMIES (312–198), SELEUCIDS (198–167), MACCABEES AND HASMONAEANS (167–37): This short period was of major importance both to the orient and the occident. Alexander the Great aimed at a synthesis in his empire of east and west, but his idea could not endure. On the contrary, attempts to Hellenize in the various oriental countries strengthened traditional elements, especially in the religious sphere. Although within Judaism a liberal reaction towards Hellenization is evident, the uncompromising elements in the fight against religious coercion and political persecution of the Hellenistic powers prevailed. The Maccabees embody this defiant attitude, and, as E. Bickerman wrote, '. . . preserved the Judaism of the Greek period from both dissolution and ossification'.

While political events of the gravest consequences were taking place ordinary life pursued its normal pattern. A treasure of silver coins found in a simple clay jug at Tel Zippor (plate 83) introduces this aspect of the Hellenistic Period. It consists of fifty-nine tetradrachms, most of them with the portrait head of Alexander the Great, some marked with Aramaic graffiti, and of four local drachms, all dated *c.* 311 BC.

The transport amphoras (plate 84) are a further witness to the intense trade of the period. The large amphora may have been used to hold wine, oil or grain, while the one at its side is probably a local 'miniature' copy. The characteristic shape, with stump base and high handles, and with Greek stamps on them, enables specialists to identify the amphoras as coming from Rhodes, the greatest Hellenistic merchant port in the Mediterranean and the Black Sea. One of the stamps reproduced in plate 85 bears the name of the Chief Magistrate of Rhodes and also the month, 'in the term of Hieron, in [the month] Hyakinthios'; the other, the name 'Sokrates', who must be either the manufacturer of the jar or the exporter of its contents. His name has been found on other amphora handles uncovered in several cities of this region. Rhodes was a flourishing exporter of amphoras between 220–180 BC but after that time the Romans, for political reasons, made Delos the new trade centre between east and west.

A series of Graeco-Roman sculptures in the Museum give us an idea of the sophisticated culture of this and the following period in the country. Slightly less than life-size, the marble statue of a dancing satyr (plate 86) from Caesarea Maritima, the seat of the Roman governors in Herodian times, represents a good Roman copy of a lost Hellenistic original, one of the many which must have existed in the region since Hellenistic rule and culture had invaded the Land of the Bible. The marble youth, drunk with wine, has placed his instrument, a syrinx, on a tree trunk, and has taken a few dancing steps to catch

83

HOARD OF ALEXANDER TETRADRACHMS

Silver coins and juglet of clay
Hellenistic Period, c. 310 BC,
Tel Zippor excavations

Coin hoards are important in determining the types of currency used at a certain period in a certain region. The different coins in such hoards also show the commercial relations of the time.

84 (*left*)

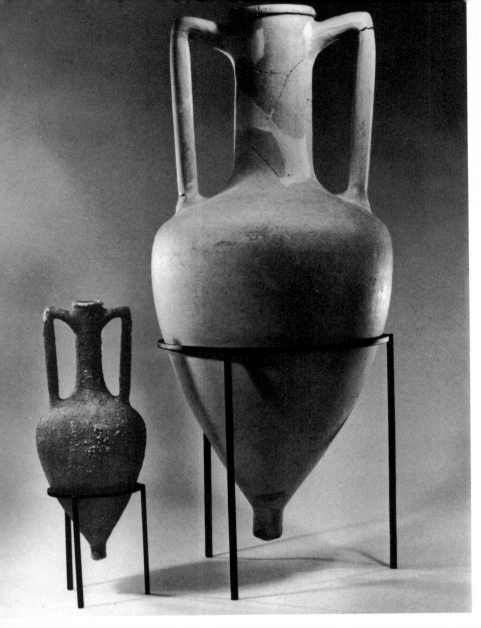

STAMPED RHODIAN JAR AND SMALL IMITATION

Pottery, Hellenistic Period, Rhodian jar from Tel Mor excavations, and imitation from Deir el-Asad

The large amphora was probably used for the transport of export goods, like oil or grain, for, until 180 BC Rhodes was a very important commercial centre.

86 (*right*)

STATUE OF YOUNG SATYR

Marble, Roman copy of Hellenistic original, Caesarea Maritima excavations

Graeco-Roman statues like this are found in all the provinces of the Roman Empire.

85 (*below*)

GREEK STAMPS ON RHODIAN JAR

Pottery, Hellenistic Period, Tel Mor excavations

The numerous stamped jar handles, found all over the Mediterranean lands, help archaeologists to date the finds in which they occur.
The jar in plate 84 was made (A) 'in the term of Hieron' (Rhodes' chief magistrate), and exported or manufactured by (B) 'Sokrates'.

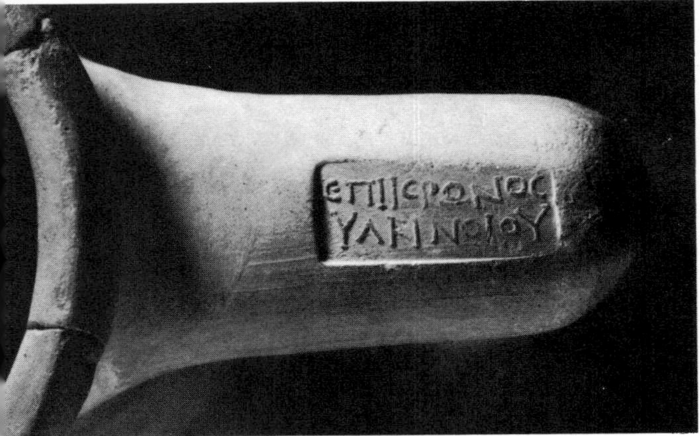

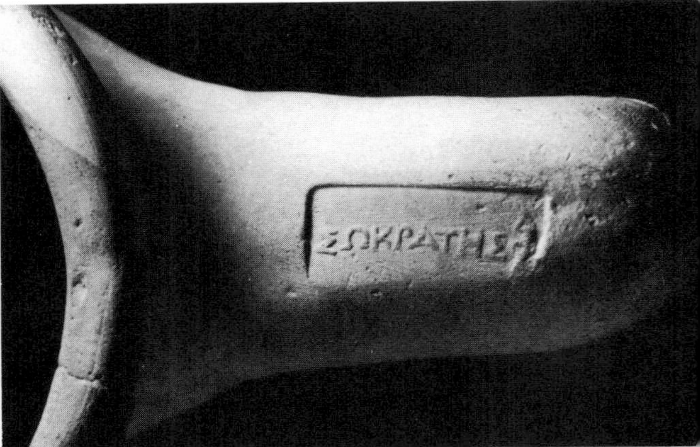

87
COIN OF MATTATHIAS ANTIGONUS
Bronze, 40–37 BC
Reverse: 'of the King' (in Greek) and menorah
(Collection of the Archaeological Institute, the Hebrew University, Jerusalem)
The menorah on this coin, minted during the time of the Maccabaean king, is the earliest known representation of Judaism's most important symbol in ancient times. Today it is the emblem of the state of Israel.

the tail of a small panther at his feet. The statue is a harmonious Hellenistic interpretation of the Dionysiac cult, which in archaic Greek art was rough and often demonic, but in Hellenistic times generally idyllic and bucolic. The statues of the period were erected in heathen temples, the palaces of rulers or the villas of nobles. For Jews these Greek depictions of the gods were graven images and idolatrous and Greek art, for this reason, was never to become established in the region. Hellenism remained a conflict-inspiring influence, eventually to become a passing episode in the history of the Land.

Anti-Hellenistic monuments of the Maccabaean Period are, naturally, extremely rare. The small coins of the Maccabees are carefully conceived representations of national and religious significance. The ordinary symbols on these coins are cornucopias, laurel wreaths, etc. However, on a coin minted by Mattathias Antigonus (40–37 BC), the last Maccabaean ruler, we see the name 'Antigonus', (the Greek name of the priestly king, written in Greek), and a depiction of the seven-branched candelabrum (plate 87). The chief symbol of Judaism until the present day, the seven-branched candelabrum was doubly significant for the Jews of that period: it was connected with the seven-branched Temple candelabrum as well as with the Channukah lamp. The Feast of Channukah was instituted in 165 BC by an earlier rebel, Yehudah Maccabee, who cleansed and rededicated the Temple in Jerusalem. In honour of this event Channukah has been annually celebrated ever since. The obverse of the coin shows the Showbread Table and the Hebrew legend 'Mattathias the High Priest and the Community of the Jews'. An analysis of the few extant specimens of this coin proves that there was less copper in their composition than in earlier mintings. This fact probably points to the inflation which then existed because of the political manoeuvres of the Romans and Parthians. But the coins are invaluable; with the exception of written documents they are the only remains of this heroic group.

PERIOD OF THE SECOND TEMPLE III (ROMAN EMPIRE I): THE HERODIAN PHASE (37 BC–AD 73) – PERIOD OF MISHNA AND TALMUD I (ROMAN EMPIRE II: AD 73 – EARLY THIRD CENTURY): During the Roman periods this region actively participated in world history more than at any previous time. The fusion of oriental and occidental cultures which began with Alexander reached its summit in the Herodian Phase, when the Roman empire replaced the Hellenistic powers. In the religious sphere, we witness the activity of the Qumran sect, the beginnings of Christianity, and the construction of the Temple in Jerusalem in the last quarter of the first century BC. Shortly after, we note the destruction of the Temple (AD 70) and the Wars of Liberation against Rome (AD 70–3 and 132–5). During this second Roman Period, the rabbinical centres moved to Yavne and Usha, and the Mishna, a collection of rabbinical interpretations and precepts on the Mosaic Law, was completed (*c.* AD 200), and several important synagogues were built in the Galilee region. These are only a few of the major events of this age of tumult, of rebels and visionaries, a time which had incalculable impact on the lives and thoughts of succeeding generations of both Jews and Christians.

Four oil lamps (plate 88) nicely represent the four major cultures during the Herodian Phase. The Hellenistic, represented by the grey 'Ephesos' lamp (bottom right), the local Herodian, commonly found in Jewish tombs (top right), the early Imperial Roman, represented by the 'discus' lamp with gladiators (bottom right), and the Alexandrian, as seen in a bronze lamp shaped like a barbarian's head. All the lamps come from the Nabataean town of Avedat in the Negev, one of the stops on a caravan road linking Egypt to the Parthian empire and to India, the Mediterranean to the Red Sea. The Nabataeans were important traders during the late first century BC and the first half of the next century.

Among the finest objects in Jewish art are the ossuaries mainly from the rock tombs of Jewish families around Jerusalem and Caesarea Maritima in Herodian times (plate 93). In the Museum these ossuaries are arranged on a platform backed by a picture of approximately the original size, reproducing an inner wall of one of these graves in the Sanhedriyah Quarter. Bones were kept in shafts (kokhim) of about two metres depth; after a year, to make room for other family members, they were deposited in the ornamented ossuaries. Sometimes the name of the deceased was written on the soft limestone in Aramaic and/or Greek. The re-burial practices were contrary to Jewish tradition and probably related to some eschatological concepts of resurrection. The custom seems to have been restricted to Jerusalem from about 50 BC until AD 70.

A rare first-century AD monument pertaining to a major figure in the Christian Gospels was found by the Italian excavators at Caesarea

89 (*right*)

GOLD EARRING

In shape of ram's head, Achaemenian workmanship, sixth-fourth centuries BC, Ashdod excavations

The sophistication of this earring suggests that it was Persian and not a local product.

90 (*overleaf left*)

GLASS VESSELS OF THE ROMAN PERIOD

(*left to right*)

TWO UNGUENTARIA, *free-blown*

JUGLET OF SIDONIAN STYLE, *mould-blown*

RIBBED BOWL, *mould-pressed*

All: Early Roman Imperial Period

The invention, probably at Sidon, of a technique for glass-making, either in moulds or free-blown, allowed for the first time the mass-production of delicate and cheap glass vessels.

91 (*overleaf right*)

GLASS VESSELS OF THE BYZANTINE PERIOD

In contrast to the functional style of Roman glass vessels, Byzantine glass is 'baroque' in form and decoration. The craftsmen no longer imitated the forms of ceramic wares, but explored the possibilities of the new medium.

88 (*left*)

FOUR OIL LAMPS

Pottery and (top left) bronze Hellenistic and Roman Periods, Avdat excavations

These oil lamps, representing the main cultural trends of the Hellenistic and early Roman Periods, come from the Nabataean town of Avdat and give further evidence of its importance as a trading centre.

92 (*left*)

FIGURINE OF DEFIANT PANTHER

Bronze, Hellenistic-Nabataean style, first century AD, Avdat excavations

A tiny masterpiece, the panther was found with other figurines suggesting that they were copies, in miniature, of originals at Alexandria, as parallel types have been found there.

93 (*above*)

OSSUARIES

Limestone, Jerusalem area, 50 BC – AD 70

Although contrary to Jewish tradition, for a short while in the area around Jerusalem, it was the custom to re-bury the dead in these ossuaries.

Maritima (plate 94). Christianity was then an underground movement and tangible remnants of the sect hardly exist in this region. The Latin inscription on the stone block reads, '. . . Tiberieum – . . . [Po]ntius Pilatus [. . . Praefectus] Iuda[ea]e . . .' which translated means, 'The Prefect (not Procurator as has been generally assumed until now) Pontius Pilate erected a building, the "Tiberieum", in honour of the Emperor Tiberius.' This document is the only known non-literary reference to Pontius Pilate.

After the Roman prefects and procurators had plundered the country during their period of rule AD 6 to 66 (except for the brief reign of the Jewish king Agrippa I), the Jews revolted. The capital was conquered and a central government set up. The top of plate 95 shows a thick silver shekel minted at this time with three pomegranates and the intentionally archaic Hebrew legend 'Jerusalem the Holy'; and on the reverse, a metal chalice and 'Shekel Israel' and 'Year Three', i.e. AD 68–9, the third year of the revolt. The emblems

95 (*right*)

COINS OF THE JEWISH WARS, AND 'JUDAEA CAPTA' COIN

(*top*) SILVER SHEKEL *of the First Jewish War* (*AD 66–73*)
Obverse: Stem with three pomegranates; 'Jerusalem the Holy'
Reverse: Chalice; 'Year Three . . . Shekel Israel'

(*centre*) BRONZE COIN
Reverse: 'Judaea Capta – S(*enatus*) *C*(*onsulto*)'
Obverse: (*not reproduced*) *Bust of Titus*

(*bottom*) SILVER TETRADRACHM *of the Second Jewish War* (*AD 132–5*)
Obverse: Temple façade; 'Simon' (*Bar-Kochba*)
Reverse: lulav; 'For the Freedom of Jerusalem'

(*All from the Reifenberg Collection, Jerusalem*)

Coins, like the lower one, bear legends such as 'For the Freedom of Jerusalem'.

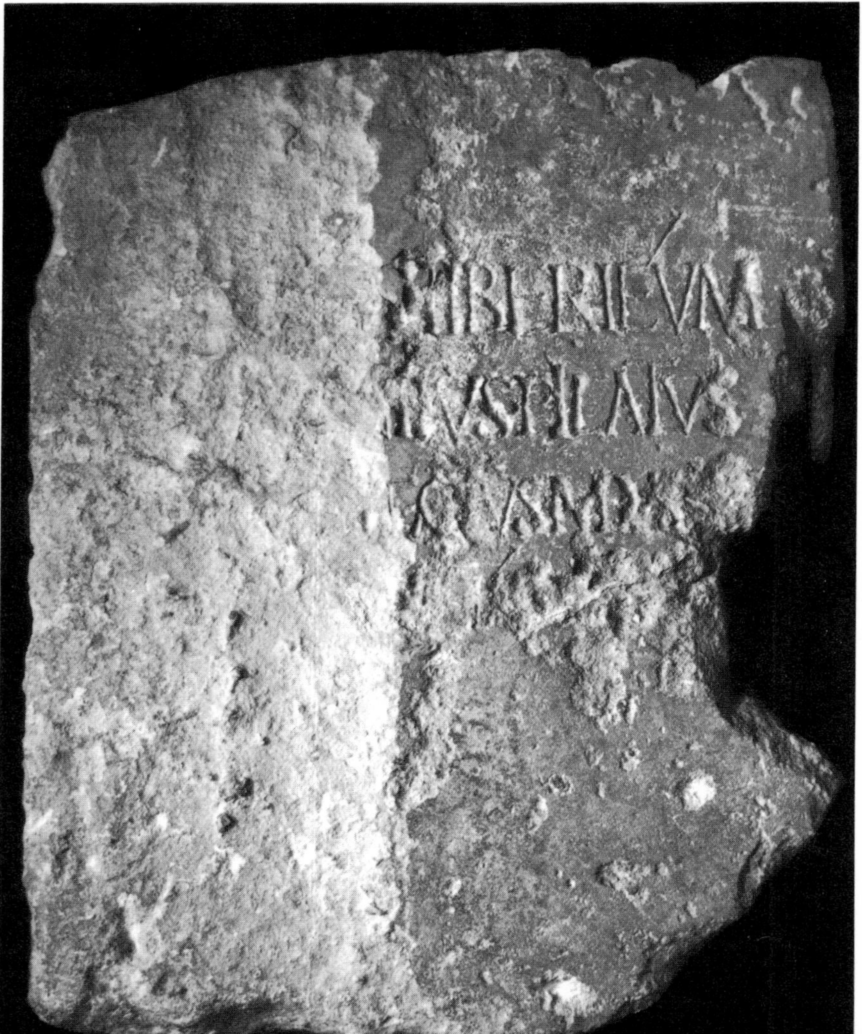

94 (*left*)

DEDICATORY INSCRIPTION OF PONTIUS PILATE

Limestone
AD 26–36, Caesarea Maritima excavations

The Roman prefect, Pontius Pilate, commemorates here completion of the 'Tiberieum', that he had built at Caesarea in honour of the Roman Emperor Tiberius.

CAPTA
SC

and legends on silver coins were neutral, but contemporary bronze coins printed clear propaganda, such as 'For the Redemption of Zion', and 'Freedom of Zion'. Pictorial symbols such as the lulav and etrog were derived from the national feast of Tabernacles, Sukkot. In AD 70 the Roman Legions, led by Titus, took Jerusalem after a five month siege. The Temple and the Holy City were completely destroyed, its citizens killed or enslaved. However, the Jewish resistance continued until AD 73 when Masada fell.

Masada stands on top of a natural rock fortress high above the Dead Sea. The site was excavated by Yigael Yadin, and with the help of the objects and photographic enlargements the Israel Museum held a comprehensive exhibition of Masada (plate 96), in 1966. The exhibition attempted to contrast the astonishing Herodian architectural feats with the pathetic remnants of the Jewish Zealots: palace architecture and once overflowing store-rooms against prayer shawls, leather sandals, iron arrow-heads, pots, baskets, ropes. These objects were all that remained of the people who committed mass suicide rather than submit to the Roman tyrants. Ten ostraca inscribed with the names of the Zealots were the highlight of the exhibition; they may refer to the ones mentioned in Josephus' *War of the Jews*: 'They then chose ten men by lot out of them to slay all the rest'. (Book VIII, Chapter IX).

To celebrate their victory the Romans minted the coin with the legend 'Judaea Capta' (plate 95, centre). A Jewish captive stands to the left of a palm tree, and to the right of the tree a personification of Judaea sits and mourns, head in hand. On the obverse, there is a profile of Titus, the conqueror of Jerusalem and later the Roman emperor. This type of coin continued to be minted after the time of Vespasian and Titus until the reign of Domitian, to 'broadcast' Roman dominance.

Only sixty years later, when the Emperor Hadrian attempted to build a sanctuary for Jupiter Capitolinus on the site of the Temple, a second armed revolt began. Led by Simon Bar-Kochba, the Jews resisted for four years (from AD 132–5) until at last the Romans crushed them. Jerusalem was destroyed again and Bar-Kochba fled with his followers to the rock-caves near the Dead Sea. In one of these almost totally inaccessible caves, where the rebels managed to survive under formidable physical conditions, the Bar-Kochba letters were found (see pages 146–7). Coins from this period also exist (plate 95, bottom). What may be the front of the Temple in Jerusalem is depicted, with the Torah shrine in the centre, and the name 'Simon', a reference to Bar-Kochba. On the right, the coin with the lulav and etrog has on it, 'Year of the Freedom of Israel'. Other Jewish coins of the period show Temple implements and local flora; all are simple and impressive in style.

96

ARTICLES FOUND AT MASADA

Even during a rebellion domestic life has to continue. That of the Zealots, during their occupation of Masada (AD 66–73), is reflected by these articles, jars, funnels, mortars, baskets and even a set of measuring cups.

After AD 135 Hadrian transformed Jerusalem into a Roman city named Aelia Capitolina. The Tenth Roman Legion remained to guard the city until the third century. In times of peace the Legion's soldiers made pottery roof-tiles, stamped with the words 'Legio X Fretensis' (plate 97). On the top right fragment we see a boar, the symbol of the Legion; in the third century, the same Legion called itself 'Antoniniana' (bottom right).

Protected by the Legions, high Roman officers, administrators and merchants adorned their living quarters, public places and sanctuaries with marble statues, ordering copies of Greek originals (creative Greek art did not outlast Hellenistic times). All the Graeco-Roman marble statues in the Museum are Roman copies of non-extant Greek originals. Statues such as the 'Artemis of Ephesus' (plate 99) or the Griffon of Nemesis (plate 98) blend Hellenistic and Roman with oriental elements, both in form and content. Although the head of the 'Artemis' has not been preserved, there is no doubt that a goddess, slightly larger than life, is intended (plate 99). She has the rigid and archaistic attitude of a cult-statue. Forty-three fertility symbols, either breasts or eggs, cover her body, and on her pectoral, a nymph

97 (*above*)

THREE STAMPED POTTERY TILES OF THE TENTH LEGION

(*top*) *fragment, stamped with a boar, first century AD, Jerusalem*
(*bottom*) *fragment, stamped 'Antoniniana', name of the Legion, early third century AD, Jerusalem*
(*left*) *complete, stamped 'Leg(io) X Fr(etensis)', third century AD, Ramat Rahel*

The Roman Tenth Legion was garrisoned at Jerusalem until the third century. The boar was the Legion's symbol.

98 (*left*)

WINGED GRIFFON OF NEMESIS, WITH 'WHEEL OF FATE'

Marble, Trajanic style (AD 98–117), found at Erez

A Greek inscription on the statue's plinth reads: 'In the year 522 (of the Seleucid era, AD 210) I, Mercury, (son) of Alexander, set up (this statue) while being a priest.'

99 (*right*)

ARTEMIS EPHESIA

Marble, Graeco-Roman style, second century AD, Caesarea Maritima

Only Roman copies of the original Hellenistic cult-statue of Artemis of Ephesus survive, but they follow closely the blend of Oriental and Hellenistic features.

and winged victory goddess are depicted in relief. On her skirt are thirty small square frames, each containing a symbol, such as a sphinx or a griffon. These ritual draperies (ependytes) belong no doubt to the Greek goddess Artemis of the Ephesians, the mother goddess originally venerated in Asia Minor, whose temple in Ephesus was one of the Seven Wonders of the Ancient World. On one of his journeys, when the Apostle Paul was attempting to convert the citizens of Ephesus to Christianity, he was hounded out of the city with the cry 'Great is the Artemis of the Ephesians!' (Acts of the Apostles, 19). Numerous Roman copies of Artemis or Diana Ephesia attest to the widespread cult of this goddess in Roman times. This statue was found in Caesarea, and is probably derived from a Hellenistic statue created in the tradition of an older cult image of the goddess.

The Winged Griffon of Nemesis (plate 98) belongs to the same category of Roman copies of orientalised Hellenistic works. The griffon is the hybrid of the body of a lioness, the head and wings of a bird of prey, and the tail of a serpent. This fabulous beast places its paw on the 'wheel of fate'. The ancient oriental concept of the griffon penetrated the Archaic Greek world in the eighth century BC and in the Classic Period the beast became merged with Nemesis, the Greek goddess of revenge and fate; her wheel symbolises destiny. The cult of Nemesis was popular in the eastern provinces of the Roman empire. If a Nemesis cult existed in this region, our griffon, a good copy of Trajan's time, may have been a cult statue for it.

The bronze figurine of a defiant panther (plate 92) with an open mouth and a raised left paw has the liveliness of a late Hellenistic original. Along with other bronze figurines of Greek and oriental divinities it was found in Avdat, the Nabataean caravan settlement in the Negev. Some of these figurines may be small-size copies of large statues; parallel types are known from Alexandria. Perhaps the panther may have belonged to a cult of Dionysus or a Hellenistic divinity of oriental origin.

During the time of the Emperor Augustus (here, the Herodian Period), several technical inventions contributed decisively to the development of the artisan's craft: clay moulds for the mass-production of relief ceramics, and a glass-blowing technique for producing free-blown and mould-blown glass. For the first time the mass-production of clay and glass vessels of high quality was possible. Arretium (modern Arezzo) was the centre of this new clay industry, and Sidon, where the famous Phoenician glass-ware was made, became the new centre of the glass-blowing industry. The Sidonian craftsmen were so proud of their invention that many vessels were signed with their names (Ennion, Artas, etc.). The glass vessèl with the palm decoration (plate 90) is such a Sidonian product, and the perfume bottles to the left are free-blown. The ribbed bowl on the right, made

100 (*right*)

MOSAIC WITH REPRESENTATION OF FISH

Fragment of mosaic floor

Fourth century AD, Bet Shean excavations

Only the wealthy Greeks or Romans could afford to have villas with mosaic paving. Although dating from the fourth century, the delicate colouring suggests a strong Hellenistic influence.

102 (*overleaf*)

SYNAGOGUE MOSAIC PAVEMENT

Byzantine Period, sixth century AD, Synagogue at Bet Shean, Bet Shean excavations

The use of mosaics instead of flagstones for the floors of synagogues was introduced by Rabbi Abun in the first half of the fourth century AD.

101 (*right*)

FRESCO FROM A BYZANTINE MAUSOLEUM

Portrait medallion of a young man

c. fifth century AD, from a mausoleum at Or-Haner (Gift of Mr and Mrs K. Sobel, Hamilton (Canada), in memory of Timothy Fenston)

The portrait, one of the few surviving frescoes in the country, combines a free almost 'impressionistic' technique with the stern frontality so characteristic of Byzantine art.

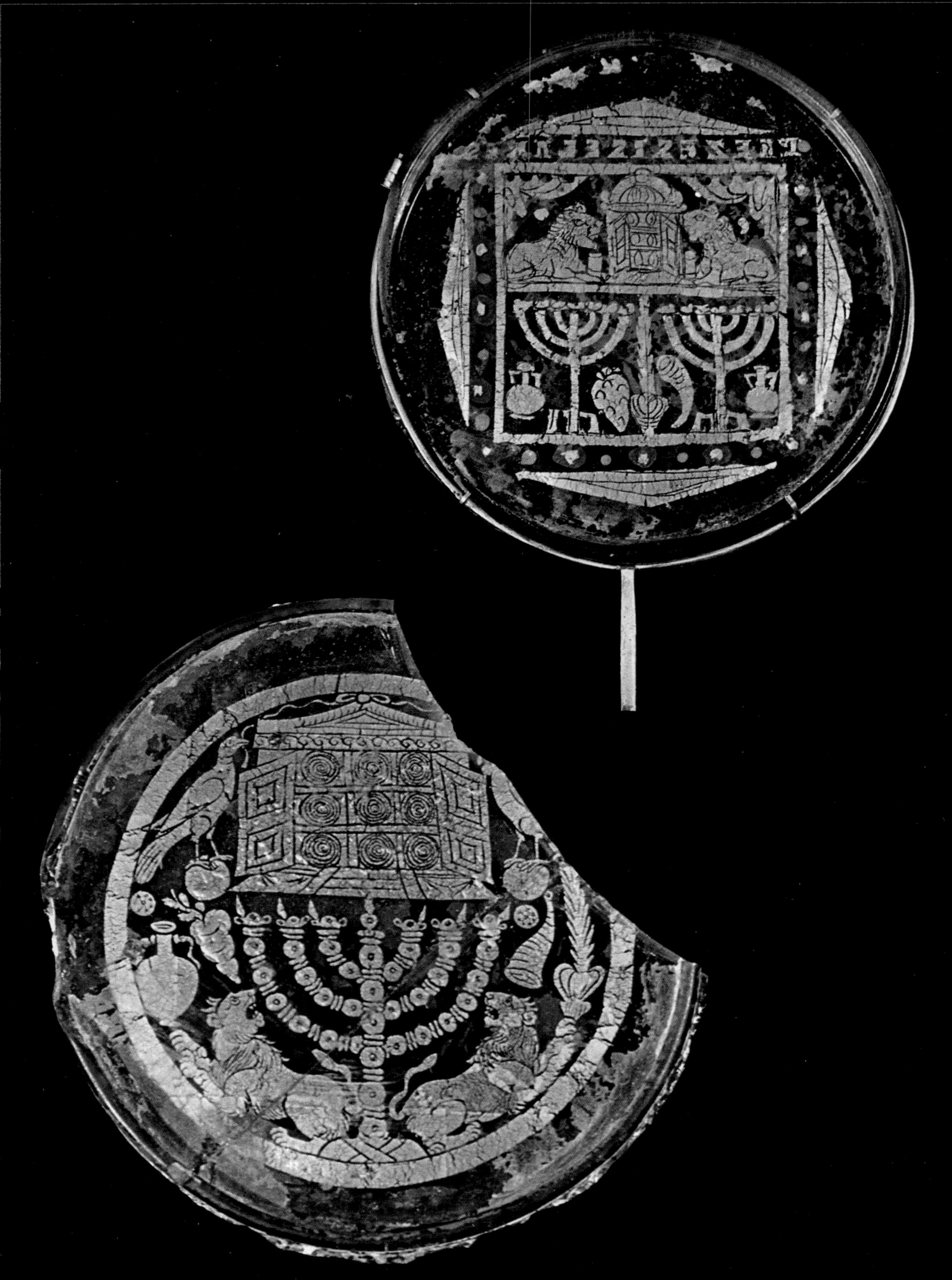

of thick glass, is mould-pressed by an earlier method. These glasses were extremely popular because they were both functional and elegant and at the same time comparatively cheap; to such an extent that they have been found throughout the reaches of the Roman empire.

PERIOD OF TALMUD II (BYZANTINE EMPIRE) – LATE THIRD CENTURY – AD 640: With the end of the Roman empire the movements toward fusion of east and west in Herodian times and toward Imperial uniformity in the Roman Period were reversed by the assertions of cultural autonomy in the provinces. The division of the empire into east (Byzantium) and west (Rome) encouraged increasing consciousness of regional traditions. Religious forces within Judaism became more intense in Palestine and in the Diaspora. The official recognition of Christianity by the Emperor Constantine was followed by the construction of ecclesiastical buildings and by formalised church programmes and concepts. The resistance which the Jews once directed against the Roman pagan forces was now redirected to challenge their successors, the Byzantine-Christian powers. This 'renaissance' in the disintegrating empire generally, and in Judaism particularly, led to the completion of the Jerusalem Talmud in *c.* AD 425 and of the Babylonian Talmud in *c.* AD 500. The Byzantine Period in Palestine ended with the conquest of the region by a new power and religious group, the Muslim Arabs, in AD 640.

Even objects of daily use reflect quite clearly the spiritual movements and trends of the period – the dying paganism and the oriental elements coming again to the foreground, the rising Christianity, and the self-renewing Judaism. If, for example, we compare the glass vessels of the Byzantine Period (plate 91) with those of the Roman Period (plate 90), the Byzantine group with its winding glass thread, its multi-coloured surfaces and bizarre forms give a 'baroque' impression. This 'barbarian' style exploits the uniquely flexible glass material more imaginatively than the functional Roman style had ever done. The older glass vessels seldom transcended the imitation of ceramic or metallic forms intended for specific uses. The glass vessels are fragile examples of the artistic creativity of the Byzantine craftsmen which was to pave the way for medieval art in the Near East and Europe.

The Byzantine Hall of the Museum exhibits three lead coffins round the central pillar, each representative of one of the three creeds of the period. For more explicit presentation only details are reproduced here. The earliest coffin, found in Jerusalem, still belongs to the latter part of the Roman Period, *c.* AD 200–250; pagan in style, it is decorated with wreaths, framed groups of Erotes, and a rope design (plate 104, top, a detail of the side). The Christian lead coffin of the

103
TWO JEWISH GOLD GLASSES
Byzantine Period, fourth century AD, probably from Jewish catacombs in Rome
(Both are the gift of Jakob Michael, New York, in memory of his wife, Erna Sondheimer-Michael)
The representation of the Ark of the Law in the synagogue is, after the menorah, the most popular theme on Jewish ceremonial objects of the Roman-Byzantine periods.

fifth century (plate 104, centre), also from Jerusalem, is decorated in relief with wreaths and ropes. The Jewish lead sarcophagus (plate 104, bottom, a detail of the side) probably dates from the fourth century AD and came from a grave in Bet Shearim. Its stamped relief friezes above and below contain amphoras, grapes and vine-leaves; the middle belt is divided into lozenges through a bead-and-reel pattern filled with petalled rosettes. A seven-branched candelabrum, the menorah, has been superimposed in ten places on the surface of the coffin. Birds drinking from a bowl and human heads decorate other portions. This profusion of mixed motifs betrays the origin of the sarcophagus. Originally it was a pagan coffin, Dionysiac in character, but through the superimposed menorah stamp, it has been transformed into something 'kosher', or Jewish. The Christian community were likewise to 'convert' sarcophagi. For instance, on a lead sarcophagus from Phoenician Sidon, identical with ours, Christian overstamps and monograms were combined with the Greek word 'fish', the cryptic symbol of Christianity. In Phoenician Sidon there was a workshop for prefabricated pagan lead coffins which could be fitted with Jewish or Christian symbols according to the client's wishes. The practice can also be seen in Byzantine lamps, glass-ware and mosaics.

For the Jew it was now permissible to portray the human face. 'The rabbis could not withstand the spirit of the times, caused by the spread of Hellenism, and made concessions in the interpretation of the commandment "Thou shalt not make unto thee any graven image" (Exod., 20:4). They laid stress on what followed: "Thou shalt not bow down to them nor serve them". So long as there was no suspicion of idolatry, they were not strict; beyond this point Judaism permitted no compromise' (N. Avigad).

A fragment of a mosaic pavement from a villa in Bet Shean (ancient Skythopolis) gives an idea of pagan art in this region. The fringe fragment (plate 100) depicts three fish swimming towards water flowers, though the naturalistic rendering of water is lacking. Another fragment of the same mosaic frieze depicts the struggle of the cranes against the dwarf people or pygmies, a subject taken from Greek mythology. The villa may have belonged to wealthy Greeks or Romans. The almost impressionistic style, with delicate colour nuances and a sure depiction of movement, seems to fit into the late Hellenistic tradition, as comparisons with earlier mosaics from Pompeii or neighbouring Antiochia show. However, this mosaic probably dates from the late third or early fourth century AD.

Plate 101 shows one of the few fresco paintings preserved in this country. The portrait medallion of a young man with, at his right, what seems to be a torch was transferred to the Museum from the wall of a Byzantine mausoleum near Ascalon, together with a female portrait. The long walls of the rectangular mausoleum hall were

104

THREE LEAD SARCOPHAGI

(top) Pagan sarcophagus
First half of the third century AD, Jerusalem

(centre) Christian sarcophagus
Fifth century AD, Jerusalem

(bottom) Jewish sarcophagus
Fourth century AD, Bet Shearim excavations

The sarcophagi represent the three main creeds in vogue during the late Roman and Byzantine periods.

105 (*left*)

CHRISTIAN CHANCEL SCREEN AND POST

Marble, Byzantine Period, fifth-sixth centuries AD

Post: from a church at Horvat Hadat

Screen: from a church at Massuot Yizhaq

Chancel screens and posts found in this region testify to the flourishing church building which began under Constantine (AD 306–37), and reached its peak in the sixth and seventh centuries.

106 (*right*)

CHRISTIAN OBJECTS

BRONZE LAMP *with cross-shaped handle, on bronze stand*

BRONZE LAMP *with cross-shaped handle and bull's head on lid*

Both: Bet Shean excavations

POTTERY AMPULLA, *decorated in relief with representation of Annunciation and Greek inscription*

Provenance unknown

CLAY PLAQUE *in shape of fish, inlaid with 'mirror' against the evil eye*

Horvat Zikrin excavations

All: Byzantine Period, fourth-seventh centuries AD

However obscure, these objects all had a Christian significance: the lamps were used for domestic and liturgical purposes, the ampulla contained holy water and the apotropaic fish was a precaution against evil.

painted with fourteen portrait medallions, eleven male and three female. One feels tempted to call this central burial hall an 'Ancestors' Gallery'. In contrast to the fish mosaic, the style of this fresco painting, in spite of the free technique, already points to the strict frontal approach, with the frozen stare to the left directed at the supernatural, so typical of Byzantine ceremonial style. The proposed date for this mosaic is the fifth century AD. Over the gate of the mausoleum hall, a Greek inscription beckons: 'Enter – no one is immortal.'

In Byzantine churches the chancel was raised on one or two steps and closed in on three sides by a solid stone fence. The officiating priests were separated from the congregation, which stood in the naves, but the fence was low enough for the congregation to watch the whole of the divine service. Plate 105 shows a marble chancel screen with wreath, leaf garlands and crosses in relief, and a typical chancel screen post with a bulbous top, both of which came from Byzantine churches of the fifth and sixth centuries. Byzantine Christian art craft developed a certain number of standard types for use in religious and daily life which were constantly subject to variations.

We can safely assume that the Christian Church was under the special protection of the Byzantine emperors. However, Christian art of the period is bound to the severe framework of the liturgy. The artist completely disappears behind his work. Even modest implements like the one shown in plate 106 have a ceremonial character. The bronze candelabrum to the front (right), with a 'Maltese' cross for a handle and a bull's head on the lid, was intended to be put on top of a candelabrum-stand, as was the lamp in the background (right). The small clay ampulla in the background (left) features the

Annunciation to Mary; the angel's words are written in Greek round the picture. This ampulla and ones like that of the Egyptian saint, Menas, usually shown with two camels, served to store holy water from the Nile or the Jordan. An even more interesting object is the flat clay fish. The small ringlets probably suggest fish scales, but the round depression in the middle is rather puzzling. In the same fifth-century grave near Bet Govrin, south of Jerusalem, where the fish was found, a cross pendant made of bronze and a disk-shaped object with a corresponding round depression were also uncovered. In this context the fish plaque is probably a Christian amulet. A series of such plaques exist, made of clay or soft limestone, with pagan or even Jewish symbols (cf. the plaque in plate 107). Remnants of glass were found in the plaques' depressions and it is now assumed that these depressions were once filled with glass and were some sort of charm 'against the evil eye, which had served their owners in life and were

107

JEWISH 'EVIL EYE' PLAQUE

Stone

Byzantine Period, c. fifth century AD

Pagans, Christians and Jews all seem to have used apotropaic devices, like this gabled plaque and the fish in plate 106, in their attempts to avert the 'evil eye'.

placed into their tombs with some hope that they might here, too, prove effective against the perils of afterlife' (L. Y. Rahmani). Just like the Sidonian lead coffins, the evil eye plaques could serve either Christian, Jewish or pagan patrons (cf. plates 106 and 107).

In the heart of the Judaean Hills, not far from Jerusalem, remains of a potter's workshop were discovered. Coins found there help to date the shop to the late third or early fourth century AD. The potter produced figurines and lamps of various types – again pagan (of Graeco-Roman and orientalised local types), Jewish and Christian. In plate 108 (top left and bottom left) we see two extremely fine pottery oil lamps; judging from the style and workmanship they probably come from the same workshop. On the lamp above, a menorah with three feet is flanked by a shofar and an incense shovel; on the lamp below, by an etrog and an incense shovel. The lamp at the right also shows the etrog and lulav. Although it is of coarser quality, it

108

THREE OIL LAMPS WITH MENORAH DESIGN

Pottery

(top and right)
From the Reifenberg Collection, Jerusalem
(bottom)
From the collection of the Archaeological Institute, the Hebrew University, Jerusalem
All: third-fourth centuries AD

The lamps at the top and bottom originated from local workshops, while the coarser quality and rather linear style of the one on the right suggests an Alexandrian origin.

109 (*left*)

MENORAH LAMP

Bronze
c. fourth century AD
(from the collection of Mrs Mizyam Shaar Schloessinger, New York. Loaned to the Museum in memory of the late Mr A. Reifenburg.)

Oil lamps were used for lighting the house, as consecration gifts for synagogues, and as funeral offerings in Jewish tombs and catacombs. This lamp, the finest extant ancient Jewish bronze lamp, certainly served a ritual purpose.

110 (*right*)

DIADEM

Gold band set with glass, stone and mother-of-pearl
Third century AD, from a tomb at Kefar Giladi

The barbarian 'polychrome' style in vogue during the latter part of the Roman Empire, and especially in the Byzantine period, was influenced by the Scythian and Sarmatian styles of jewelry.

is particularly interesting because its linear style suggests an origin in Alexandria, which in Hellenistic times had been the largest Diaspora community. However, when this lamp was made, during the third to fourth century AD, Alexandria was no longer a spiritual centre of Judaism. Finds of this type in Israel are a testimony to the trade relations of this land with the Diaspora communities. Another oil lamp, from Ascalon, featuring a menorah not reproduced here, belongs to a fourth century Carthaginian type, a specimen of which has been discovered in Trier, one of the Roman centres in the Rhineland. This lamp seems to be one of the earliest indications of Jewish life in the Rhineland. It is now generally assumed that Jews had settled in the Rhineland cities, especially Cologne, since late Roman and early Byzantine times as potters, glassmakers or goldsmiths.

Plate 109 reproduces the finest of all extant menorah lamps. This bronze lamp has a handle in the form of a menorah with cross bar, supported by a shofar (to the right) and an etrog and lulav (to the left); the original hinged lid is missing. The lamp would have 'sat' on a stand (cf. plate 106) and probably dates to the fourth century AD.

Plate 102 looks like a carpet but is a reproduction of a mosaic made up of thousands of tiny stones of various shapes and colours, giving an organic effect even to the columns and metal implements. This large and bright mosaic came from a pavement in a basilica style synagogue in Bet Shean of the sixth century AD. The design is framed on all sides with a broad, braid-like pattern; on three sides a spiralling wavy ornament has been added. In the centre, two columns support a gable and a raised curtain reveals an arched depiction of the Ark of the Law. Two monumental seven-branched candelabra flank the Ark. The remaining space is symmetrically filled with a shofar, incense

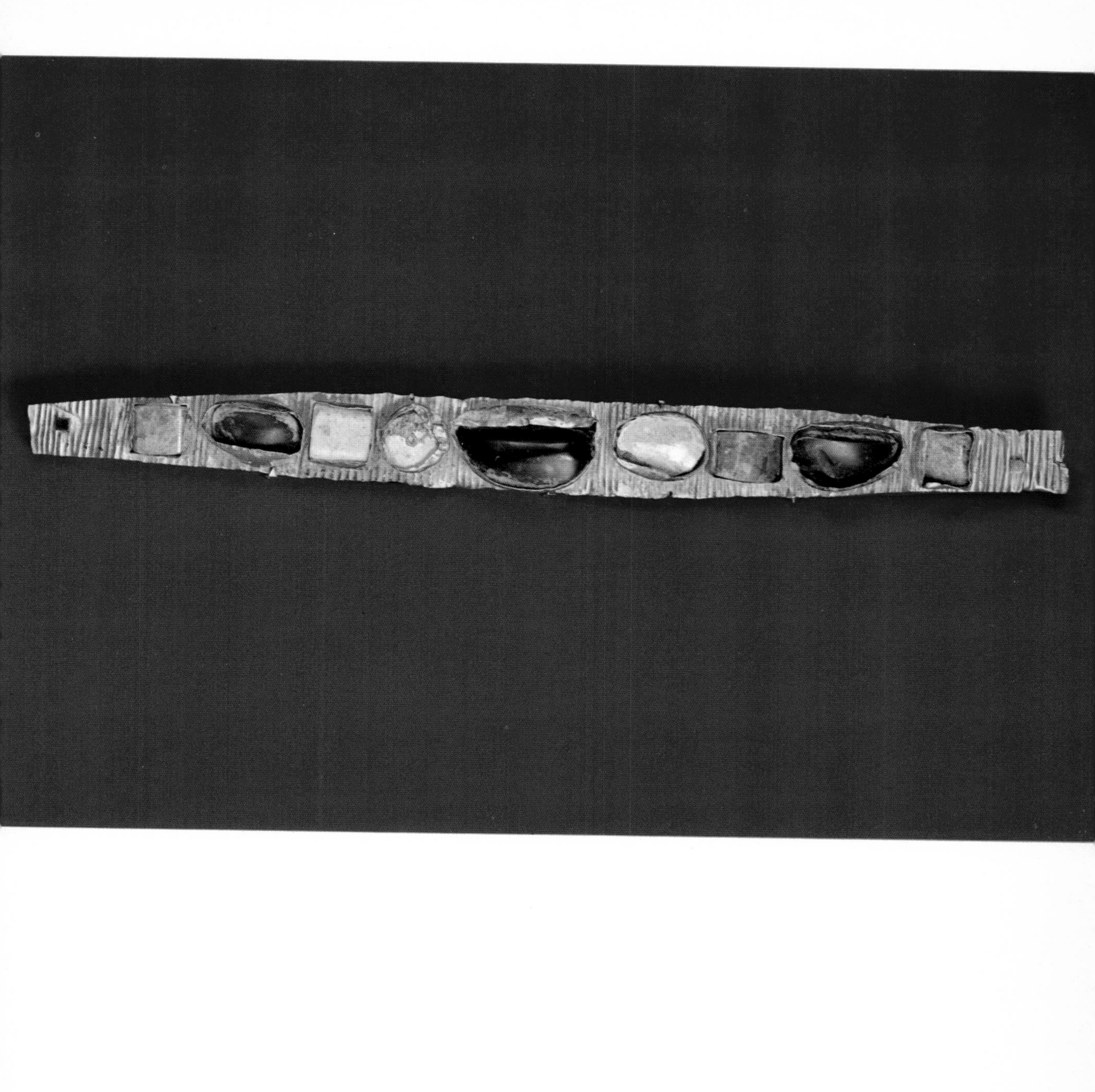

shovel and patterned ornaments. The spreading of cult implements and designs on a free surface contrasts with the somewhat realistic, two-layered architectural depiction in the centre. The style of spreading ritual objects on the surface to form an overall pattern is the compositional type of many depictions of synagogues in mosaics or gold glass. It is not clear whether the artist intended to depict a synagogue realistically or symbolically or whether he intentionally fused both concepts.

A similar style exists in the Museum's two gilded glasses (*fondi d'oro*) from the fourth-century Jewish catacombs in Rome. In plate 103 (top), we can see a depiction of the synagogue appurtenances divided into two registers: above, the open Ark of the Law contains the Scrolls and is guarded by two lions – statues of lions have actually been found in synagogues, as in Capernaum and Kfar Baram; below, we see two candelabra with burning lamps, lulav, shofar and etrog, and at the far corners two amphoras for oil. Above the rectangular frame a Greek drinking toast has been transliterated into Latin: 'Drink and live, Elares!' On the other gold glass the same implements plus a pair of birds on globes are arranged without a dividing line inside a circular frame. The gold glass was actually the gilded base of a drinking vessel with cut-out gold leaf placed between two layers of glass. It was a custom among the early Christians and the contemporary Jews to impress small objects, including drinking vessels, into the mortar of the freshly closed tomb wall for the easy identification of deceased relatives. As from Herod's time the Jewish community in Rome was large, the demand for ritual implements was great and it is assumed that the gold glass was produced by Jewish glass-makers there.

We now turn to Byzantine ceramics, the work done by simple potters for the daily use of the community, objects which in so many ways are invaluable to the archaeologist. Typical ceramics of this period are informally arranged in the Museum with a potter's wheel in two parts on the right (plate 112). The surprising feature of this pottery is that it has no similarity to the ceramics of the preceding periods, with their fusion of western and eastern stylistic elements; rather, it is reminiscent of the solid, earthy vessels of the Israelite period, although the pronounced ribbing adds a baroque element. The twenty-two rooms in Bet Shean, where these objects were found, contained large quantities of ceramics, bronze, iron, glass and stone implements, and an installation of a well, water supply and other conveniences, indicating a comparatively high standard of living in Byzantine Palestine.

At no other time in antiquity or in the ensuing Middle Ages was the country so densely populated as in Byzantine times. Several Byzantine objects (plate 113) allow us to have a glimpse into the life of a Jewish farmer who lived in Even Menahem, in the Galilee region.

111

ARAB GOLD JEWEL HOARD

Found in glazed pot the hoard includes:

SIX LARGE GOLD BEADS, *with granulation*

SIX FILIGREE GOLD BEADS, *globular and biconical*

(*right*) BEADS, *carnelian and glass*

(*left*) BRONZE AMULET, *with a Koranic verse*

Caesarea Maritima

The superb craftsmanship of the articles found in the hoard, gives a good indication of the highly civilized Islamic city culture in medieval times.

That the paterfamilias was a farmer we can infer from the remains in his grave, such as the iron farm implements to be seen on the floor of the showcase. His name was inscribed in Greek over one of the burial niches: 'Joseph's kokh' (see the photograph in the showcase). To the right, we see a selection from over seven hundred small objects found on the burial site. Over a hundred coins permit us to date the grave to the end of the third century AD.

The 'royal' aspect of Byzantine life can only be suggested by the glittering diadem in plate 110. Taken from a grave of the third century AD, this gold jewel has nine different precious stones inserted into the ribbed gold band. Of uneven size and form, baroque in colour and shape, the gems contrast strikingly with the simple gold band. The Byzantines borrowed this 'barbarian' idea of adornment from the Scythian and Sarmatian peoples of southern Russia. The 'polychrome style' existed during the Roman empire, particularly in Syria, but reached the heights of its achievements in the sixth century AD at the imperial court in Constantinople. The wall-mosaic of the distinguished Empress Theodora, wife of Justinian, in San Vitale, Ravenna, artistically expresses the connection of royalty with representational jewelry, symbol of imperial power.

We shall conclude our survey of the archaeological division of the

112

BYZANTINE POTTERY

TWO JUGS

ONE MUG

(*right*) POTTER'S WHEEL OF STONE

All: Byzantine Period, Bet Shean excavations

Although solidly functional and obviously intended for daily use, the ribbed almost 'baroque' style of this pottery is reminiscent of the decorative Byzantine glass.

113
SHOWCASE: A JEWISH FARMER'S TOMB
(left to right)
POTTERY LAMP
AGRICULTURAL IMPLEMENTS OF IRON
GLASS VESSELS
JEWELRY AND COINS
Byzantine Period, fourth century AD
The photograph in the showcase shows the name of the deceased: 'Joseph's kokh' (i.e. burial niche or grave). The agricultural tools found in the tomb indicate that Joseph was a farmer.

Israel Museum with a glimpse at early Arab and Crusader antiquities. These are two periods which so far it has not been possible to arrange properly pending expansion of the Museum.

The golden jewelry of the Fatimid Period (AD 969–1171) is totally different from the Byzantine diadem but equally alluring. Found in Caesarea Maritima (plate 111), it was hidden in a small green and brown glazed pot, probably from the time of the Crusader siege of the Arab fortress in AD 1101. The six large beads, made of beaten gold-leaf and decorated with granular work, hang from the pot, with two large filigree gold beads and a large biconical bead. Behind it are three linked biconical beads, similar to the previous one but much smaller in size. To the right are carnelian and glass beads and to the left a bronze amulet with a verse from the Koran. In contrast to the 'barbarian' but sophisticated diadem of the Early Christian Period, this Arab gold adornment looks admittedly highly civilised, the creation of a ripe, urban civilisation, but nevertheless still carries an aura of *A thousand and one nights*. The Crusader Period is represented by an acanthus capital of the eleventh century AD from the Church of the Annunciation at Nazareth (plate 114). The grotesque face with bulging, penetrating eyes, a broad open mouth, a protruding tongue, and the teeth of a beast of prey, reminds us of gargoyles, the water-

114
CRUSADER CAPITAL (*Detail*)
Stone
Eleventh century AD, from excavations at the Church of the Annunciation, Nazareth
A striking piece of medieval architectural sculpture, this grotesque head was probably made by a French sculptor taking part in the Crusades.

spewing monsters of French cathedrals. This similarity is no product of chance; like the Church of the Holy Sepulchre in Jerusalem, the Church of the Annunciation in Nazareth was built with the help of French sculptors who took part in the Crusades and created or influenced the style and ornamentation of the building.

The display scheme of the Archaeological Museum was prescribed by the fact that ninety-five per cent of the exhibits are from scientific excavations. Situated in a country with a copious and vital archaeological past, the Museum is, most fortunately, independent of the vicissitudes of the international art market. The curators have first-hand information from excavators on the objects earmarked for exhibition, this permits a display based on historical principles – either by periods or typologically. So far the Museum has favoured the first method, adding a few systematic sections, such as a survey of documents written in ancient Hebrew, local coins in antiquity, and objects from neighbouring cultures. Considering that almost all the exhibited objects are from excavations conducted since 1948, we can confidently look forward to the future expansion and development of this central Museum for Biblical archaeology.

Magen Broshi **Scrolls from the Dead Sea**

One day in 1947 a Bedouin shepherd boy, searching for a stray goat, entered a cave near Khirbet Qumran and stumbled upon some jars containing ancient manuscripts (plate 116). In this way were discovered the seven Dead Sea Scrolls, which were to have such a revolutionary impact on historical and theological scholarship throughout the western world.

The Shrine of the Book (plates 117 and 118), the D. Samuel and Jeane H. Gottesman Centre for Biblical Manuscripts, keeps and exhibits these two thousand year old manuscripts. They came from three sites on the western shore of the Dead Sea – Khirbet Qumran (plate 115), the oldest and most important (*c.* 100 BC – AD 68), Masada, and the Cave of Letters in Nachal Hever.

115 (*left*) The Essenes, the sect that lived in the Khirbet Qumran region, would have had much the same view from the caves as present-day visitors: the hills and Dead Sea in the background and in the left foreground the monastery, though this is now in ruins.

The first seven scrolls were brought by the Bedouin to Bethlehem and Jerusalem for sale. Professor E. L. Sukenik of the Hebrew University was the first to identify them properly and in the same year that they had been discovered was able to purchase three. The other four were acquired in New York in 1954 by Professor Yigael Yadin with the help of the late D. Samuel Gottesman. All seven are now on display in the Shrine of the Book. The other documents displayed in the Shrine were found by Professor Yadin in the Cave of Letters (1960–1) and in Masada (1963–5).

These seven manuscripts cover a period of two and a half centuries, a period crucial in the history of the Jewish people, for it includes the end of the Second Commonwealth and the sixty-five years immediately following the destruction of the Second Temple. The period also saw the rise of Christianity and the ministries of John the Baptist, Jesus Christ and the Apostles and is, as well, distinguished by two major rebellions against the Romans in Palestine: the Great Revolt, from AD 66 to 73, and the Bar-Kochba Revolt, from AD 132 to 135.

116 (*below*) Two of the jars in which the seven Dead Sea Scrolls were found at Khirbet Qumran, measuring 65.7 cm. and 47.5 cm. in height, they had lain undisturbed in the cave from the time of the Great Revolt, circa AD 70, until their discovery in 1947.

Before discussing the Dead Sea Scrolls, however, a few words must be said about the Dead Sea Sect. This Jewish sect, which flourished during the last two centuries before the destruction of the Second Temple (AD 70) is known to us both from its own writings and from archaeological remains in Khirbet Qumran. Near the caves where the scrolls were found, a building was unearthed which must have served as a centre for the sect (plate 115). It is of a monastic type, made for communal life (as may be inferred, for instance, from the assembly-hall-refectory). It had workshops, store-rooms, and a scriptorium, with the benches and inkwells that one expects to find in such a place. The outstanding features of the site are the water installations and the seven cisterns, which must have been used for ritual baths.

The sect's ideology was based, generally speaking, on two main principles. The first was what can only be called an avid expectation

117 (*left*) The lower hall in the Shrine of the Book displays finds from the time of the Bar-Kochba revolt. The rough-hewn stone walls contrast with the symmetry of the central dome of the Shrine, and give a feeling of the natural rock walls of a cave.

of the apocalyptic 'End of Days'; the second, a deterministic division of the world into the 'Sons of Light' (that is, the Sect, who are the 'elect') and the 'Sons of Darkness' (the rest of humanity). As a logical consequence of these beliefs, they retreated into the desert and there founded their settlement '. . . separate from the habitation of ungodly men . . . into the wilderness to prepare the way of the Lord . . .' (The Manual of Discipline, 8:13). Most scholars identify this sect with the Essenes, a Jewish sect already known to us from ancient historians.

The seven original Dead Sea Scrolls may be divided into two main groups, Biblical and Sectarian. The two Biblical manuscripts are both texts of the Book of Isaiah. The first is the largest and the oldest of the scrolls (it dates from *c.* 100 BC). Consisting of seventeen leather sheets, it contains the complete book of Isaiah (chapters 1–66). It is 7·34 metres long and is well preserved though it had obviously been heavily used (there were two tears in it which had been carefully repaired). It was actually in use for about one hundred and fifty years before being hidden in the cave. There are some minor differences in wording between this text and the standard Massoretic text, and the spelling is quite different, being the 'full', vowelled type. The second is a smaller fragmentary scroll. It is not nearly so well preserved (the next to the last sheet is the only one that has remained whole and only fragments of other sheets remain) but bits of as many as thirty-eight pieces of Isaiah appear. The great importance of these scrolls lies in the fact that they are two thousand years old – at least a thousand years older than the oldest Hebrew text extant.

The four Sectarian scrolls are the 'Manual of Discipline', the 'Thanksgiving Hymns', the 'Habakkuk Commentary' and the 'War of the Sons of Light against the Sons of Darkness'.

118 (*right*) The focal point of the Shrine of the Book is the raised platform upon which is displayed the scroll of Isaiah. This version, written in about 100 BC is 7.34 metres in length and is displayed fully opened around a drum, above which is an enlarged representation of a Torah scroll handle.

119 (*overleaf left*) The Habakkuk Commentary is the oldest known attempt to interpret the words of the Prophet as applying to actual events. Beside each verse the author explained events as he knew them in relation to the words of the Prophet.

120 (*overleaf right*) Among the objects found in the Cave of the Letters were several fragments of textile. This woollen kerchief, patterned in red, yellow and blue, might have been used as a wrapper for a Torah-scroll.

פשרו על כול עושי התורה בבית יהודה אשר X
יצילם אל מבית המשפט בעבור עמלם ואמונתם
במורה הצדק ואף כיא הון יבגוד גבר יהיר ולוא
ינוה אשר הרחיב כשאול נפשו והואה כמות לוא ישבע
ויאספו אלו כול הגואים ויקבצו אלו כול העמים
הלוא כולם משל עליו ישאו ומליצי חידות לו
ויומרו הוי המרבה ולוא לו עד מתי יכביד עלו
עבטט פשרו על הכוהן הרשע אשר
נקרא על שם האמת בתחלת עומדו וכאשר משל
בישראל רם לבו ויעזוב את אל ויבגוד בחוקים בעבור
הון ויגזול ויקבוץ הון אנשי חמס אשר מרדו באל
והון עמים לקח לוסיף עליו עון אשמה ודרכי
תועבות פעל בכול נדת טמאה הלוא פתאום יקומו
נושכיך ויקיצו מזעזעיכה והייתה למשסות למו
כיא אתה שלותה גואים רבים וישלוכה כול יתר עמים
... ל הכוהן אשר מרד

נגועי במשפטי רשעה ושערוריות מחלים X
רעים עשו בו ונקמות בגוית בשרו ואשר
אמר כי אתה שלותה גוים רבים וישלוכה כול
יתר עמים פשרו על כוהני ירושלים
האחרונים אשר יקבצו הון ובצע משלל העמים
ולאחרית הימים ינתן הונם עם שללם ביד
חיל הכתיאים כיא המה יתר העמים
מדמי אדם וחמס ארץ קריה וכו[ל] יושבי בה
פשרו על הכוהן ה[ר]שע אשר בעוון מורה
הצדק ואנשי עצתו נתנו אל ביד אויביו לענותו
בנגע לכלה במרורי נפש בעבור אשר הרשיע
על בחירו הוי הבוצע בצע רע לביתו לשום
במרום קנו להנצל מכף רע יעצתה בשת
לביתכה קצות עמים רבים וחוטי נפשכה כיא
א... כפיס מעץ ...
... אשר ...

לחיות אבנו ...
אשר קצות עמ ...
פשרו הוא ב ...
משפטו בתו ...
ובתוכם ירשי ...
בונה עיר ב ...
הנה מעם י ...
ולאמים בדי ...
פשר הדבר ...
לבנות עיר שו ...
בעבור כבודה ...
במ... שקר ...
למשפטי אש ...
כיא תמלא ה ...
יכסו על ה ...

121 (*left*) The preservation of many of the articles dating from the Bar-Kochba revolt, 132–5, is extremely good; the mirrors, jugs and key still retain much of their freshness, little damaged by the passing of time.

122 (*below*) The Nachal Hever caves where many of the Bar-Kochba objects were discovered. Although protected from the weather, excavations were hampered by the lack of light, suffocating dust and the difficulties in bringing in equipment.

The 'Manual of Discipline' (known also as the 'Rule of the Community') is a compilation of the rules and regulations of the sect and an exposé of its ideology. It is made up of eleven pages, written on much-used sheets, and is apparently not complete. It draws the picture of a select community which initiates into membership only those who pledge themselves to follow the laws of God given 'through Moses and through all his servants, the prophets'; who adhere to a special calendar; and who contribute to the community all that they have. The scroll goes on to describe the actual initiation ceremony for new members, and the oath they had to take. It deals with conduct at communal meals, when the priest shall first 'stretch out his hands to bless the first portion of the bread and wine', and lists punishments – such as stopping part of a person's rations for ten days – for any infringement of the Code.

The Thanksgiving Scroll shown in plate 123 contains about forty hymns, stylistically similar to psalms but written in the first person singular. Most of the hymns open with the phrase 'I give thanks unto thee O Lord', and it is from this that the scroll has been given its name. In them the author praises the Lord for electing him and his brethren

123 (*left and right*) The work of opening the jars and unrolling the scrolls requires great skill and patience. Over the years the parchment dehydrates and becomes so fragile that the sudden exposure to light and air and any rough handling may cause it to crumble to dust. As these two photographs show, archaeologists were able to open the Thanksgiving Scroll successfully.

and endowing them with divine grace. He feels that he has been appointed by God to be 'a banner for the righteous and an interpreter of knowledge', and is clearly a teacher with many disciples. Persecuted by his enemies and driven by them from his country he can continue to live and work only because God helps him. Hints of some doctrinal struggle, embracing opposing groups of people, show through the intensely personal atmosphere of these Thanksgiving Hymns.

'The War of the Sons of Light against the Sons of Darkness' describes the Final War, a war to be fought between the sect and its enemies which was to last forty years. Even though victory would

eventually be given to the sect, it was necessary to prepare the Sons of Light for the conflict to come and to make a general plan for the war. The scroll contains nineteen columns of text on five sheets and is the only extant comprehensive description of Jewish military tactics and regulations at the end of the Second Commonwealth. It describes in great detail the procedure for recruiting, the signalling system, the organisation and equipment of the heavy and light infantry and the cavalry units, the various formations to be taken up by the front line, the weapons and general tactics – even the qualities of the horses are discussed. The scroll concludes with the prayers to be said before,

124 The excavated synagogue built by the Zealots at Masada, where some of the scrolls were found. The precipitous nature of the site is clearly visible.

during and after battle. The prayer before battle is especially moving, invoking as it does one of the central symbols of Jewish historic existence:

> . . . Goliath of Gath a mighty man of valour
> Thou didst deliver into the hands of David,
> Thy servant,
> Because he trusted in Thy great name
> And not in sword and lance;
> For the war is Thine.

The Bible was more than a sacred legacy to these men of two thousand years ago. It was a living force, whose words had a bearing on their own present-day problems. One of the four scrolls acquired by Dr Yadin has been given the name of the Habakkuk Commentary (plate 119). It is an attempt, in a way hitherto unknown, to interpret the words of the prophet, treating the verses as relating to contemporary events. The author quotes the first two chapters of the prophet, verse by verse, adding after each his own explanation and interpretation (thus incidentally providing us with a Biblical text approximately a thousand years older than any extant copy of this prophet). In chapter 2 of Habakkuk we are given a detailed attack on the 'Wicked Priest', who had been pure of heart when he first took office, 'but when he ruled over Israel . . . he abandoned God' and persecuted the Teacher of Righteousness (the leader and probably founder of the sect) and his followers.

The Genesis Apocryphon (strictly speaking not a Sectarian composition) is in Aramaic – the other scrolls are in Hebrew – and is an expanded version of several episodes from the Book of Genesis, beginning with the birth of Noah and going on through the prophecy of

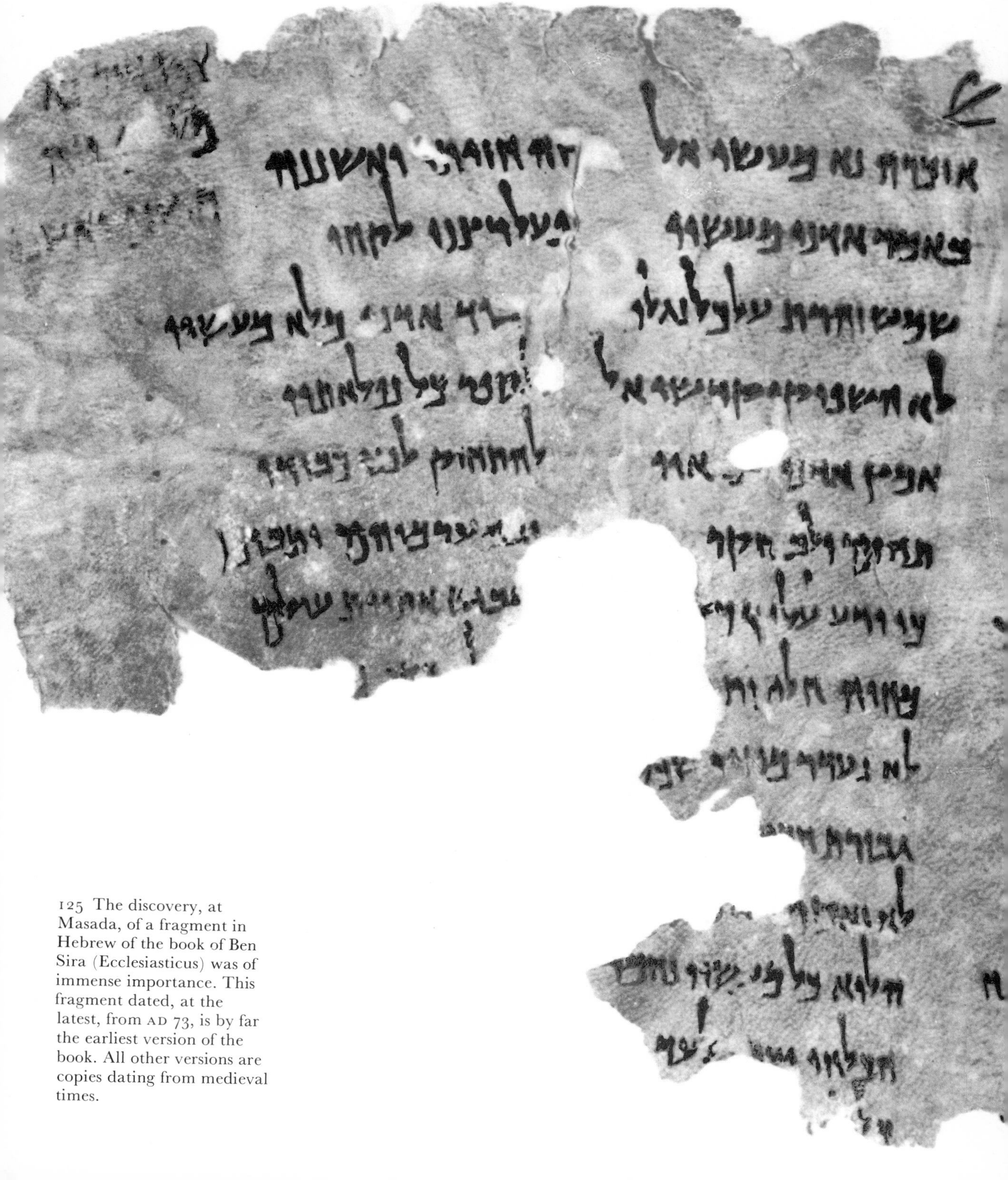

125 The discovery, at Masada, of a fragment in Hebrew of the book of Ben Sira (Ecclesiasticus) was of immense importance. This fragment dated, at the latest, from AD 73, is by far the earliest version of the book. All other versions are copies dating from medieval times.

Isaac's birth to Sarah. The heroes of the Bible were not merely symbols to these Jews of the Second Commonwealth. A vivid and artistic imagination was clearly at work in this retelling of Genesis, with a strong desire to invest its characters with new life. The Bible, for instance, tells us that Sarah is beautiful; the scroll describes how beautiful she was, and in marvellously elegant prose:

> . . . how fair indeed are her eyes and how pleasing her nose and all the radiance of her face . . . how beautiful her breast and how lovely all her whiteness. Her arms goodly to look upon and her hands how perfect . . . how fair her palms and how long and fine all the fingers of her hands . . .

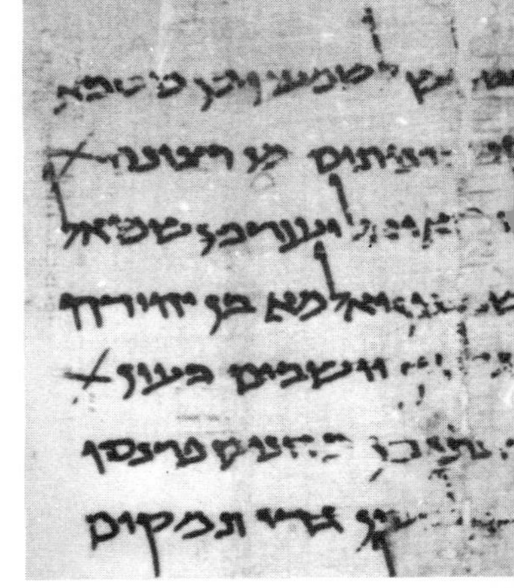

126 Land-lease in Hebrew from the Bar-Kochba revolt, found in the Cave of Letters. The deed (written on papyrus) regulates the distribution of lands which had been leased from Bar-Kochba's administration.

Masada, that tremendous rock fortress, is the southernmost site where scrolls were found. It took the superbly organised work of two thousand volunteers, working for six months in both 1963–4 and 1964–5, to excavate and explore King Herod's terraced palace and the store-houses, fortifications and living quarters of Masada (plate 124). These excavations have supplied answers to several puzzling problems raised in connection with the scrolls. Here we can mention only that fourteen manuscripts were discovered on this site – Biblical, Apocryphal and Sectarian. Besides the interest in the actual contents of the scrolls they are of great importance as comparative material, as their date can be accurately fixed between the years AD 66 and 73. Seven hundred ostraca (inscribed potsherds) were also discovered in Masada. The biggest and most spectacular discovery, however, was that of a first century AD copy of a part of the lost Hebrew original of Ecclesiasticus, the book of Ben Sira (plate 125), composed twenty-two centuries ago. In the past Ben Sira was known only in Greek, Syriac and Latin versions, medieval manuscripts of a Hebrew version having been discovered only towards the end of the nineteenth century in the Cairo Genizah. The Masada Hebrew fragment, which cannot be dated later than AD 73 and which is almost identical with the text from the Cairo Genizah, proves that the Cairo fragments were copies of the Hebrew original and not translations from the Greek.

While the Second Jewish Revolt was being cruelly subdued by Hadrian's legions, some of the Jewish inhabitants of the oasis of En Gedi fled to a cave in Nachal Hever (plate 122). The cave, now called the Cave of Letters, must have seemed a safe hiding-place – plenty of room inside but with an inconspicuous entrance in the cliffs, hundreds of metres above the river-bed. But the refugees did not escape the Romans for long and all, apparently, met their death here, leaving behind them their well-hidden belongings: two groups of manuscripts (the Bar-Kochba letters (plate 126) and Babata's archive) and many humble items for daily use.

127 Several of the Khirbet Qumran caves. These caves, unlike those on the mountain slopes which are natural, are artificially dug out of the soft marl.

The Bar-Kochba letters are military despatches sent from HQ by the commander-in-chief to his lieutenants in En Gedi. They deal with

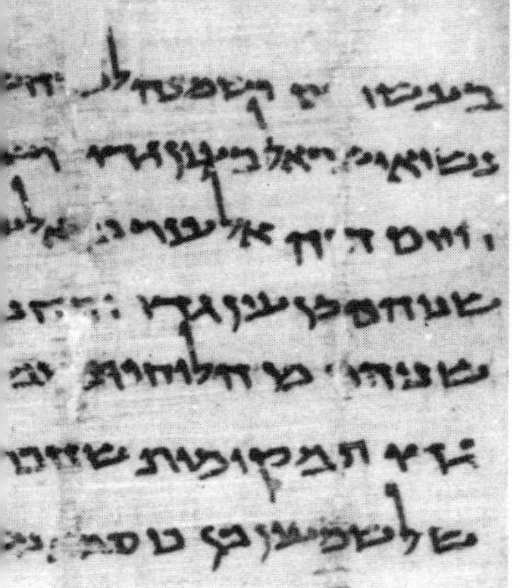

supplies, matters of discipline, and other related matters. A typical letter starts with a rebuke for the delay in sending supplies:

> From Shim'on Bar Kosiba to the
> men of En Gedi
> to Masabala and to Yehonatan
> Bar Ba'ayan, peace. You
> sit, eat and drink from the property
> of the house
> of Israel, and care nothing for
> your brothers.

The second group, the Babata archive, is a mine of information about life in the region of the Dead Sea at the end of the first and the beginning of the second centuries AD. Babata was a wealthy woman, twice widowed, who spent a great deal of her time in civil courts, sueing and being sued. Invaluable data can be gleaned from these documents, about the economy, laws, history, geography and the languages spoken in southern Palestine at that time.

The objects from the Cave of Letters (plate 121) are also of great importance. It is a collection of finds unique in several respects. First, they were found in a marvellous state of preservation, an unusual thing in the Palestine climate. Secondly, they can be dated accurately to the year AD 135 or perhaps a little earlier, and accurate dates are extremely rare in this country. Moreover, we know exactly who the owners were, while most of the finds in Palestine are, as one knows, anonymous. There are baskets made of palm leaves; a copper mirror mounted in a painted wooden case; a jewel box; household utensils (knives, wooden dishes, cooking pots); an extremely well-preserved glass bowl; and textiles, one of the oldest and most precious collections of ancient woven fabrics in existence (plate 120). The colours, which include thirty-three shades, are all made of three primary fast colours, blue, yellow and red.

These then are some of the treasures in the Shrine of the Book – a wonderful and memorable collection, strikingly housed in a shrine whose architecture seeks to express the continuity implicit in rebirth. From the grandeurs of Isaiah, through the spiritual dedication and otherworldliness of the Sons of Light, to the charm and naïveté of the Genesis Apocryphon and the touchingly humble items from the Cave of Letters, a journey is made which brings Israel's past into sharp and clear focus.

Karl Katz **Jewish Tradition in Art**

The spiritual concepts promulgated in the Bible begin with dialogues between God and the Patriarchs, Abraham, Isaac and Jacob (plate 130), but it is with Moses and the 'Giving of the Law' that the actual precepts and foundation of Jewish ethics, law and tradition were formulated.

From the latter half of the second millennium BC the journeyings and other historical events of the Hebrews and Israelites – the People of the Book – were elaborated on and eventually written down. The alphabet (the Greek word for the first two Hebrew letters, *alef* and *bet*) was an innovation of this epoch, which made it possible for people to record and transmit ideas to a large public. The resulting written collection, in abbreviation called TANACH in Hebrew, consisted of the Pentateuch (Five Books of Moses), the Prophets, and the Hagiographa writings, and formed the basis of the Jewish faith. In the early centuries of our era, rabbinic interpretations attempted to regulate the life of the Jew by the addition of a body of interpretive material (Mishnah, Talmud, Shulchan Aruch). These subsequent texts evolved from the oral code of this nomadic people and provided precise and exact injunctions for the regulation of Jewish life. But it is the Scroll of the Law (Torah), containing the Five Books of Moses, which is the nucleus of the Jewish religion as well as the focal point of Jewish worship.

Early in the Hebrews' history, the Tables of the Law, which Moses received on Mount Sinai (plate 128), were enshrined in a portable tabernacle which the Jews took on their wanderings. Eventually taken by Joshua into the Promised Land, this Ark of the Covenant with its precious contents was later placed in the Holy of Holies in Solomon's Temple. Possibly the Law in scroll form was to be found in the Second Temple, and weekly portions were read to the congregation. At that time there was no formalised popular prayer; sacrifices and tri-annual pilgrimages marked the national and agricultural celebrations of the Jewish calendar.

With the destruction of the Second Temple in AD 70 a new mode of life and worship was forced to develop (although there were precedents for this new way of life as early as the period of the Babylonian exile, for example, the Temple at Yev). Never again was there to be a Temple in Jerusalem at which sacrifices were offered. To replace this sacrificial form of worship, the practice of praying in synagogues (the Greek word for 'House of Assembly') developed. The scroll form of the Five Books of Moses was placed within each of these 'meeting places of God' (Psalms, 74:8) and was contained in the Ark of the Law. Three times a day a minimum of ten Jewish males over thirteen years of age would gather to pray, often led by the rabbi, a learned layman.

128 (*opposite*)

REGENSBURG PENTATEUCH

Parchment – 246 leaves
Germany, Bavaria (Regensburg), c. 1300

Moses is seen receiving, descending, and delivering the 'Law' to the Hebrews assembled at Mount Sinai.

אנכי לא תרצח
לא יהיה לך לא תנאף
לא תשא לא תגנב
זכור את לא תענה
כבד את לא תחמד

129 (*left*)

VITTORIO VENETO SYNAGOGUE

Wood, gilt, brass and silver
Italy, Vittorio Veneto, 1701
(*Gift of Mr Jakob Michael, New York, in memory of his wife Erna Michael*)

A diminutive house of prayer combining the Baroque and Neo-Classic traditions. In this small community, the men prayed on the ground floor, facing the Ark, and the women were seated behind the lattice in the gallery above.

130 (*right*)

THE YAHUDA HAGGADAH

Parchment – 40 leaves
Southern Germany, mid-fifteenth century
(*Gift of Mrs Rachel Ethel Yahuda, Conn.*)

A towering angel, the divine intermediary of the Lord, is earthbound and confronts Joshua in a conversation.

Special prayers were recited for the Sabbath, which was inaugurated at sunset on Friday and concluded after sunset on the following day. For the Sabbath, and on some other occasions, the Pentateuch was ceremonially taken from the Ark and a portion of the Law was read. From the third century AD, the orientation of prayer was towards the Ark, which was in or on the wall in the general direction of Jerusalem. So wherever the worshippers were in the Diaspora, they faced the city of David, the setting of the Temple of God and their spiritual home. All that remained of that glory was the Western Wall of the Second Temple enclosure, and this became a symbol for Judaism and for the return to the Holy Land. Although synagogues had been built before the destruction of the Second Temple (such as the one at Masada), after the destruction of this great edifice Jews of the Diaspora built their houses of worship wherever they wandered; and always enshrined the Pentateuch and prayed towards Jerusalem.

In mosaics, frescoes and gold glass of the second to the seventh centuries AD, in Palestine and in the neighbouring Mediterranean countries, the Ark of the Law, or Torah shrine, containing the Scrolls is represented. In these works of art, the Ark of the Law is most often flanked by guardian lions which in turn are surrounded by objects symbolic of the Jewish people: the menorah (seven-branched candelabrum), the lulav (date-palm branch) and etrog (citron), the shofar (ram's horn), and the incense shovel. These motifs, with variations, are still in use today.

At the beautiful third-century synagogue at Capernaum, on the shores of the Sea of Galilee, a fragment of a stone frieze was excavated; it bears, in relief, what is probably a representation of the Ark of the Covenant on wheels – a mobile Torah shrine. A representation of this concept can be seen in the frescoes from the synagogue at Dura Europos, which dates from about AD 245 and was part of a Syrian caravan city built on the Euphrates river midway between Baghdad and Aleppo. Here, as in Capernaum, the Ark of the Covenant is depicted as a gabled, portable shrine on wheels, equipped with a handsome coffered double door and richly draped (plate 139). In this same third-century synagogue, which manifests so strongly the influence of the Hellenistic-Parthian style, there is a niche which may have been used as a Torah shrine (plate 138). Above it there is a representation of the façade of the Temple almost exactly like the one appearing on the Bar-Kochba tetradrachm silver coins, struck between AD 132–5 (plate 95). These architectural forms are related to the representation seen on the relief at Capernaum. We can, then, surmise that the Ark of the Covenant was a roofed structure with a panelled door. Speculations regarding the Temple suggest that it followed a similar architectural format. Torah shrines in later times sometimes echo this ancient structure. The columns flanking the entrance and supporting the gables in many of these works of art are reminiscent of the pair of portal columns Solomon had placed in his Temple (cf. 1 Kings, 7:21).

This simple format can be seen in the third to fourth century Jewish gold glass discovered in the catacombs of Rome (plate 103), and the Byzantine Period mosaic floors of the synagogue of Bet Alpha (plate 131), Tiberias and Bet Shean (plate 102). In some of the representations, there is even a curtain which either covered the panelled doors or was placed behind the wooden doors to veil the interior niche which contained the Scrolls, a tradition which has tenaciously survived.

The gradual disappearance of the tangible remains of Jewish tradition, an inevitable loss due to constant wandering or wanton destruction, has made the creation of a department in the Museum dedicated to Judaica a necessity and a challenge. Assembling these

131
BET ALPHA SYNAGOGUE FLOOR
Diagrammatic reconstruction
Mosaic
Israel, sixth century

The thousands of tesserae of natural stone forming the scene of the sacrifice of Isaac, and the Zodiac represent a turning point in the history of late Roman-Byzantine art.

objects of our Hebrew heritage in order to preserve and exhibit the most complete representation is an exciting, difficult and at times poignant task and many of the stories of their acquisition bear retelling.

In 1964 an extraordinary opportunity presented itself. The Venetian Jewish Community and the Fine Arts Commission of Venice approved the sale and transfer of a small synagogue located in Vittorio Veneto, a village once called Ceneda located sixty kilometres to the north of Venice. There has been no Jewish community in Vittorio Veneto since the latter part of the nineteenth century, and apparently, the last service held in this diminutive late Baroque synagogue, dated 1701, may have been a military one, on the successful conclusion of the First World War. A newspaper of 1918, headlining the War's termination, was found on the synagogue's lectern, covered under nearly fifty years of dust. The Jewish community of Venice consented to the synagogue's new venue at the Israel Museum (plate 129) and saw historic justice rendered, since some years previously the Ark of the Law from the neighbouring village of Conegliano had reached Jerusalem as well. After making careful architectural plans, renderings, perspectives, and taking colour samples of flooring and even studies and measurements of the intensity of light filtering through the windows, the synagogue was packed into seventy-two large crates. The Israel Museum built a shell to the specifications of the Ceneda synagogue, including the women's gallery. With the help of the Italian architect who had dismantled the synagogue and expert artisans who recreated the old stencil patterns on the walls, the Vittorio Veneto house of prayer was installed in the Israel Museum, a fine example of a late Baroque synagogue.

The women's gallery is now used as exhibition space for illuminated and illustrated marriage contracts and for brocade and embroidered textiles. There is a small foyer at the entrance to the synagogue, next to the flight of stairs which leads to the women's gallery. In this foyer there is a show case where superb examples of Jewish ceremonial works of art made in Italy in the seventeenth and eighteenth centuries are displayed. Visitors looking at the synagogue and the vitrine nearby have no difficulty in visualising the rich and lavish beauty of the north Italian Jewish tradition.

A study of the Vittorio Veneto Ark of the Law reveals some rather interesting vestiges of antiquity. As previously pointed out, the Graeco-Roman representations of the Tabernacle, Temple façade and the Ark always showed these structures with gabled roofs. Here, in the Vittorio Veneto Ark, we see a gable as a split pediment, very much 'in vogue' in the Baroque period, but certainly somewhat incongruous against the more formal architecture of the rest of the synagogue. There is a fascinating echo from the past in the façade of the Ark. The Ark is divided into three vertical sections, but only the central section

is functional. It is opened to receive the Torah; the other two sections are decorative. Each part, however, is flanked by applied columns with classical capitals. If the rows of these columns were to be extended into space, the resulting structure would be the traditional Roman basilical form of the early synagogue, with a central nave and two aisles – another remarkable example of the tenacity of tradition.

Another synagogue rarity in the Museum are the great panelled double doors of the Fatimid Period, coming from the Ben-Ezra synagogue of Fustat, Egypt, (Cairo's neighbouring city which was abandoned in the medieval period). The doors, which date from the twelfth century, have panels and are reminiscent, coincidentally no doubt, of the type seen on Temple or shrine portals in frescoes, mosaics, reliefs, and gold glass. The carving is purely Islamic and is very similar to the work done for the western Palace of the Fatimid caliphs (plate 132).

A thirteenth-century Hebrew inscription associated with the synagogue was located in New York almost at the same time as the appearance of the doors on the European market in 1958 (plate 132). The inscription was published and recorded as lost, and until 1958 the fragment in the Islamic Museum, Cairo, was thought to be the only section to have survived. Our inscription reads: 'Our master and teacher, Solomon, who died in his youth, may God let him rest in peace and console his brother's heart.' From numerous sources, it can be ascertained that these sumptuous doors and the inscriptions were the portals of an inner room of the Fustat synagogue in which the great Rabbi Maimonides may have prayed.

In Jewish ceremonial art, there is a distinction between those objects used for the Torah or in a synagogue context and others. The accoutrements used to embellish the Scroll of the Law form the entire class of 'sacred' objects, and all the rest are objects of 'deed'. This distinction is another affirmation of the special status of the Torah. Rigorous rules regulate the scribes' writing of the Scroll of the Law. Its Hebrew text cannot vary one 'jot or tittle' from the ancient prototype. This purity and simplicity are in direct contrast to the frequently ornate and elaborate decorations which adorn it. The juxtaposition of the unembellished leather or parchment scroll fixed on wooden rollers, and the rich trappings used to 'dress' and adorn the Pentateuch are interesting to note. In studying these 'sacred' or holy objects, two observations can be made. First, an historical fact emerges and that is, that there are practically no ceremonial and ritual works of art that can be dated prior to the Renaissance. We conjecture that the objects we have are in direct continuity, with variation, to previously used accoutrements. If this speculation is incorrect then were there no scroll accoutrements until the period of our earliest known objects? Certainly, much patient archaeological

132

SYNAGOGUE DOORS

Carved wood panels
Egypt, Fustat, twelfth century
(Acquired with the aid of Baroness Alix de Rothschild, Paris, and donated by Mr Astorre Mayer, Milan, in memory of his father Sally Mayer)

Pitch-pine panels, similar to the ones used for the palace of the Fatimid caliphs, are decorated with animals, birds and a lute player and dancer.

LINTEL

Carved wood
Egypt, Fustat, thirteenth century
(Gift of Mr Jakob Michael, New York, in memory of his wife Erna Michael)

A fragment in fine Hebrew square letters of a larger dedication inscription which framed the doors or was above them.

work, research into literary records and representations in manuscripts will be necessary if we are to confirm or deny these speculations. But the chances of earlier material appearing are, apparently, very slight and at this time there can be no real doubt that a gap exists in 'Judaica' material between the Roman-Byzantine Period and the Gothic-Renaissance Period.

The second fascinating fact which can be observed when studying Jewish ceremonial objects, both in terms of form and content, is the lack of homogeneity, a lack resulting from the dominant influences which diverse environments exercised on the creations of the Diaspora artist or craftsman. Of course, this is even more striking in the case of 'ritual' creations made by non-Jews for Jewish patrons. However, even when these two factors are taken into consideration – the lack of historical continuity and the heterogeneous nature of the art – we are nevertheless dealing with a fascinating corpus of material which has important historical significance and immense emotional meaning. From an art historian's point of view, there is a measure of fascination in these very problems, and one certainly finds a great deal of beauty, both sophisticated and naïve, in this ceremonial and ritual art.

The oriental and occidental Jewish traditions vary in some respects. In regard to the Scroll of the Law there is an interesting difference. The oriental scribe, after fixing the leather scroll on the two rollers, places it in a 'tik', a cylindrical wooden or metal container; when it is being used he simply opens the container – standing it vertically so that the reader can see the Scroll facing him – and turning to the next column by winding the rollers from the outside. The western tradition 'dresses' the parchment scroll, making it, in a sense, the personification of the high priest. It is clothed in rich brocades and adorned with a crown, breastplate, and a 'sceptre' made of gold, silver and precious stones. But in this case, when the Scroll is read as part of the synagogal ritual, all its decorations are removed, and it is laid down on the reader's table which is covered with a fine cloth so that, symbolically, it is kept away from 'unclean' things. At the conclusion of the reading it is held aloft without its accoutrements, spread open and shown to the congregation as the 'scroll placed by Moses before the Israelites' (plate 134). The reader and those attending the service are not permitted to touch the Scroll itself. As an added mark of respect, when the Torah is taken from the Ark and replaced, the congregation, eastern or western, rises in deference to its sanctity, frequently kissing the textile mantle or wooden or metal receptacle in which it is contained.

Each appurtenance used in the adornment of the Scroll of the Law, the embellishment of the Torah Ark, or the enrichment of the simple ceremonies and traditions of the Jew is full of historic and symbolic significance, such as the Krakow Torah Ark doors (plate 133). The

133

TORAH ARK DOORS

Painted lead on wood
Poland, Krakow, early seventeenth century

(Gift of H. Jacobowitz in memory of Mr and Mrs Mathatias and Havah Rivka Jacobowitz)

Many of the ritual utensils used in the Temple as described in the Bible are seen in appliqué relief.

parchment Scroll is clothed in a silk brocade or velvet mantle. Often the abbreviated version of the Ten Commandments or a suitable Biblical inscription, sometimes ending by mentioning the donor, is embroidered on the textile's surface. The Scroll is carried from the Ark and heads the procession. A crown is placed on top of the two rollers (called 'etz chaim' – the tree of life), attesting to the majesty of the Pentateuch. At times, depending on the tradition, there are finials, used either in conjunction with the crown or separately, each one being placed on one wooden dowel used as a handle for the rollers. In an earlier period these handles were plated and decorated, but eventually these decorations became removable and separate objects in themselves. The finials are called 'rimmonim', the Hebrew word for pomegranates. In antiquity, the High Priest who carried out the rituals in the Temple wore a robe, the hem of which was trimmed with pomegranates made of precious metal alternating with golden bells. This tradition is preserved in these finials, which are frequently fitted with bells. The form of these rimmonim seems to have an extensive history. One of the few early objects preserved from mid-fifteenth-century Sicily is a pair of finials having a tower-like shape and fitted with bells. They are now in the Cathedral of Palma de Mallorca.

Suspended by a chain over the wooden handles and lying on the mantle is the 'tass', the breastplate or shield. Its origins may also go back to the time of priestly ritual when the High Priest performed ceremonies wearing the 'choshen' or breastplate, with twelve precious stones called 'Urim and Tummim', one gem for each of the Israelite tribes (who were originally the sons of Jacob). In the oriental tradition, the tass is rarely found. Though the concept is probably ancient it is assumed that the breastplate is a relatively recent western innovation in the repertoire of accoutrements for the Scroll of the Law. One explanation for the origin of the breastplate, as a plaque for information, seems to have merit. Very often, there is space on the tass for an interchangeable plaque. If the synagogue is wealthy enough to own more than one Torah Scroll, the plaque in the breastplate would indicate the specific holiday on which a particular Torah would be used, implying that the Scroll was already rolled to the part of the Law to be read on that particular celebration (plate 135).

As we have just mentioned, the Torah Scroll is holy and therefore its parchment cannot be touched. When it is placed on the table, a special cover is put down, and when it is carried it is clothed in a mantle; when it is read from, a 'yad' or pointer is used to indicate the place. This pointer is often made of precious metal and takes the form of a stylised hand with one finger outstretched, on an attenuated handle. In the Ashkenazic tradition this, too, is suspended over the roller onto the outside of the Scroll of the Law. A fully adorned Torah would therefore consist of a Torah binder, very often gaily

134 (*right*)

THE YAHUDA HAGGADAH

Parchment – 40 leaves
Southern Germany, mid-fifteenth century
(*Gift of Mrs Rachel Ethel Yahuda, Conn.*)

A rare representation of the Scroll of the Law, rather than the two Tablets of the Law, being received by Moses on top of Mount Sinai.

135 (*overleaf left*)

GERMAN TORAH GROUP:

MANTLE

Velvet with silver thread embroidery, Germany, 1749

RIMMONIM

Silver, partly gilt, Germany, early nineteenth century
(*I.R.S.O.*)

POINTER

Silver gilt, Germany, Nuremburg, early seventeenth century
(*Gift of Mrs Joseph Hirsch, Jerusalem, in memory of her husband*)

TASS

Silver, partly gilt, Germany, early eighteenth century

ARK CURTAIN

Brocade, silver lace, silver thread embroidery on damask, Silesia, Glogau, 1795

In the east and west European Jewish tradition torah scrolls usually have these accoutrements; the only variation is that sometimes a rimmonim may be replaced by a crown.

ובדברי צדיקים תתברך ובלשון חסידים
תתרומם ובקרב קדושים תתקדש:

ובמקהלות רבבות עמך בית ישראל יתפאר
שמך מלכנו בכל דור ודור
שכן חובת כל היצורים לפניך יי אלהינו ואלהי אבותינו
להודות להלל לשבח לפאר לרומם להדר לברך לעלה ול
ולקלס על כל דברי שירות ותשבחות דוד בן ישי
עבדך משיחך:

ישתבח שמך לעד מלכנו האל המלך
הגדול והקדוש בשמים ובארץ
כי לך נאה יי אלהינו ואלהי אבותינו שיר ושבחה
הלל וזמרה עז וממשלה נצח גדלה וגבורה
תהלה ותפארת קדשה ומלכות ברכות והודאות
מעתה ועד עולם ברוך אתה יי אל מלך גדול ב
בתשבחות אל ההודאות אדון הנפ
הנפלאות הבוחר בשירי זמרה אל חי העולמים:

כתר תורה
בשנת תקט
לפק

זה השער לה׳ צדקים יבאו בו

136 (*preceding pages right*)

ITALIAN TORAH GROUP:

MANTLE

Silk with gold thread embroidery Italy, seventeenth century

(*Gift of Mr Jakob Michael, New York*)

TASS

Silver, Italy, 1776

CROWN

Silver, partly gilt, Italy, 1742

FINIALS

Silver, Italy, Padua, eighteenth century

(*Gift of the Paduan Jewish Community*)

ARK CURTAIN

Italian silk, with silver and silk thread embroidery, Turkey, eighteenth century

Fine repoussé silver work characterises Italian-Jewish ritual art. The inscription on the torah curtain reads 'This is the gateway to God only the righteous will enter'.

137

NORTH AFRICAN TORAH GROUP:

MANTLE

Velvet, with gold and silver thread embroidery, leather-backed
Morocco, nineteenth century

FINIALS

Silver, partly gilt and enamel North Africa, nineteenth century

The textile mantle is a translation of the oriental wood or metal case, and the finials are minarets in miniature.

painted or embroidered with genre scenes related to the donor's name and date of birth (this is mainly a German or northern Italian custom), a richly embroidered mantle of some precious textile, a silver or gold crown, finials, a breastplate and a pointer. This would be the general appearance of the Torah in the western tradition.

The Italian Torah Scroll does not in most cases have a breastplate, or has only a small one, but it would frequently have both a crown and finials, a union of Sephardic and Ashkenazic tradition, whereas the western Torah might use just one or the other. The Italian mantle may be a textile version of the solid cylindrical oriental cases (plate 136).

The Torah Ark curtain reproduced in plate 136 comes from Turkey and preserves a motif which pre-dates it by more than twenty-five centuries. Again one sees an example of persistence in the Jewish tradition. The two columns, which appear so regularly in Jewish ceremonial art and which were seen in the Capernaum synagogue relief, the mosaic floors, and other related material, may in fact be the pair of free-standing pillars called Yachin and Boaz which flanked the entrance to Solomon's Temple. This simple architectural reminiscence of the Temple, whose destruction is an ever-present theme in the Hebrew tradition, can be seen with great frequency on such diverse objects as Ark curtains, Channukah lamps and bookcovers. The use of the spiral columns may be based on the Colonna Sancta in Rome.

The North African tradition is somewhat like the Italian style, a synthesis of east and west, as in the group of North African objects shown in plate 137. The textile Torah mantle is an imitation of the cylindrical form of the containers. The breastplate is most often absent in the oriental tradition; if used at all it is understated. The finials reflect the oriental tradition in shape, but they are less ornate and are fixed onto the wooden rollers in a western manner. The crown, again if it is used at all, certainly reflects the western tradition but its construction is much closer to the Italian style than to anything else.

Is it true that the oriental Jewish ritual art objects reflect more faithfully the actual forms of comparable objects from antiquity? The answer is not clear. Different environments imposed variants on fairly constant factors, and both traditions most probably preserve reflections of the past, both having a certain historical relevance.

In the Dura Europos frescoes one can see both an actual niche and a representation of the Ark of the Covenant on wheels. We know that the Ark was a movable piece of furniture, but where and when did it become an integral part of the architecture of the synagogue? The occidental Scroll makes one suspect that the Ark was movable, whereas the oriental Torah in its wooden case, often overlaid with some precious metal or textile, seems far more suited to a niche. The Torah Scroll cases in plate 140 come from Iran and India, and are fine

138
DURA EUROPOS
Fresco
Syria, AD 245
A double-doored portal, flanked by pairs of columns, is painted above a niche which may have contained a Pentateuch scroll.

139

DURA EUROPOS

Fresco
Syria, AD 245

The return of the Ark of the Covenant from the hands of the Philistines. (I Samuel:6)

examples of oriental ornamental work. When the two halves of the cylinder containing the Scroll are closed, the split finials in the centre of the case unite to look somewhat like a miniature crown in the form of a single finial. In turn, this is flanked by two 'rimmonim', sometimes set off at angles to the body of the container. It is treated with an overall pattern, an aesthetic approach very much a part of oriental taste. Hebrew inscriptions, lozenge and ogive patterns cover the body and the inside of these beautiful Scroll containers.

Central to the Jewish faith everywhere is the unadorned Torah, but the superimposed variants reflect the cultural differences and influences that the Jews living in the Diaspora faced.

There is an ancient pagan precedent for the idea of the Sabbath, but the Hebrew version was a revolutionary one. It meant a compulsory day of rest for man and his servant, a liberation from the mundane and a turning to the sacred. Gradually the idea of the Sabbath became connected with sanctification; the individual was to dedicate this day to God, the creator of the world, who had rested on the seventh day and demanded of his creation that they do likewise. Its observance is a constant affirmation of the relationship between God and the Jews. It is a day of prayer and of rest, of spiritual rededication and religious contemplation. It is a day 'where one postpones concluding the Sabbath and rushes to inaugurate it' (from the Sabbath Prayer Liturgy). The inauguration is carried out by the woman of the house who kindles the Sabbath oil lamp or candles. In some cases the lamp is shaped like a star or the radiating points of the light of the sun.

The separation (havdalah) ceremony divides the Sabbath from the other days of the week. Before the Sabbath can be gracefully concluded, three stars must be clearly visible on the Sabbath night, unequivocal testimony that the sun has set and that the day of rest has ended. A goblet of wine, a braided candle and a spice container are the three objects required in the western tradition for the separation ceremony (plate 143). With each special event in the life of the Jew, the 'kiddush' or sanctification blessing is made over a cup of wine (plate 144). The shadow cast by the cupped fingers over the palm in the candle ceremony is symbolic of the division between day and night, between light and dark. To add a lingering pleasure to this parting from the Sabbath, aromatic spices are introduced. Their fragrance is inhaled as the box is passed from hand to hand among the participants, while God is blessed as the 'Creator of the varieties of spice'. The service is a domestic one and the spice containers are often delightful pieces of decorative art (plate 141).

The burning of some fragrant substance was frequently used in worship, and what is thought to be an incense shovel may be the object represented on mosaic floors, gold glass, oil lamps, and other archaeological objects. Because of the rarity of spices, which most often

140
TORAH SCROLL CASES
(*left*) *Silver, partly gilt*
India, nineteenth century
(*Gift of the Beth-El Synagogue, Calcutta*)
A hammered silver case from India.
(*right*) *Velvet-covered with silver and partly gilt decorations*
Iran, 1799
Velvet and brass studs in a decorative pattern cover this Iranian scroll case.

came from the Near and Far East and which in ancient and medieval times were extremely valuable, the container for the spices used in the separation ceremony often takes the form of a tower or campanile. There is a fortified aspect to the spice container. A delightful whimsy can be found in these little spice boxes, sometimes guarded by diminutive knights and Biblical heroes. Since the object is a domestic one, with the simple function of containing spices permitting one to enjoy the pleasures of the scent, there is a wealth of inventiveness in the forms which this box assumes. Apart from the tower shapes, one finds flowers, birds, fruits and even windmills and locomotives (plate 141).

The idea of sacred light has permeated the Jewish tradition from the very outset of the faith, and this concept of divine illumination is frequently given form in the field of Judaica. God commanded Moses to commission Bezalel ben Uri ben Chur to make a lampstand with three branches on either side and a central shaft (Exod., 25:31). This seven-branched lighting fixture was called the 'menorah', and it was placed in the tabernacle which stood on the south side of the sanctuary. Pure olive oil was used for the lamps and the light was to burn from evening to morning. Aaron, Moses' brother, after being solemnly consecrated, was required to enter the Tabernacle and light the menorah. Later other High Priests continued this practice in the Temple (plate 152). After the destruction of the Second Temple, an 'eternal light' was placed in synagogues in front of the Torah Ark (Lev., 24:2), a scene sometimes shown in ancient mosaic floors.

The earliest representation of the lampstand with seven lights can be found on a small bronze coin of the Hasmonaean Dynasty, struck by the Maccabean ruler, Mattathias Antigonus, 47–40 BC (plate 87); it is possible that it takes the form of the menorah made for the Tabernacle and later used in the Temple, as described in the Books of Exodus and Leviticus. Probably the most famous of all representations of the holy menorah used in the Temple rebuilt by Herod is depicted in relief on the Triumphal Arch of Titus in Rome, built in AD 94 by the Emperor Domitian to commemorate the destruction of the Temple and the capture of Jerusalem by forces headed by Titus during the reign of Vespasian. It is this 'Romanised' representation, with its many-sided base, which is so frequently reproduced. However, the earliest actual menorah is in the Israel Museum. It was unearthed in the early part of this century in a synagogue excavation on the shores of the Sea of Galilee, near Tiberias (plate 142) and may well be the oldest ritual object in existence. Only recently a large fragment of a beautiful stone menorah was uncovered in the ancient synagogue of Sardis in Asia Minor. The Tiberias example is a simple stone relief of the second to third century AD and preserves on its branches representations of alternating flowers and knobs which are described

141

SPICE BOXES:

BIRD'S WING SPICE BOX

Silver

Poland, late eighteenth century

BELL-TOWER SPICE BOX

Silver

Germany, early nineteenth century

ROSEWATER SPRINKLER SPICE BOX

Silver

Germany (?), eighteenth century

(Gift of Mr A. Burstein, Lugano)

CASTLE SPICE BOX

Silver, partly gilt

Germany, seventeenth century

(I.R.S.O.)

From left to right, the wings of the bird, the door of the bell-tower, the top of the rosewater sprinkler, and the gates of the castle all open to receive the fragrant scent used in the separation ceremony.

142 *(above)*

MENORAH

Limestone, Israel, Tiberias, second to third centuries

This limestone menorah probably had ceramic oil lamps in the seven shallow receptacles, which terminate each branch. The hole at the base of the centre branch suggests that it stood on a socle.

143

HAVDALAH GROUP:

CANDLE HOLDER

Silver

Germany, Frankfurt, first half eighteenth century

(Acquisition by Mordechai Narkiss Fund)

KIDDUSH GOBLET

Gold

Germany, early seventeenth century

(I.R.S.O.)

143 *(continued)*

SPICE BOX

Silver, and partly gilt

Austria, 1817

The little figure supporting the candle holder has a spice box in his left hand, and in his right, a goblet very much like the golden one next to it, depicting scenes from the Old Testament; here, Jacob wrestles with the angel.

ברוך אתה יי׳ אלהינו
מלך העולם
בורא מאורי האש
ברוך אתה יי׳ אלהינו מלך
העולם המבדיל בין קדש
לחול בין אור לחשך ובין
ישרא׳ לעמים ובין יום
השביעי לששת ימי המעש׳
בין קדושת שבת לקדושת
יום טוב הבדלת ואת יום
השביעי מששת ימי המעש׳
קדשת הבדלת וקדשת את
עמך ישרא׳ בקדושתך

144 (*left*)

THE YAHUDA HAGGADAH

Parchment – 40 leaves
Southern Germany, mid-fifteenth century

(*Gift of Mrs Rachel Ethel Yahuda, Conn.*)

Here, a star-shaped oil lamp is used instead of a braided candle by the worshipper in the separation ceremony.

145 (*right*)

SABBATH LAMP

Silver repoussé
Italy, eighteenth century

This fine specimen was used either in a domestic setting for the Sabbath and Holidays, or else in a synagogue as an 'eternal light'.

146

CHANNUKIOT

(left) Bronze
France, fourteenth century

Surmounted by a trefoil and pierced by a rose window, the façade rests on a running arcade of horseshoe arches.

(right) Bronze
Italy, sixteenth century

(Gift of Mr Nafi, Rome)

This open-work building has a central and two flanking towers not unlike the silhouette of a fortified castle.

147
ROTHSCHILD
MANUSCRIPT 24
Thin vellum – 473 leaves
Italy, Ferrara (?), c. 1470
(Presented to the Museum anonymously)
As a marginal illustration to the story of the Hasmonaeans, a bearded man is seen lighting the Channukah candles perched on the top of a classical capital.

so carefully in the Old Testament specifications (Exod., 25:33). Generally, there are very few in the round examples of seven-branched candelabra to be found in Jewish ritual art. It is not surprising, since this particular object had its function within the context of the Tabernacle and the Temple and with the destruction of the Temple it no longer had ritual meaning. In addition, its exact reproduction was forbidden by Mishnaic law. However, it is frequently represented as a decorative, symbolic or apotropaic device.

The general interdiction against making the menorah form was observed and by a simple expedient; a very similar form with eight branches was introduced into the synagogue, and at times into the home. This eight-branched candelabrum is annually used during the holiday of Channukah, often referred to as the 'Festival of Light'.

In 165 BC, led by their military leader Judah the Maccabee, the Hasmonaeans overwhelmed the Seleucids and reconsecrated the Temple. Tradition recounts that a measure of oil sufficient for only one day burned for eight, and because of this the ceremonial object used to commemorate this holiday has places for eight lights, which are lit each night – the number lit corresponding to the day of the holiday – with the help of a 'servant' lamp (shammash) which is set off from the others, often placed at the side. This feast too is primarily a domestic holiday, and again the Channukiah assumes a multitude of forms, all related to the artistic conventions and influences of the people who made and used them. It is quite fascinating to see the variety of shapes which the Channukah lamp takes.

Since the traditional miracle of this holiday took place in the Temple in Jerusalem, the artisan, whether eastern or western, often used this architectural fact as a point of departure for his aesthetic fantasy when fashioning a Channukah lamp. In one case we see the façade of a French medieval cathedral with an arcade and rose window (plate 146); in another, the crenellated towers of a castello in north Italy (plate 146); in yet another, we find a magnificent two-floored Moorish palace, topped by a star and crescent (plate 148). In an eighteenth-century Polish example there is a delightful synthesis of what appears to be the entrance to the Temple and a rural synagogue complete with chimneys (plate 148). Each one is apparently the artist's naïve way of representing the Temple.

In a group of oriental Channukah lamps (plate 149), we find a variety of traditional near eastern ornaments merging with symbols frequently found on Jewish objects. All three metal lamps are adorned with a profusion of birds. The bird can often be found in Islamic art and is traditional in the oriental repertoire, as are the crescent and star, and the stylised hand – a common device for protection from the 'evil eye'. But what is really fascinating is the mélange of motifs one sees in the perforated back panel of one of the Moroccan lamps – the

150 (*right*)

ROTHSCHILD MANUSCRIPT 24

Thin vellum – 473 leaves
Italy, Ferrara (?), c. 1470

(*Presented to the Museum anonymously*)

One page from this profusely illustrated Miscellany, containing over fifty religious and secular works illuminated by at least three artists.

148 (*left*)

CHANNUKIOT

(*left*) *Brass, Poland, eighteenth century*

(*Gift of the Burstein Collection, Lugano*)

A lion holds the servant lamp, and rampant birds sit on the roof in this fanciful Polish Channukiah

(*right*) *Copper and brass, Algeria, late nineteenth century*

(*Gift of Mr Z. Schulmann, Paris*)

The servant lamp is in the central window on the second floor, and each of the eight Moorish arches accommodates one oil lamp.

149 (*left*)

ORIENTAL CHANNUKAH LAMPS

(*left*) *Brass, Morocco, Tetouan, nineteenth century*

(*Gift of Mr Z. Schulmann, Paris*)

A seven-branched menorah forms the central motif for the eight-lamped Channukiah

(*centre*) *Brass, glass, oil containers*
Iraq, Baghdad, eighteenth century

(*Loan from the Ticho Collection*)

Water was placed in the glasses, and oil was poured in to float on top. A wick absorbed the oil, and the flame was lit.

(*right*) *Brass*
Morocco, Fez, nineteenth century

(*Gift of Mr Z. Schulmann, Paris*)

Birds merge into foliage in a pierced background of arabesques.

הלכות חמץ ומצה
מהרמב"ם ז"ל

פרק ראשון · ט' האוכל כזית חמץ בפ
בפסח מתחלת ליל חמשה
עשר עד סוף יום אחד ועשרים בניסן
במזיד חייב כרת שנ' כי כל אוכל חמץ

הסדר של פסח והגדה

קדש ורחץ · כרפס יחץ · מגיד רחצה · מוציא מצה ·
מרור כורך · שלחן עורך · צפון ברך · הלל נרצה ··

אחר

קדוש נטילה · כרפס יבצע · הגיד והרחיץ נטילה המוציא
מצה ומרור טבל ·· קנך יהנה וגו' ··

בערב פסח סמוך להתחלת ראשון לא יאכל אדם עד הראשון ובעזיזו הבית
ראשון · והמזגין לו כוס ראשון ··

אחר תפלת ערבית צריך עדיין להמתין עד שיהיה ודאי לילה · ואז יסדר
השלחן ומסדרין כוס לפני כל אחד ואחד ואפי' הקטן בן יומו ומיחדין לו כוס
ולפני בעל הבית יסדרו גם הקערה ובה הג' מצות המשמורות ולשם ג'
מיני · והמצה שיש לה ג' סימנים ישים תחלה בקערה כדי שתהיינה תחתונ'
והיינו העליונות השלישית · והמצה שיש לה ב' סימנים ישים עליה והיינו
העליונות האמצעית · והמצה שיש לה רק סימן אחד תהיה עליונה ·
גם יהיו בקערה מיני הירקות · והיינו מרור שקורי' לטוך · וגם ירקות
אחר קורי' ... שקורי' לויך · גם יהיו בה השני תבשילין
... ביצה צלויה והחתיכת בשר המורוע ... אחת · גם
יהיו בה כלי עם חרוסת · גם יסדרו לפניו המים חוץ בכלי · לטבל ראשון
ויטלו לטול ידיהם קודם שיסבו ... בלא ברכה · וכל אחד ואחד מוזג
לעצמו · והיו הטעמיו כוס ראשון ... · והתחיל בעל
הבית והקדוש ·· וזה נוסח הקידוש ·· יום הוא
שבת יאמר תחלה
ויכלו

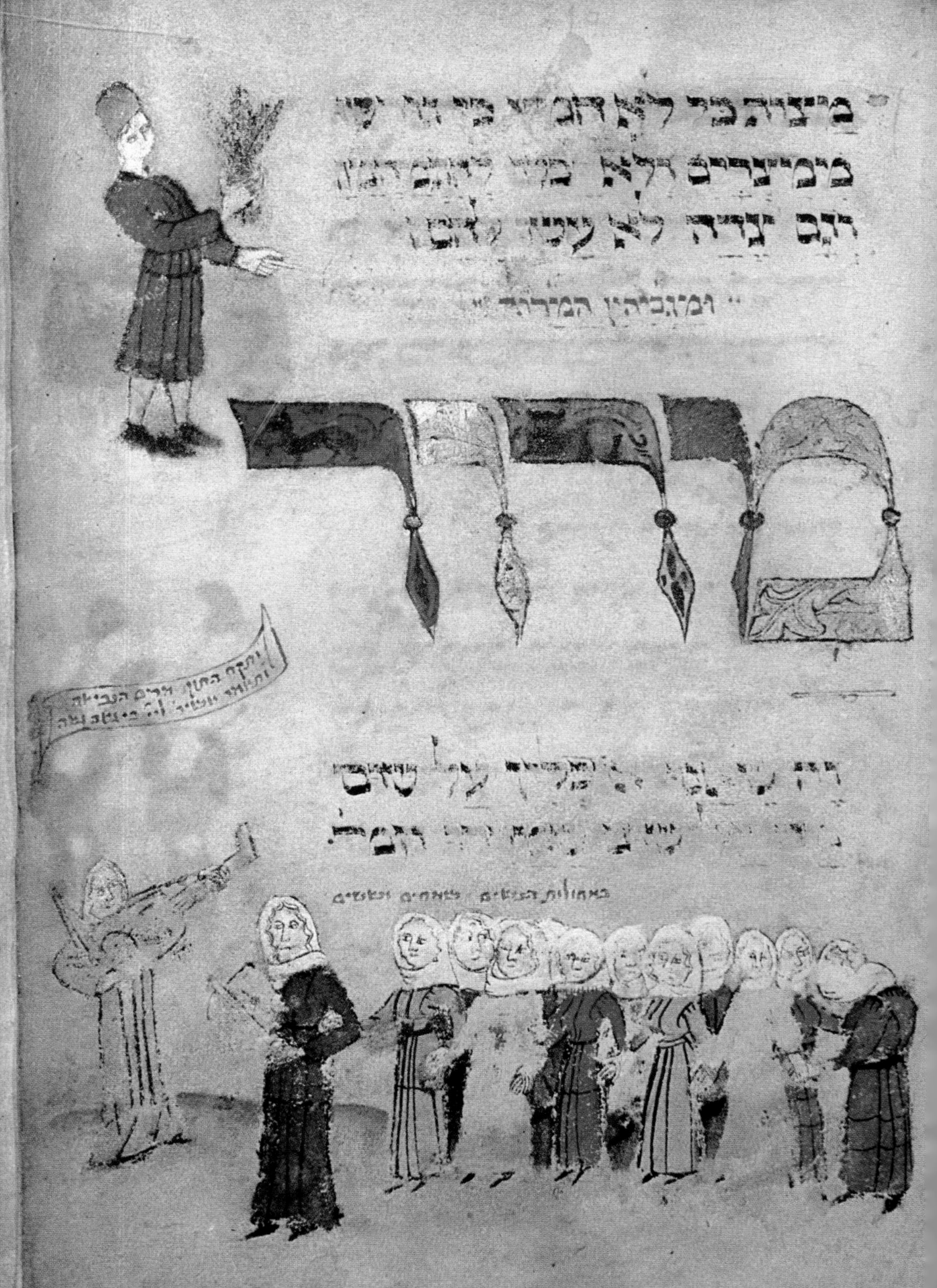
וגם צדה לא עשו להם
ומגביהין המרור
מרור

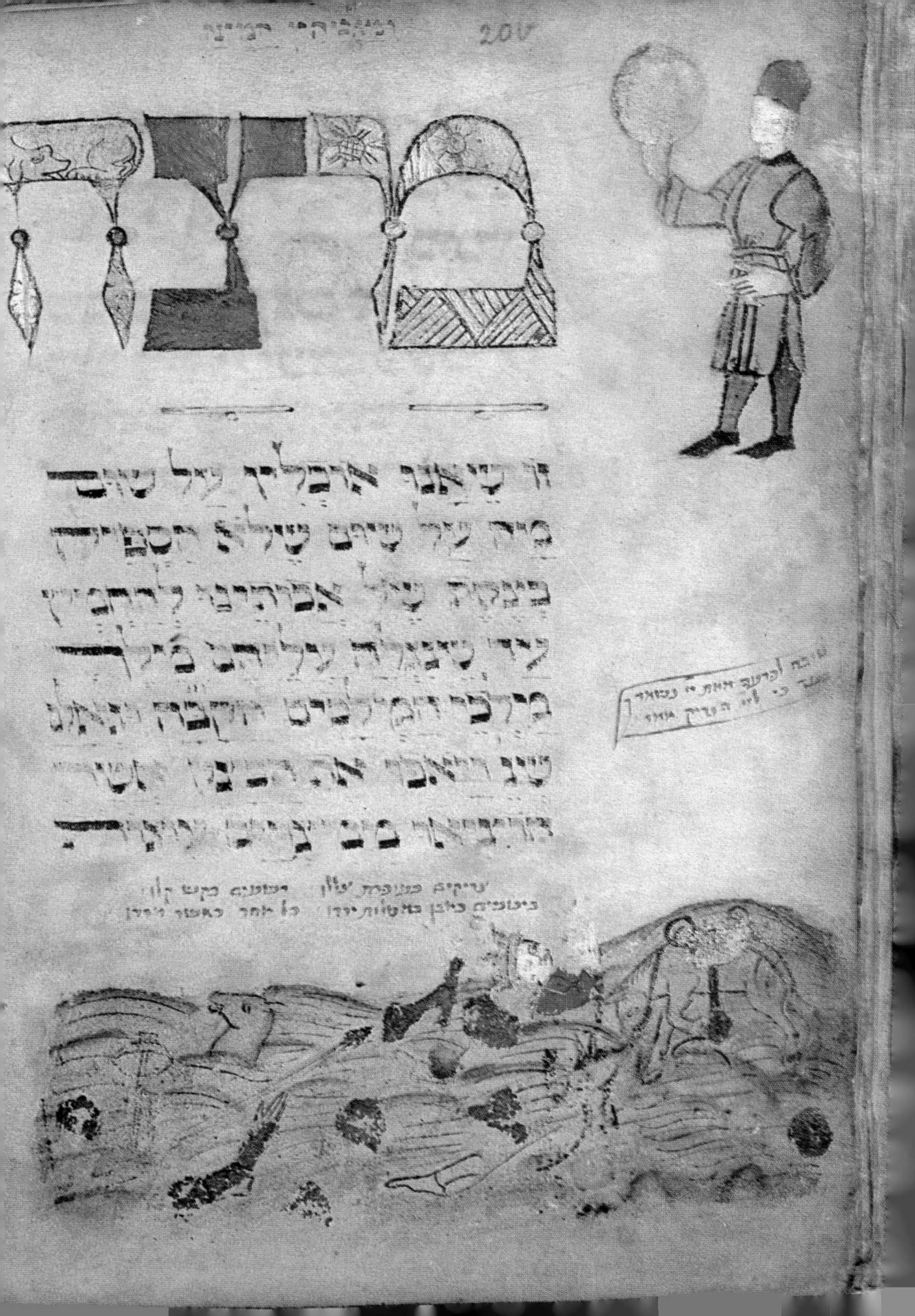

זו שאנו אוכלין על שום
מה על שום שלא הספיק
בצקם של אבותינו להחמיץ
עד שנגלה עליהם מלך
מלכי המלכים הקב"ה וגאלם
שנ' ויאפו את הבצק אשר
הוציאו ממצרים עגות

להתמהמה וגם צדה לא
עשו להם׳

מרור זה שאנו אוכ
אוכלין על
שום מה על שום שמררו
המצריים את חיי אבותינו
במצרים שנ׳ וימררו את
חייהם בעבודה קשה בחומר
ובלבנים ובכל עבודה בשדה
את כל עבודתם אשר עב
עבדו בהם בפרך׳

בכל דור ודור חייב
אדם לראות את עצמו כ
כאלו הוא יצא ממצרים
שנ׳ והגדת לבנך ביום ההו
ההוא לאמר בעבור זה
עשה יי׳ לי בצאתי ממצרי׳

לא את אבותינו גאל
הקב״ה בלבד אלא
אף אותנו גאל עמהם ש
שנ׳ ואותנו הוציא משם
למען הביא אותנו לתת
לנו את הארץ אשר נשבע
לאבותינו׳

151 (*preceding pages*)

THE YAHUDA HAGGADAH

Parchment – 40 leaves
Southern Germany, mid-fifteenth century

(*Gift of Mrs Rachel Ethel Yahuda, Conn.*)

Because of some archaisms and naïve renditions, scholars consider the illuminations and illustrations of this manuscript to be the work of a Jewish artist.

154 (*right*)

CHANNUKIAH

Bronze
Germany or Holland, 1574

The lamp was made by Meïr Heilperin. The first line of the inscription reads 'These lights we kindle in commemoration of the miracles, the acts of salvation, and the wonders which Thou didst accomplish for our forefathers through the medium of the holy priests.'

152 (*left above*)

REGENSBURG PENTATEUCH

Parchment – 246 leaves

Germany, Bavaria (Regensburg), c. 1300

Aaron, surrounded by the appurtenances of the Tabernacle, wearing a mitre on his head, Urim and Thummin on his chest, and the robe of the ephod, is seen lighting the seven-branched menorah.

153 (*left*)

THE BIRDS' HEAD HAGGADAH

Vellum – 47 leaves
Germany, upper Rhine, c. 1300

(*Gift of Mr H. Cohen with aid of Mr Fred Monosson, in memory of of Dr Ludwig Marum, Karlsruhe, Germany.*)

The bird-headed figures are used to avoid depicting human features, and the conical hat of the men was made compulsory for Jewish males in Germany in the year 1215.

menorah is flanked by what appears to be amphoras (seen on ancient Jewish coins) and the entire composition is framed by those not infrequently used columns. It strikes one as an interesting juxtaposition when one notes that the seven-branched menorah, used decoratively forms the central motif for the eight-lamped Channukiah. For instance, an early eighteenth-century German Channukah lamp (plate 155) has the menorah and the canonical flower and knob on its branches occupying the central panel, with Aaron and Moses on either side of the seven-branched candelabrum. Heroes, animals and appropriate inscriptions populate this interesting silver specimen. Some are extremely austere, one of the finest in that class being an example, probably from Holland, and dated 1574 (plate 154), which uses simply the attractive form of the Hebrew letter as the decorative feature for the back panel, at the same time utilising the inscription for the appropriate chant which is sung nightly while lighting the Channukah lamp.

When the holiday was celebrated in a synagogue setting the problem of including the 'forbidden' menorah into the house of worship was solved by installing a large eight-branched menorah. Very often, it was placed to the right of the Ark of the Covenant, corresponding to the original menorah's place in the Temple. The Museum owns a large Channukah lamp for synagogue use which is in the form of an eight-branched menorah. It also has a smaller version, apparently a domestic one, with the heroine Judith on the pinnacle of the central shaft (plate 156), clutching the head of the Syrian general, Holofernes in one hand and in the other a sword.

155 *(left)*

CHANNUKIAH

Silver, partly gilt – $R^3$731
(CP) *mark*
Germany, Augsburg, early eighteenth century
(Gift of Mr Ignazio Bauer, Madrid)

The prayers for the kindling of the Channukah lights and the traditional chant are inscribed on the back of this example flanking a seven-branched menorah.

156 *(left)*

CHANNUKIAH

Silver – mark: BD
Germany, Augsburg, 1759
(Gift of Mr Jakob Michael, New York, in memory of his wife, Erna Michael)

This graceful, more than 200-year old Channukah menorah bears the mark of the master BD, an Augsburg silversmith.

157

SUKKAH *(right)*

Painted wood
Germany, Fischach, first half nineteenth century
(Formerly owned by Mr Abraham Deller of Fischach and acquired by the late Dr H. Feuchtwanger)

A simple wood dwelling with charming naïve paintings depicting the village of Fischach and a visionary Jerusalem.

If we return to the earliest motifs seen in Jewish art, we can notice that the branch of a palm and a citron frequently appear in archaeological contexts such as mosaic floors and coins. These two agricultural symbols are used in the celebration of the Feast of the Tabernacles (Sukkot), which coincides with the end of summer and the beginning of the autumn harvest (plate 158). In the Museum we have a rare example of the temporary booth (sukkah), which is erected for this seven day holiday. In a naïve and delightful style the artist's longing for Jerusalem is given sensitive expression (plate 157). A family living in the village of Fischach in Swabia, southern Germany,

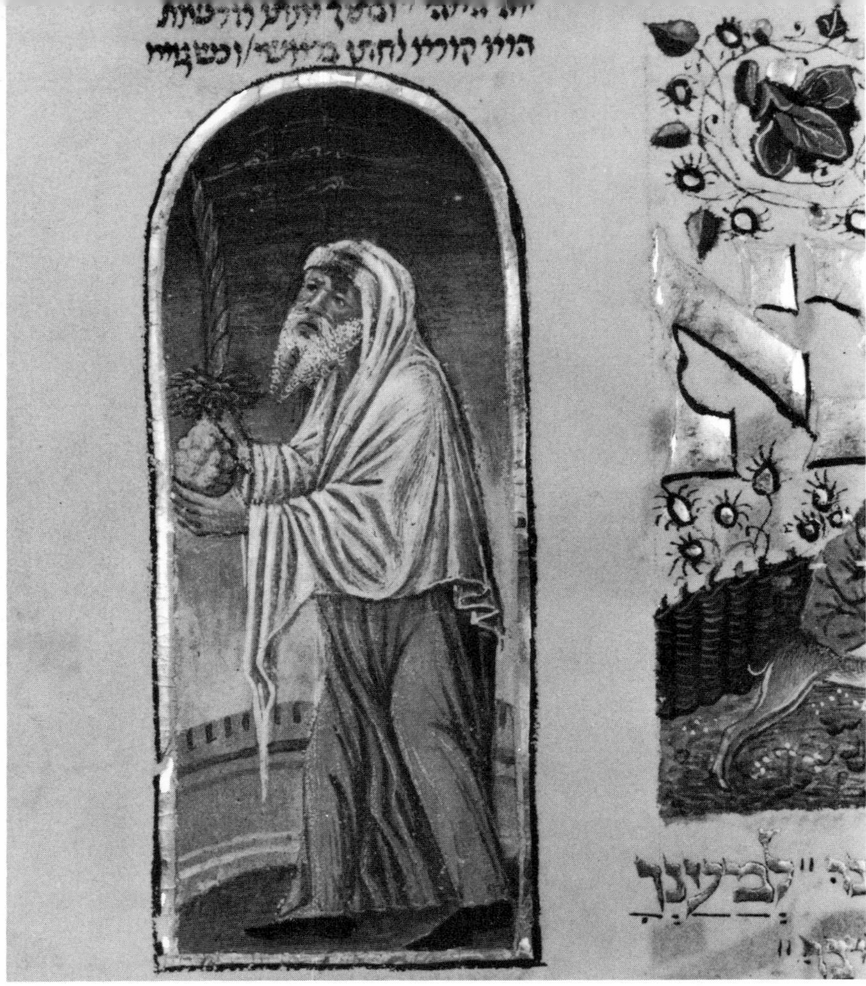

158 (*left*)
ROTHSCHILD MANUSCRIPT 24
Thin vellum – 473 leaves
Italy, Ferrara (?) – c. 1470
(*Presented to the Museum anonymously*)
In his left hand, an etrog or citron, and in his right, the lulav or date-palm branch; which together with myrtle and willow leaves, are used in the celebration of Sukkot.

159 (*right*)
ERNA MICHAEL HAGGADAH
Parchment – 77 leaves
Germany, middle Rhine, c. 1400
(*Gift of Mr Jakob Michael, New York, in memory of his wife, Erna Michael*)
The towers of this medieval gateway are also prototypes of the spice boxes illustrated earlier.

commissioned for the walls of this temporary dwelling, which commemorates the wandering of the Jews in the wilderness, a visionary Jerusalem; the painted wooden wall with its imaginary view of David's city was probably placed so that it faced the Wailing Wall. The other walls of this sukkah have genre scenes of the early nineteenth century, portraying life in this small community. It is certainly remarkable that though the climate in Fischach in early autumn is not conducive to outdoor living, and the palm-branch and citron are not indigenous, the Jews' longing for their land, and for Jerusalem, and for a life based on a calendar and an agricultural timetable appropriate to their ancient homeland's near eastern setting, lead them to celebrate Sukkoth in the appointed season even in this southern German village.

All the holidays derive either from the Pentateuch or from the early and formative period immediately post-dating the destruction of the second Temple. The biblically prescribed Feast of Passover is probably the richest and certainly one of the most specialised holidays in the Jewish year. It marks the triumphal occasion of the Exodus, when the Hebrews left Egypt and their bondage of four hundred years, and received the law. It is a holiday of liberation which has taken on profound meaning in contemporary Israel as a celebration of inde-

חמודה על הזהב אשר
לא ירשו ועל מלכה
אשר בשמו לא קרא״

160 (*left*)
SEDER PLATE
Majolica
Spain, c. 1450
(*Gift of Mr Jakob Michael, New York, in memory of his wife Erna Michael*)
It is difficult to justify the orthographic errors on this plate, and the speculation advanced is that the lettering was made by a non-Jew, or a descendant of one who had been forcibly converted and practised his faith secretly.

161 (*below*)
SIDDUR OF THE RABBI OF RIZIN
Parchment – 365 leaves
Southern or eastern Germany, c. 1460
(*Formerly in the possession of the nineteenth-century Hassidic Rabbi Israel Friedman of Rižin*)
The verdant and hilly landscape of southern or eastern Germany is the setting for the miraculous crossing of the Red Sea, and the wanderings in the wilderness with Moses leading the Israelites.

pendence. It is not only a festival for traditionally religious Israelis, it is celebrated by everyone, and has taken on a real national significance, even though it commemorates a series of miraculous happenings which occurred almost thirty-five centuries ago.

We can trace the story of Passover through some of the finest works of Jewish art in the Israel Museum. By examining a variety of objects, the events marking this festival of freedom from Egyptian bondage are illustrated. Central to this spring-time holiday is the special feast which is called 'Seder' (order), when the book, 'Haggadah', containing the required texts, is read. It is written in the form of a lesson, a pedagogical exercise meant to instruct the children of the house and remind them of this fateful period of their ancestors' redemption from slavery.

The Haggadah, which takes the form of narratives, prayers, hymns, songs and riddles, was at times richly illuminated and illustrated. It was always a domestic text and never used in synagogue worship. Consequently, some of the finest works of art in the Jewish tradition are these lavishly produced Passover feast manuscripts.

Intent on freedom, Moses threatened Pharaoh numerous times, demanding that the Hebrews be allowed to leave Egypt. Finally, after the Ten Plagues, they succeeded in escaping. Moses, their leader, was commanded to head the Exodus. One of the first problems he faced was the crossing of the Red Sea (a mistranslation of the Hebrew words 'Yam Suf' or 'Sea of Reeds'). With Egyptian chariots pursuing Moses and the Israelites, it was necessary to cross the sea, and:

> . . . the Lord said to Moses, 'Stretch out your hand over the sea that the water may come back upon the Egyptians, upon their chariots and their horsemen.'
> . . . But the people of Israel walked on dry ground through the sea, the waters being a wall to them on their right and on their left (Exodus, 14:26, 29).

In one fifteenth-century Haggadah an angel, the Lord's intermediary, guides Moses' hand, and a stylised path appears through the waters ready for the miraculous crossing (plate 161). In a Passover manuscript from the Rhineland, this incident of the crossing of the Red Sea is more animatedly depicted (plate 151), and Miriam, having crossed the sea, appears playing the timbral (Exod., 15:20) and accompanied by a lute player, leads the Israelite women in song and dance. In the upper right and left hand sides of the manuscript pages, there are two representations of foods that are required eating for the Passover Seder. They are symbols associated with this holiday. On the right hand page, we see a figure holding a round, flat, unleavened bread called 'matzah'. For the eight days of this holiday, ordinary leavened bread cannot be eaten. This is to commemorate the 'bread of affliction' that the Hebrews made when they precipitously left Egypt to embark on their forty-year desert wanderings. On the upper left hand of the manuscript page the bitter herbs, 'maror', are held aloft. They are eaten to remind the participants of the bitter times the Israelites suffered in their bondage. These are two of the symbolic foods traditionally placed on the Seder table (plate 151).

In order to make certain that the Jewish home is devoid of all leaven, a special ceremony of ritual cleansing and burning of the leaven takes place the night before the evening of the Seder meal. In one of the most sumptuous Hebrew manuscripts known, the Rothschild Ms 24, a north Italian Miscellany of about 1470 (plate 150), we see three phases of these Passover preparations. An old gentleman is seen with a candle in his hand ceremonially searching for leaven. Below that is a scene depicting the careful preparation of the dough for making matzah. And finally, we see the men and women preparing these flat, round, unleavened pieces of bread and stippling designs on their surface before putting them in the oven for baking.

Another manuscript from the Rhineland (perhaps the earliest known illuminated and illustrated Haggadah), shows the charming domestic scene of women kneeding dough, flattening and baking the matzah. In this manuscript, called the 'Birds' Head' Haggadah (plate 153), dated *c.* 1300, the artist, probably in order to avoid painting Jews' faces, resorts to a circuitous approach. All the Jews in this Haggadah are represented as birds, and only the few non-Jews, such as Pharaoh and his charioteers and even angels, are endowed with human features. By doing this, he skirts the injunction against making 'a graven image, or any likeness of anything' (Exod., 20:4).

In the Erna Michael Haggadah is depicted a group of men seated round the table ready to start a Seder. They are wearing the pointed hats characteristic of Jews in central Europe during medieval times. Beautiful objects are being carried towards the table, on which have already been placed some lovely golden vessels (plate 167). The whole setting within the framework of a medieval city, probably in the Rhineland, is one of the richly illuminated pages in the manuscript.

Over four hundred years later, a seated group portrayed on a pewter Seder plate from Germany, full of provincial charm, gives an even more intimate glimpse of the Passover feast as a family occasion. Father, mother and their four children all sit very properly round the table on which the required foods are set out – shankbone, egg, chopped nuts and fruits, matzah, bitter herbs and parsley. In this domestic setting of starched linen and polished brass, the German-Jewish family is carrying out the commandment of 'recounting the story of Passover' (plate 162).

These illuminated and illustrated Haggadot give some fascinating insights into Jewish life of the medieval, renaissance and subsequent

162

SEDER PLATE

Pewter
Germany, early nineteenth century
(*Gift of Mrs Marianna Baer, in memory of her mother*)

The eight words on the rim of this plate mark the highlights of the Passover Seder Feast which starts with the Paschal lamb and ends with the hymn of thanks.

periods. Of course, one must always remember that calligraphy played a very important role in the Hebrew tradition, as it does in all near eastern cultures. This emphasis on the beauty of the written letter is a significant feature in these manuscripts. Plate 166 is a page of one of the manuscripts: it has no narrative or symbolic significance, but it has a delightful rhythm based on the calligraphy and the playful art of the illuminator.

The opening page of a book is often called a 'sha'ar', or gateway. In a number of cases the artists working on a manuscript will take this idea of a gateway and translate it literally into a formal architectural structure, into which they frame the text. In the Erna Michael Haggadah there is a page, not even a frontispiece, simply the beginning of a chapter of the text, which actually utilises the form of a medieval gateway surmounted by towers (plate 159). Massoretic texts were often called 's'yag la-Torah', or fences for the Pentateuch, meaning that to prevent people from inadvertently transgressing a commandment, another law was propounded which would make it even more difficult for the individual to reach that point of possible sin. These written 'fences' which are incorporated into the margins of manuscripts, often take on the actual appearance of a barrier, and here again we see the translation of words into form.

Plate 163 is of a tiny manuscript which is called a Psalter, a rare chattel of the rich Spanish tradition that was almost obliterated. Apparently, this little vellum Book of Psalms with 'fences' was written in pre-expulsion Spain just a few decades before the end of the fifteenth century. After the Jews' expulsion and the destruction of their culture, this manuscript somehow survived, to reappear in Italy in 1519 where a wealthy Jewish family acquired it. They have placed their family crest on the frontispiece and cover.

The Museum is fortunate in having recently acquired another object from pre-expulsion Spain, in this case possibly from Valencia. In 1903 it was exhibited in the Louvre and reappeared only quite recently. There are some fine manuscripts which are undoubtedly Spanish in origin, but as we have already mentioned, with the exception of the pair of Torah finials from Sicily in the sacristy of the Cathedral of Palma da Mallorca, there are almost no movable works of art attesting to the ancient Sephardic tradition. Recently however, and on permanent exhibition in the Museum, a Hispano-Moresque Seder plate has been added to this rare group (plate 160). The vessel is made of terracotta and glazed in lustre gold and blue. On it are inscribed the words 'Seder Pesach Matzah Maror' (with orthographic errors – which may suggest a later dating); clearly this plate was for the varieties of foods used at the Passover feast and was meant to be placed on the Seder table.

Naturally, the blessing over the wine, and the injunction to drink

163
DEBRY PSALTER
Vellum, velvet binding with silver, applied niello decorations Spain, late fifteenth century
(Gift of Mr Jakob Michael, New York, in memory of his wife, Erna Michael)
It is suggested that this Psalter belonged to the wealthy Jewish banking family of da Norsa, who lived in Mantua and Ferrara. On their family badge is the saying 'This is my name forever, and this is my remembrance for all generations.'

four cups during the course of the reading of the Haggadah, prompted artisans to make wine cups for the Passover holiday and patrons to order them. A cup, often of the finest workmanship and filled to the brim with wine, is put on the Seder table. It is called 'Elijah's cup'. As we have already noticed in other objects which have a purely domestic function, the further removed an object is from religious ritual, the greater the freedom of artistic expression. During the course of the Seder, while reciting the Haggadah, the significance of the Passover is discussed as it applies to the 'wise man', the 'wicked man', the 'fool', and 'the one who cannot ask questions'. It is interesting to observe that on the 'Elijah' wine goblet (reproduced in plate 164) the 'wicked man' is depicted as a warrior, the figure being based on an earlier printed prototype. Jewish tradition has always had somewhat of an aversion to military heroes; those few who are revered, like Joshua, David and Judah Maccabaeus, are not really professional warriors but individuals from the ranks who, by virtue of their position or as a result of chance and divine intervention, were called upon to assume leadership.

Many laws in the Jewish tradition are associated with food, with prohibitions and specific injunctions relating to clean and unclean animals which can be eaten or are forbidden. Only certain animals, slaughtered under special conditions, can be eaten. But even more important are the holidays, and their specific connections with the

164
WINEBOTTLE
Polished glass, silver and gilt handle, lid, and base
Austria, Eisenstadt, 1740
(Formerly owned by the Austerlitz family and donated by Dr Moshe Atlas, Jerusalem)
SEDER CUP
Silver, partly gilt
Germany, late seventeenth century
(Permanent loan from Mr and Mrs Victor Carter, Los Angeles, ex-Sholom Asch Collection)
At times, by merely adding Hebrew inscriptions, an object of general use such as this wine decanter becomes an object used for Jewish ritual purposes. At other times, the entire work of art from its very inception is created as a Jewish ceremonial object, like this beaker.

family gathering round the table to eat. As we have already mentioned, each ritual meal is initiated with a blessing over the wine. On the Sabbath three meals must be eaten. The entire Passover holiday uses symbolic foods, the matzah serving as a reminder of the feast's origin. Tabernacles places the family round the feast table in a temporary dwelling; over the years, similar traditions have evolved around many of the other holidays in the Jewish year.

As there are feasts, there are also fasts, and the 'Sabbath of Sabbaths', the day most holy to the Jews in the calendar of holidays, is Yom Kippur, the 'Day of Atonement'. It is observed in the autumn, ten penitential days from the beginning of the Jewish New Year. It is a solemn day devoted to prayer; from sunset to the following nightfall, eating or drinking is forbidden. During the New Year's holiday and the Day of Atonement, a special instrument is introduced into the synagogal ritual. Following the destruction of the Second Temple, the rabbis forbade the use of musical instruments during worship. The only exception to this is the appearance of the shofar or ram's horn (plate 165) in the New Year's service. This primitive instrument has an archaeological prototype and can be seen in the mosaics and gold glass in the early centuries of our era. The horn used on this High Holiday is most often that of a ram, but at times of an ibex, goat or sheep (plate 168). In antiquity it was used for calling the people together for announcements of great importance. People were led to war by the sound of the shofar, and proclamations were preceded by the blowing of the horn. On Yom Kippur, a long blast of the shofar concludes this Day of Awe.

Gravity and solemnity distinguish the Day of Atonement. Exhilaration and uninhibited joy characterise Purim, the Feast of Lots. The book associated with this holiday is in the last of the five rolls of the Hagiographa. The setting is Susa, in Persia, capital of the Achaemenians, during the fifth century BC, the Purim heroes are Esther and Mordechai, and the villain Haman. Esther becomes a queen and succeeds in saving the life of her cousin and of the Jews living in that great empire. She does so by exposing Haman's plot to destroy them and has him hanged, along with his ten sons, instead of Mordechai. The Feast of Lots is a time for great rejoicing, and the story, in an undecorated Esther roll narrative, is read in the synagogue. Haman is vilified and the heroes are blessed. On this holiday, the rabbis ruled it as permissible even to become 'lightheaded through drink'. Gifts are exchanged, and the triumph of Mordechai and Esther over Haman, who has come to personify all Jewish oppressors, is fancifully depicted in personal scrolls which, like the Passover Haggadot, are often wonderful examples of Jewish art, sophisticated or naïve. A traditional gift of bride to groom was a decorated metal or wooden container which housed the Esther scrolls. The Museum has a

165

ROTHSCHILD MANUSCRIPT 24

Thin vellum – 473 leaves
Italy, Ferrara (?), c. 1470

(Presented to the Museum anonymously)

Following the tradition of many centuries, the rabbi is shown sounding the shofar.

166

SIDDUR OF THE RABBI OF RIZIN

Parchment – 365 leaves
Southern or eastern Germany, c. 1460

(Formerly in the possession of the nineteenth-century Hassidic Rabbi Israel Friedman of Rižin)

Five hundred years ago this manuscript was probably used by a wealthy family living in Germany. A human touch can be seen in the rubbed corners of the pages, marginal notations and the wine stains in the section of the Passover Haggadah.

ליל
ערבים

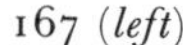

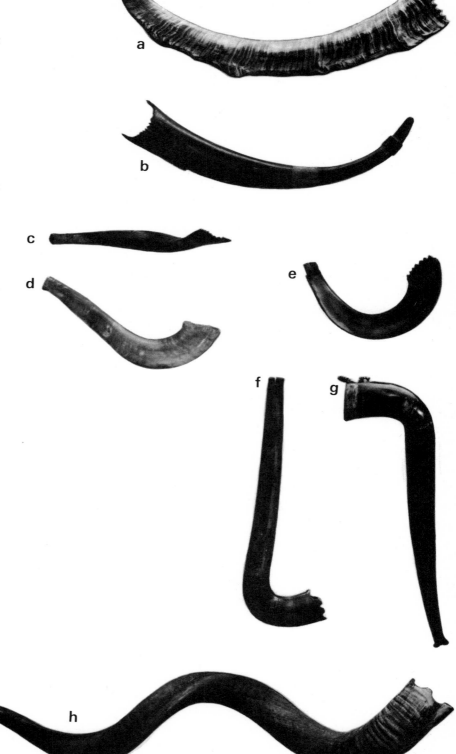

167 (*left*)

ERNA MICHAEL HAGGADAH

Parchment – 77 leaves
Germany, middle Rhine, c. 1400
(*Gift of Mr Jakob Michael, New York, in memory of his wife, Erna Michael*)

Hanging above the Seder table is a star-shaped oil lamp. The participants wear the required Jewish conical hats, here somewhat stylized.

168 (*right*)

SHOFARS

(*from the top, left to right*)
(a) *Ram's horn*
Yemen, nineteenth century
(b) *Horn*
Central Europe, early nineteenth century
(c) *Horn*
Tripoli, early nineteenth century
(d) *Horn*
Morocco, Fez, c. nineteenth century
(*Gift of Mr Z. Schulmann, Paris*)
(e) *Horn*
Algeria, nineteenth century
(*Gift of Mr Z. Schulmann, Paris*)
(f) *Horn*
Germany, eighteenth century
(*Burstein Collection, Lugano*)
(g) *Horn*
Hungary, early nineteenth century
(h) *Horn*
Yemen, eighteenth century
(*On loan from Hechal Shlomo Museum, Jerusalem*)

Some examples of the varying types of the traditional Shofar horn.

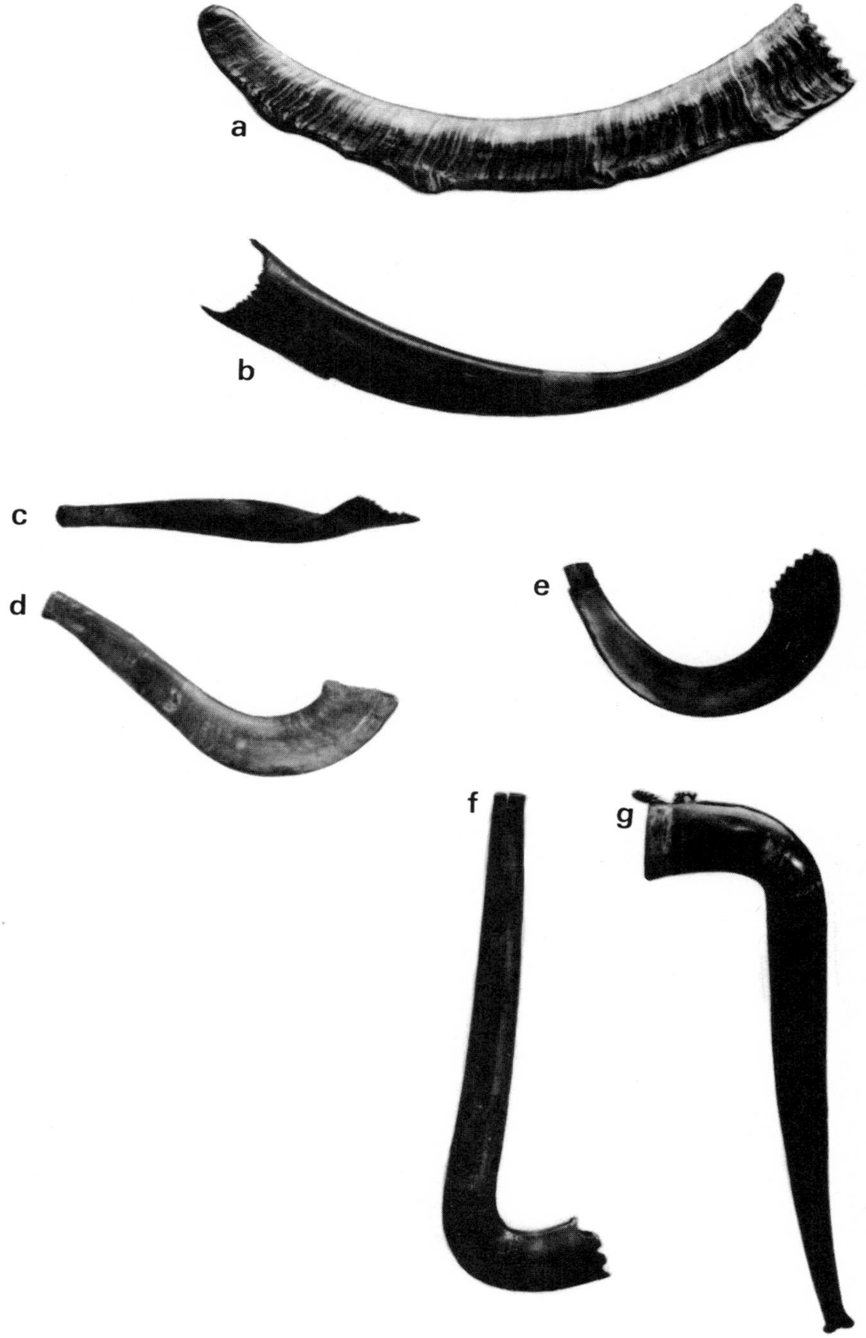

considerable number of attractive silver examples. The scroll reproduced on plate 176 is Alsatian, and the detail here, showing a three-piece string ensemble entertaining a festive group seated around a holiday table, can only hint at the charm of the manuscript and the joyful aspect of this holiday.

We have seen how the Torah scroll is richly embellished with textiles and silver accoutrements, and how the Esther roll is placed into a richly ornamented container. This manner of housing and covering sacred writings is indicative of the respect and love given by the People of the Book to their Books. And it is consistent with this approach that prayer books for the Sabbath and holidays should also be covered in an attractive and pleasing way. The silver-gilt, filigree book cover on the right in plate 169 is from Italy and dates from 1771; it was most probably used by a woman for the Sabbath. This cover, with another one in the Museum's collection, is one of the earliest metal Jewish bookbindings known. The repoussé silver bookbinding on the left has on it an inscription which dates it to 1753, in Italy, and once more we see the use of the seven-branched menorah as an ornamental device. The openwork bookbinding from Galicia in the lower half of the plate in all probability once covered a High Holiday prayer book, used on New Year's Day and the Day of Atonement. On one side there is a representation of Jacob's dream and on the other a representation of the sacrifice of Isaac. Both of these Biblical episodes, which are reaffirmations of God's covenant with His People, were popular themes in the Jews' artistic repertoire.

There are customs and rules which permeate every aspect of the religious Jew's life, from the moment he rises until the time he retires, and from the day of his birth – and even prior to that – until his burial. Every phase of the Jew's life is regulated by commandments and tradition. To live within this faith is a way of life, and there are beautiful and precious objects to accompany each of its significant occasions.

As we have seen in various other contexts, the near eastern genesis of the Jewish faith had a profound effect on the art forms and iconography in occidental as well as oriental Judaica. We have noted the persistence of tradition, the continuity of motifs, the tenacious reliance on oriental elements, giving a Mediterranean overtone to many objects which are Jewish.

Let us trace the life cycle of the Jew through the objects connected with those highlights which are given specific artistic expressions. Even before the child is born, the mother, if she comes from the Near East or cultures affiliated with the Sephardic rite, will wear amulets – superstitious protective devices for good health and to ward off the evil eye – to assure the wearer of safe-keeping and to guard the mother from the dangers of childbirth, and later the male child during the days before circumcision. Naturally, these magical objects do not

169

BOOKBINDINGS

(*right*) *Silver, gilt and filigree*
Italy, 1771
(*Gift of Mr A. Burstein, Lugano*)

(*centre bottom*) *Silver*
Galicia, early nineteenth century

(*left*) *Silver*
Italy, 1753
(*Gift of the Jewish Community, Rome*)

Any religious text in manuscript or print is holy in the Jewish tradition, and if it is not serviceable, it cannot be destroyed, and must be burned or secreted away. Removable precious bookbindings take that fact into account.

bear mundane texts, but secret Hebrew symbols and special groupings of effective letters carrying cabbalistic meanings, which are inscribed or placed on or into these amulets. Plate 175 shows five types, each one having its own significance. Looking at them clockwise, we see a torque with several objects dangling from chains. Two of the most powerful names of God are inscribed on these hanging, coin-like objects. There is a hand – frequently used in the orient to ward off the evil eye – and a rattle, an object which has a long association with magic. In the amulet below that, the tinkling sound of the diminutive bells had in all probability a certain magical significance. The actual text for the amulet was inserted in the hollow space below the carnelians which decorated the container.

The golden medal on the lower left-hand side is one of the finest examples of its kind; it was made in either Holland or Germany, probably in 1665. On one face there is a representation of David being anointed, and on the other we see David playing the lyre and dancing before the Ark of the Covenant, which is being carried by the priests. This medal was probably placed above a baby's crib, the child's name certainly being David. Directly above the golden medal is a silver pendant, a Shiviti amulet from Persia, on which is incised the menorah and a number of superscriptions and acrostics. The top of it bears the first half of Psalm 16:8, 'I have set the Lord always before me', and the tetragrammaton is in the upper centre. Psalm 67 and Genesis 49:22 are incorporated into the amulet by using the first letters of each of the words. Often the name of the owner appears on the reverse of these pendants, which are intended to be worn as parts of necklaces.

The elaborate amulet in the upper left-hand corner is typical of the Italian style. It is generally called a 'shaddai', the holy name of God, here incised in the heart-shaped upper part of the case. Often, small ornaments are applied in the round or in high relief, such as the Tablets of the Law, menorah, high priest's hat, censers, and sometimes objects which can be interpreted as fertility symbols, such as the bunch of grapes suspended from the bottom of this beautiful object.

For the superstitious, an amulet is to the wearer as the mezuzah is to the Jewish home, which is popularly believed to protect the house and its occupants. The Bible commands that each Jew profess his love of God and His Unity – 'Hear O Israel, the Lord our God, the Lord is One' (Deuteronomy, 6:4), and when in prayer to wear phylacteries on his arm and over his head every day except the Sabbath and holidays (Deut., 6:8, and that the essence of God's commandment be an integral part of his home. To carry out this last commandment, the tradition-orientated Jew places the mezuzah at the entrance to his home – 'And you shall write them on the door-posts of your house and on your gates' (Deut., 6:9) (plate 170). An attractive container is fixed

170
ROTHSCHILD
MANUSCRIPT 24
Thin vellum – 473 leaves
Italy, Ferrara (?), c. 1470
(*Presented to the Museum anonymously*)
No Renaissance mezuzah cases survive and this depiction is a rare example of a door-post amulet installed in a Jewish home in northern Italy.

obliquely to the right-hand door-post, and a parchment containing Deut., 6:4–9 and 11:13–21 is placed in the container which has the 'shaddai' name of God appearing through an aperture. On the right-hand side of plate 171 we see an example from Russia, made of silver, with the small doors actually opened to reveal 'Shaddai'. The porcelain mezuzah is from Germany and dates from the eighteenth century; it is rare as most mezuzot are made of either metal or wood.

In God's Covenant with Abraham (Gen., 17:1–10, 21:4) the initiation of every Jewish male consisted of circumcision, a rite found in many societies. This ritual operation is performed when the boy is eight days old. Plate 172 shows the ceremony depicted in a special 'Brit Milah' circumcision manuscript made in Germany in 1729. Below it are the various surgical devices necessary for this operation required by the Bible. Numerous other objects have evolved around this ceremony besides the knife, clamp and flask shown.

171 (*left*)

MEZUZOT

(*left*) *Porcelain*
Germany, eighteenth century

(*right*) *Silver, Mark: 84,* HK, *1873* AD
Russia, 1873
(*Gift of Joseph Wilenski, Petah Tikva*)

Ranging from the most simple container to elaborate and artistic examples such as these, every traditional Jewish home or institution has a mezuzah at least at the entrance, and on the door-posts of some rooms.

172 (*right*)

MOHEL MANUSCRIPT

Parchment
Germany, Hamburg-Altona, 1729
(*Gift of Mr Joel Snoman, Tel-Aviv*)

CIRCUMCISION FLASK

Silver
France, nineteenth century

CIRCUMCISION KNIFE

Steel and porcelain
Bohemia, 1813
(*Gift of Mr Jacob Tedesco, Paris, in memory of his father*)

(*left*)

CIRCUMCISION CLAMP

Silver with lacquer paint
Morocco, nineteenth century
(*Gift of Mr Z. Schulmann, Paris*)

(*bottom*)

CIRCUMCISION KNIFE

Steel, silver and amber
Near East, 1819

The mohel, the person performing the circumcision, sits in the seat named after Elijah the prophet and carries out the operation as Abraham the patriarch had 'circumcized his son Isaac.'

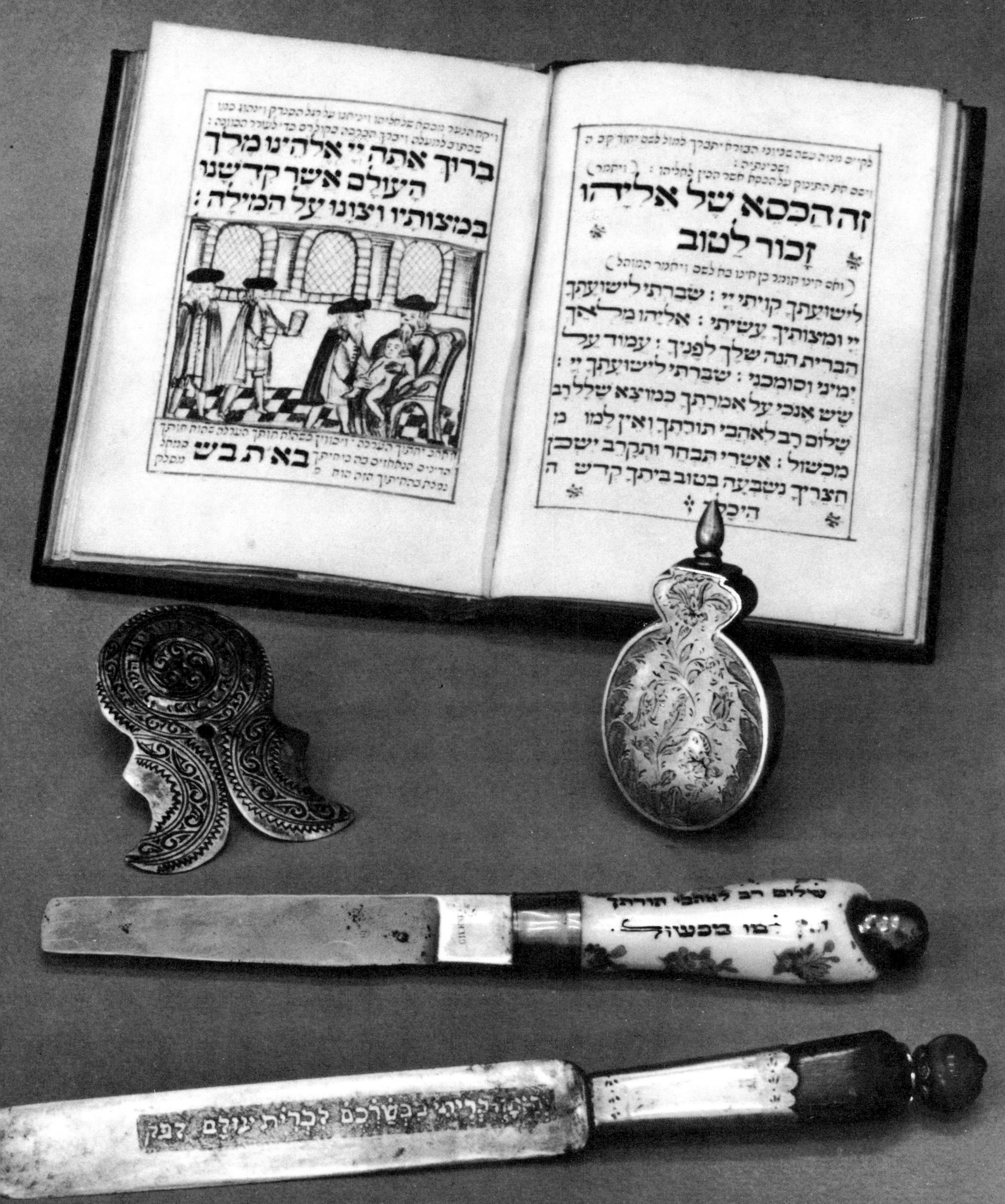
ברוך אתה יי אלהינו מלך
העולם אשר קדשנו
במצותיו וצונו על המילה:
זה הכסא של אליהו
זכור לטוב

173 (*left*)
COFANETTO
Silver, partly gilt, niello
Italy, Ferrara, second half fifteenth century
(*Gift of Mr Astorre Mayer, Milan*)
The inscriptions near each of the depictions of the deeds for the married woman are in Hebrew, while the linen list and the numeration are in Italian, but written in Hebrew letters.

174 (*right*)
KETUBAH
Parchment
Holland, Rotterdam, 1648
(*Gift of Mr H. Gans, Amsterdam*)
Name of Groom: Isaac Pareira.
Name of Bride: Rachel, daughter of Abraham da Pinto.

Marriage in the Jewish tradition is a simple ceremony. There is the sanctification over the wine, six other benedictions, a simple vow stating intentions 'according to the laws of Moses and Israel', the giving of a simple ring, which should be 'worth at least a penny', and a contract, or 'Ketubah', witnessed and signed by two males of the community.

The Israel Museum possesses a fine collection of objects associated with Jewish married life. One of the rarest is a silver and niello cofanetto (plate 173) from northern Italy, *c.* 1470. The scene which decorates the front panel of the casket, in which keys and precious objects were kept, shows (from right to left) the three duties incumbent upon every Jewish woman: baking bread for the Sabbath and symbolically sacrificing a piece, ritual bathing, and kindling of the Sabbath and holiday lights. The Ketubot – marriage contracts – show, almost more than anything else, the diverse aesthetic influences at work in Jewish art. The text for the contract is much the same in all the countries of the Diaspora, the only difference being the name of the bride and groom, the year, the date and place of marriage, and the amount of money in the dowry. But when it comes to the illumination and illustration of the contract, these marriage contracts reflect the diverse artistic trends of each community (plates 174 and 177–179).

At the conclusion of the marriage ceremony, the groom breaks a glass. There is a certain amount of discussion as to the significance of this act. Some see it as a symbol of the destruction of the Temple; others, as a sacrifice of a precious object. In Germany, synagogues

175 (*overleaf left*)
AMULETS
(*upper left*) *Silver*
Italy, nineteenth century
(*Collection Mr A. Burstein, Lugano*)
(*upper right*) *Silver, semiprecious stones*
Kurdistan, eighteenth century
(*centre left*) *Silver*
Iran, eighteenth century
(*bottom right*) *Silver, carnelian stones*
Yemen, eighteenth century
(*bottom left*) *Gold*
Holland, Amsterdam, 1665
(*Gift of Mr Moshe Oved, London*)
Amulets, words of power, special symbols or colours, in an extraordinary variety of forms, help ward off the 'evil eye' and protect the wearer from a multitude of dangers. These are some of the Museum's extensive collection.

בסימנא טבא ובמזלא יאה ובסיעתא דשמיא אורה
לחתן הבחור ולכלה הבתולה בשם אר אלהי

176 (*preceding pages right*)

ESTHER SCROLL CASES

(*left to right*)
Silver filigree
Turkey, nineteenth century

Silver
Russia, nineteenth century

Silver
Salonica, nineteenth century
(*Gift of Mr Sistero, Rome*)

Silver gilt, with polished coral
Italy, c. nineteenth century
(*Gift of Henry M. Rein, New York*)

Silver, partly gilt
Italy, late seventeenth century

ESTHER SCROLL

Parchment
Germany, Alsace, eighteenth century

At the top, a delightful scroll from Alsace-Lorraine with many gay genre scenes, and below are some examples of the charmingly decorative cases used for the Esther scrolls.

177 (*left*)

KETUBAH

Paper
Iran, Isfahan, 1860
(*Gift of Mr Eliezer Ben Dov, Teheran*)

Name of Groom: Ezekiel, son of Joseph.
Name of Bride: Leah, daughter of Elijah.

178 (*right*)

KETUBAH

Parchment
Italy, Rome, 1857

Name of Groom: Daniel Joseph, son of Yehuda.
Name of Bride: Bolisa, daughter of Moses, son of Zonamma.

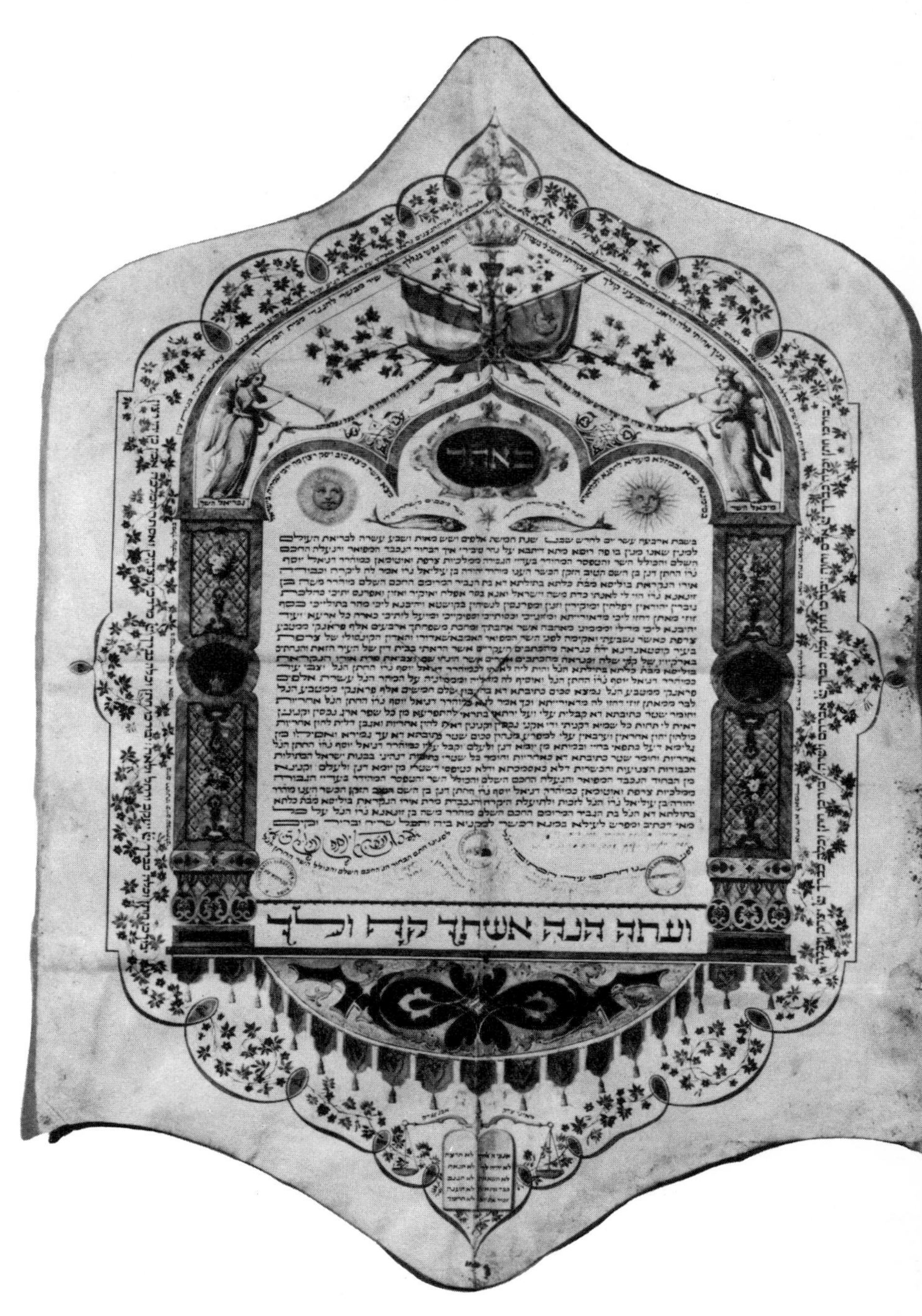

בשם רחמן
בשם אשר לו הגדולה ומרומם על
כל ברכה ותהלה בשיר
מצא אשה מצא טוב ויפק רצון מה' בית והון נחלת
אבות ומה' אשה משכלת

180 (*above*)
ENGRAVING BY PUSCHNER
From a book by Paul Christian Kirchner, Jüdisches Ceremoniel, Nürnberg, c. 1730
The bridegroom, during the wedding ceremony, breaks a glass against the marriage stone.

179 (*left*)
KETUBAH
Parchment
Yemen, San'a, 1794
Name of Groom: Abraham, son of Hanukkah, son of Yichyah.
Name of Bride: Romaya, daughter of Abraham.

had marriage stones built into one of their exterior walls. Plate 181 shows one from the community of Bingen on the Rhine in Germany, dated 1700. As one can see from the engraving (plate 180), the groom throws the glass at the stone, which has on it two cornucopias – symbols of plenty – and in the star-shaped motif the first letters of the phrase, 'The voice of mirth, and the voice of gladness, the voice of the bridegroom, and the voice of the bride'.

'Repentance', 'prayer', and 'charity', are the three practices which can alter the final judgment. This phrase is repeated every year during the Day of Atonement, when each soul is weighed and judgment made. Charity boxes are household objects in the Jewish home, and they are frequently seen during a Jewish funeral. Plate 182 shows a brass charity box with an inscription noting the charity – to help the infirm in the community of Reggio in Italy. The box is dated 1830 but it was probably first used in the eighteenth century. Placing money in a charity box allows the donor to remain anonymous, which is considered the highest form of charity. To the left of this alms box is a Bohemian

181 (*left*)

MARRIAGE STONE

Red sandstone
Germany, Bingen, c. 1700
(Gift of the Jewish Community, Cologne)

The mnemonic inscription on the stone is from a pessimistic prophecy of Jeremiah (7:34), but it is neatly edited to make it an optimistic one.

182 (*right*)

BURIAL AND CHARITY BOXES:

(*right*) CHARITY BOX

Bronze
Italy, Reggio, end of seventeenth century
(Gift of Mr and Mrs Siegfried Kramarsky, New York)

Charity boxes such as this one are not only found at funerals, but in synagogues and at every joyous occasion as well.

(*left*) 'HOLY BURIAL SOCIETY OF PRAGUE' GLASS

Glass with enamel painting
Bohemia-Moravia, 1713

This is one of the four known rare Holy Burial Society glasses, all of them from Bohemia, this one probably from Prague. The oldest one of the three dates from 1692; the others, 1784 and 1787.

glass, dated 1713, which was used annually by a 'Holy Burial Society' (in Prague) on their annual feast celebrated on the traditional date of Moses' death. The society, which was organised to take care of the funerals in the community, was composed of distinguished individuals who held this feast, at which time these great glass beakers were used. On this burial society glass a scene from a funeral procession is depicted (plate 183), with the distinguished gentlemen marching behind a group of mourning women, the last one carrying an alms box, as are the first two men in the procession. One of the men is seen saying to the other, 'Charity will save you from death'.

Were we to go backwards in time to Joshua, David, or even Solomon, then the minimum number of years which we can reckon on as the span of Jewish history is more than three thousand; and yet in over thirty centuries the sum total of the objects which can be connected with the Hebraic religious tradition is extremely limited. There are almost no objects made of precious metals, although there are a number of small movable works in relatively ordinary materials, and there are not many architectural landmarks. All this is understandable when one considers the innumerable invasions and subsequent devastations of the Holy Land, and the forced wanderings and ordeals which the Jews in the Diaspora had to endure.

The vast majority of the objects discussed above cannot be classed in the category of great art. They do not aspire to this special status, and the patrons who ordered them, and the artisans and artists who created them, were probably not even trying to requisition a masterpiece or fashion a memorable creation. The desire to beautify the Holy Scroll, the wish to embellish the festivities of their holidays, and the need to enhance day to day occasions which had religious significance, inspired and prompted the patrons' commissions. For the artisan

and the artist the motivation was the desire to shape and fashion a beautiful work of art. With naïveté and enthusiasm, with untutored abilities and zeal, the Jewish craftsman or artist responded to the best of his ability to the patron's order. He combined a variety of elements, possibly not in the manner most fashionable at the time, but in a way which was full of human expression and beauty. For the Jewish creative person was very often not part of the artistic mainstream, membership in the craftsmen's guilds being denied to him. As a result of his status within the community we see certain aspects appear-

183

'HOLY BURIAL SOCIETY OF PRAGUE' GLASS

The full scene, shown in a rolled-out form, that decorates the glass shown in plate 182.

ing in Jewish art, motifs and methods which were passé by the time they were created. But what we have is an art made from love and enthusiasm, integrity and deep religious commitment. It is a living art, responsive to a living religion, and so there is no final chapter. Although we have not shown any of the contemporary material which the Museum possesses in small quantities, with the new influences at work in Israel and the Diaspora today there will most certainly be many new developments in the creation of Jewish ceremonial and ritual works of art.

Karl Katz

World Art in Jerusalem

Archaeology is a national pastime in Israel, and vast numbers of people visit archaeological sites and museums. The interpretation and scientific understanding of the objects and artifacts of hundreds of thousands of years which have been discovered in this land require much scholarship and specialised knowledge, but the fact that they are there, under one's feet, almost like natural resources, means that they can be found and cherished by everybody. Pagan objects, Jewish, Christian and Muslim fragments are to be found by anyone in Israel, at any time – while planting a tree, laying a road, excavating foundations for a house, or even just walking along the sea-shore. A special fondness is felt for these pieces from the past which makes them a significant part of the present and a fascination to all.

We have already mentioned certain motifs that regularly appear in Judaica, but it would be going too far to isolate the objects carrying these symbols and to label them 'Jewish art'. Certainly, there are superficial resemblances uniting these heterogeneous objects of the Jewish tradition, but there is no homogeneous style. Because of this the Museum displays Jewish ritual and ceremonial material together with some ethnological exhibits that can be clearly identified with the Jewish people, conveniently calling this assemblage 'art and art-craft in the Jewish tradition'. To Jews these works associated with their religion and tradition do not appear either foreign or strange, and though an occidental Jew may look at an oriental object without fully understanding its aesthetic approach, a genuine rapport does exist between a majority of the inhabitants of the country and the many different creations made within the context of the Hebrew faith. To many of the visitors, a large portion of the Museum's archaeological and ritual art galleries are meaningful. In the total concept of the Israel Museum the general art section is certainly as important as its specialised sections but, to the specific public it serves, these areas may be less understandable.

In the introductory chapter, we spoke of the Yemenite family, the Bokharan couple and the Arab parents, and the confrontations which occurred on first visiting the Museum, when they came across strange objects, very different from what they were used to. The ethnological section of the Museum, where costumes and jewelry of the Jews of the Near and Middle East are exhibited, was discussed briefly as one of the means through which these visitors gradually became more accustomed to the Museum, eventually to become regular visitors.

The Yemenites are without doubt the most exotic of the far-flung Jewish communities. One tradition puts them in this mountainous region of the south-western portion of the Arabian Peninsula immediately after the destruction of the First Temple (586 BC). Whether one

184 (*opposite*)
YEMENITE BRIDE
Brocade, silver and gilt beads, white pearls, corals, bead embroidery Yemen, San'a – modern reconstruction of traditional costume
A number of prescribed costume changes are made during the two-week wedding celebrations. This is the richest of them all.

185

NORTH AFRICAN GROUP

Black costume

Velvet, embroidered with ribbon, lace and golden thread, silver filigree buttons, large Muslim sleeves, golden thread woven girdle

Morocco, Tetouan, late nineteenth – early twentieth centuries

(Gift of Mr Z. Schulman, Paris)

Elements of modesty, conspicuous wealth, subtle decorative devices and symbolic ornament are all interwoven in middle eastern costumes.

accepts this date or the late first century AD (after the destruction of the Second Temple), they certainly represent an extraordinary group, which has survived under most trying conditions. Although at one period (in the sixth century) in their two thousand years or more in the Yemen they even rose to political power, their stay in that remote country has for the most part been a difficult one. From the beginning of the Islamic Period thirteen hundred years ago, they were forced to assume an inferior status. It was during one period of persecution directed by the Abbasids in Baghdad, that the great Rabbi Maimonides, himself a refugee from Spanish persecution, wrote the famous 'Letter to the Yemen' (1172), explaining to his fellow Jews the reason for their suffering. In general, they were stratified within the total society as artisans, craftsmen, tinkers and merchants. Their crucial position in the Yemenite society became clear when in 1949–50 nearly all of them emigrated to Israel, completely depriving the Yemen of craftsmen. It is no idle claim that almost all indigenous Yemenite crafts are the work of Yemenite Jews. In the late 1920s and 1930s, the Hamburg geographer and ethnologist, Carl Rathjens, made four expeditions to the Yemen. As a result of his fieldwork, thousands of objects were collected and evenly divided between Hamburg and Jerusalem – a collection acquired and permanently lent by the Schocken family to the Bezalel Museum. In the Museum's collection, one of the mementoes of this culture is seen in the Yemenite bride display, decked in precious cloths, silver, and silver-gilt jewelry (plate 184). During the two-week wedding ceremony, several costumes would be worn by both the bride and the groom; the one shown in the plate is from San'a and was worn by the bride in the Sanctification and Union ceremony. The superb jewelry and the brocaded coat would have been borrowed for the occasion. The costume consisted of the coat and two dresses, with brocaded leggings underneath, a tiara covered with pearls, small semiprecious stones, filigree work and flowers, and traditional jewelry. Yemenite families continue these wedding customs in Israel.

The North African Jews settled along the entire coast of that continent from Morocco to Libya in Graeco-Roman times (they had established themselves in Egypt before this period). As in so many other areas where various religious groups held sway, they were persecuted under numerous rulers during the course of their long stay in the 'Maghreb'. In the fifteenth century, the Jews had been expelled from Spain and in the sixteenth century, Leo Africanus, a Jewish traveller, recorded that the Jews were the only masons, locksmiths, goldsmiths, metal-founders, potters, silk-weavers, painters and minters in North Africa. There were important centres of learning in Morocco and Tunisia; Maimonides himself lived in Fez for some time before he moved to Fustat in Egypt.

The costumes of the North African Jews (plate 185) show strong influences from Spain, which is quite understandable given the propinquity of the Iberian peninsula and the fact that refugees had come to North Africa from Spain in various waves during the twelfth, fourteenth and fifteenth centuries as a result of persecution and expulsion.

Whether the Bokharan Jewish community (which lived in what is now Uzbekistan) settled there ten, twenty or twenty-five centuries ago is a problem which scholars have not yet been able to solve. In the early Islamic period, traders from northern Persia and probably from Bokhara and Samarkand made their way to the Imperial Court of China; in T'ang tomb figurines we can see representations of Semitic merchants. If we assume that the general Jewish culture of northern Iran applies to the Bokharan Jews, then the observations of the traveller Benjamin of Tudela (*c.* 1161–73) regarding the Jews of Khazvin and Nishapur apply also to the Jews of Uzbekistan. He reported that these Jews were well-established and that they maintained friendly relations with the nomadic Turkish tribes of the region. In the early nineteenth century, an English missionary observed that the Jews were '. . . mostly dyers and silk merchants; they wear a small cap, and a girdle around the chest, in order to be distinguished from the Mohammedans.'

The beautiful robes, jewelry (plates 17 and 187) and other wearing apparel, are all testimony to the extraordinary wealth and sumptuous beauty of the central Asian Jewish tradition. One can find parallels for the motifs used in the art of migratory tribes from the fifth century BC and in Mongol and Turkish tribal decorations. Since it was on the Silk Route, it is not surprising to find in the Bokharan repertoire far eastern motifs merging with Persian and central Asian art.

These are the costumes and jewelry of the parents, grandparents and remote ancestors of our regular visitors and their children. As we have already said, once they have seen this section and are made to feel at home by these familiar things, it is not long before they are investigating the rest of the Museum. Naturally, more knowledgeable visitors find this ethnological section extremely enlightening, and gain added admiration for their fellow citizens whose backgrounds are near and middle eastern. Both groups profit from this rich display of ethnological material. In the future, the Museum hopes to enlarge this section to include an exhibition of indigenous ethnology of the village and city Arabs, the Bedouin and Druze and also, if possible, material from the European Diaspora.

As we have already mentioned, the Museum regularly collects and exhibits archaeological works of art from neighbouring cultures. In order to increase appreciation of local antiquities, it is essential to understand the diverse influences which have gone to make the many

186

HUNTING SCENE PLATE

Silver with gilt, repoussé
Persia, c. fourth-fifth centuries, Sassanian

(Anonymous collection, permanent loan)

Hunting was a royal sport in the Sassanian Period. The lion being shot is represented as dead below the king, who is mounted on a horse in a flying gallop.

archaeological finds in the Holy Land what they are. Two such galleries can be visited at the Museum. One of them is dedicated to the rich Iranian culture, an area of tangential influence on Israel's archaeology compared with Egypt and the Aegean, but certainly containing material of great beauty.

There are similarities to the Achaemenian gold ibex (plate 188) in the exhibits at the Berlin, London and Washington museums. In all the examples it would appear that these beautifully arched and magnificently graceful animals were in fact handles of large vases. Some of the ibexes are winged; others, like this one, have stylised bodies in which parts of the physique, such as the rib-cage, the forelegs and the hind quarters, are deliberately emphasised. These articulations are transformed into decorative elements, so that in spite of the unnatural exaggeration they are harmoniously united in an elegant and satisfying whole. The Museum owns a silver Achaemenian vase on which the handles are a pair of lions grasping the rim with their forepaws and the body of the vase with their back legs. The ibex must have been used in a similar way on a golden vase. In this connection it is interesting to note that on the great stairway leading to the grand audience hall at Persepolis are figured, in low-relief, processions of people bearing gifts and tributes to the King of Kings. The rulers Darius I, Xerxes I and Artaxerxes, received these representatives of the various lands which lay within their hegemony. The gift-bearers represented bring presents typical of their regions or precious works of art. One Lydian bearer can be seen carrying a vase with animal handles comparable to the golden ibex in the Museum.

There are also numerous parallels to the rhyton reproduced in plate 189. These drinking horns, which can be seen with either ibex, lion, ram, bull or griffon heads, exist in ceramic, bronze, silver and gold, and are found widely distributed throughout the Near and Middle East. The type shown here was first commonly seen during the reign of Sargon II of Assyria (721–705 BC).

After the destruction of the Achaemenian empire and the devastation of their capital city Persepolis by Alexander the Great in 330 BC, there followed a long period of Graeco-Roman influence. Then an indigenous Iranian dynasty, the Sassanians, rose up and vanquished the Romans, to rule a large portion of the ancient Near East for a relatively short but significant period (AD 224–651). The new dynasty utilised Achaemenian motifs to affirm their continuity with the authentic Iranian tradition (plate 186). It is only recently that the art of this culture has been seriously studied. In the last decade, vast amounts of newly unearthed Sassanian material have appeared in the world markets, considerably broadening our knowledge of their art.

In a comparison between two works of art which utilise the same motif, we can see another interesting example of the persistence of

187

BOKHARAN JEWELRY

Gold and semiprecious stones

'Pirkhona' ornament for the forehead and earrings for a Jewish woman of Bokhara.

188 *(overleaf left)*

IBEX HANDLE

Gold

Persia, Achaemenian, c. fifth century BC

(Anonymous collection, permanent loan)

The essence of a mountain goat, a graceful example of the sumptuous art of the Achaemenian Period, created by artists who stylized their observations with great skill.

189 *(overleaf right)*

RHYTON

Gold

Persia, Achaemenian, c. fifth century BC

(Gift of Mr A. Rabenou, Paris)

A drinking horn in the shape of a horned ibex-head.

190 (*left*)

BOWL

Terracotta, champlevé ware, green glaze
Persia, Yasukand, c. eleventh-twelfth centuries

(*Gift of Mr and Mrs Edward M. M. Warburg, New York*)

The eagle as a decorative element, stylized, flattened, but still reminiscent of the imperial eagle on the Sassanian plate.

190 (*continued*)

CUP

Terracotta, overglaze painted
Persia, Rayy, c. thirteenth century

(*Gift of Mr and Mrs Edward M. M. Warburg, New York*)

Mounted riders in a procession, polo players or falconers, created in the colourful 'minai' style.

191 (*below*)

PLATE WITH EAGLE

Silver repoussé
Persia, Sassanian, fourth-fifth centuries

(*Anonymous collection, permanent loan*)

The eagle, a symbol of empire, courage and military prowess, is powerfully represented on this plate.

tradition. In plate 191 is reproduced a Sassanian silver dish on which an eagle is represented in repoussé work, and in plate 190 a champlevé technique green glazed ceramic bowl made about five hundred years later. The ceramic version, potted in north-western Iran during the eleventh or twelfth centuries, may in fact be based on a metal prototype. The wings are merely large curved shapes accommodating foliate forms, turning this powerful bird into a decorative object. The leaf pattern is also in the body of the eagle; this combination of animal and vegetal motifs into inseparable decorative patterns was a major contribution of the Islamic style. The bird is also flattened; the shape of the bowl predominates, forcing the form of the eagle to accommodate the bowl's carinated profile. In the silver plate, the Sassanian eagle shows the strong influence of its Graeco-Roman predecessor as seen through the eyes of an indigenous Iranian artist. There are specific stylisations around the eyes and feathers which mark it as an Iranian work of art, but the naturalism and the modelling, the sense of illusion and the highly specific detail show it to be a synthesis of the Graeco-Roman tradition and the art of Iran.

The mounted riders trotting in a procession on the little cup reproduced in plate 190, have precedents in Iranian art going back at least two thousand years. These riders (possibly polo players) mounted on their steppe ponies, were created under Mongol influence and are related to miniature painting. The cup is painted in the very colourful 'minai' or seven colour style.

The only two religions to have a relative direction of prayer rather than an absolute one are Judaism and Islam. The Jews, as we have observed, no matter where they are, orient their prayers toward Jerusalem. The Muslims face Mecca, the city which Muhammed established as the focal point of Islam, and the mihrab or prayer niche indicates the compass direction of their prayer. The example reproduced in plate 193 comes from the Safavid city of Isfahan and dates to the reign of Shah Abbas. It is made up of thousands of interlocked pieces of ceramics which fit together like a jigsaw puzzle. Above and around it, in beautiful calligraphy, are quotations from the Koran (sura number ninety-six across the top and in the niche suras forty-eight and eighty-nine). Non-figurative art is the only form permissible in the mosque.

Certainly the Museum's position in the centre of the Middle East must be affirmed, but it cannot lose sight of the diversity of man's creation in every place and in all periods. In the planned expansion of the Museum, galleries are to be built which will house far eastern art, primitive arts from Africa and the South Seas, pre-Columbian art, as well as an enlarged section for near and middle eastern art.

With regard to western art, period rooms are one of the means which the Museum uses to achieve this broader aim. The eighteenth-century

192
SALON (*Detail*)
Wood, painted and gilt, gobelins and paintings
France, Paris, eighteenth century
(*Gift of Baron Edmond de Rothschild, Paris*)
Formerly in the home of the Parisian banker, Samuel Bernard, a brilliant ambiance of the period of King Louis XVI.

French room (plate 192) already mentioned has a superb interior, and once belonged to the French banker Samuel Bernard. The sumptuousness of the room captures the essence of an entire epoque and gives the visitors, particularly the youngsters, an extraordinary opportunity to relate to the atmosphere and the mood through the art of this rich period of Louis XVI. Visitors can make interesting comparisons between this room and the decoration in the 1701 Vittorio Veneto synagogue, and in the near future the Museum plans to install a seventeenth-century Dutch room, and a fifteenth- to sixteenth-century Italian-Spanish room. It will be in these galleries that the youth studying European history, and the citizens who have not had contact with the west, will gain insight and understanding of these periods in history which have had such significant effects on the lives of us all.

The Israel Museum was established too late to be a great general art museum. No royal family patronised the masters of the past and thus accumulated treasures; vast sums of money could not be expended on works of art when – and so rarely if – they were available for purchase; and conquerors did not bring back the spoils of war. Consequently the collections of pre-nineteenth century paintings, sculpture, drawings and decorative arts in the Museum are not evenly balanced, and often there are great gaps in this early and essential material. The creation of the general art section has been and continues to be a triumph of interest and generosity, warmth and good-will, among people of all faiths from all over the world, and particularly the artists who see in this Museum 'an oasis in the Middle East'.

The ideal (for us) combination of a Biblical subject by a master artist can be obtained only on rare occasions. It is the Museum's policy to acquire, when possible, this type of art, though fine works in general are the Museum's ultimate goal. The specific aim must not be misunderstood as a narrow point of view – it is simply that paintings representing scenes from the Old Testament find a sympathetic audience in Israel, who immediately appreciate the subject matter. Happily, this union can be found in a few paintings in the Museum. For example, *The Destruction of Pharaoh's Host in the Red Sea* by Rubens (1577–1640) (plate 194), depicts a traditional subject which we have even seen in Hebrew illuminated manuscripts (see plate 161). Naturally, unlike the miniaturist, Rubens relies on drama and scale, drawing the viewer into the scene and overwhelming him with his vision of the miraculous drowning of Pharaoh and his army. The painting was originally attributed to Van Dyck and was thought to be *The Horses of Phaeton*, but because of the virtuoso rendering of the four horses and the heavy overpainting, this attribution was questioned. It was X-rayed, cleaned and only then identified as a lost Rubens. Full of brilliance and power, it is now assigned to the young Rubens, who probably painted it in 1604–5 in either Mantua or Rome, at a time when he was under the influence of the sixteenth-century Venetian masters, Titian and Tintoretto. It is a work which stands by itself, but the subject, together with the quality of the painting, makes it ideal for the Museum.

The Limoges cofanetto (plates 202 and 203) is a superb example of the same approach in the field of decorative arts. Here, in rich detail and sumptuous colours, we see the story of Joseph. In eight parts – the four sides, two scenes on the lid and two half-circles at the sides – the entire narrative is shown. The small arched scene on the side of the lid shows the young Joseph with his older brothers and their sheep, describing the two dreams he had (Gen., 37:7–9). In one dream, his brothers' sheaves of wheat bowed down to his; in the other, the sun, moon and stars made obeisance to him. Below, we see a favourite

193
PRAYER NICHE
Glazed ceramic mosaic tiles
Persia, Isfahan, seventeenth century
(*Gift of Mr A. Rabenou, Paris in memory of Khalil Rabenou*)
The niche gives the direction to which the Muslim prays, Mecca. The elegant calligraphy is a portion of the Koran and serves as visual instruction as well as a decorative element.

194 (*left*)
PETER PAUL RUBENS
Destruction of Pharoah's host in the Red Sea
Oil on canvas, Flemish, c. 1604–5
(*Mr and Mrs Philip J. Goldberg, London*)
Detail of a larger work, done by Rubens in Italy, and influenced by Tintoretto.

195 (*below*)
REMBRANDT VAN RIJN
The Healing of Tobit
Pen, bistre and wash drawing, Dutch, c. 1642–4
(*Gift of the Schocken family*)
Sketchy and modest in size, this drawing still evokes the atmosphere of the apocryphal scene.

subject of Baroque and Mannerist painters as a slightly more mature Joseph escapes from the advances of Potiphar's wife (Gen., 39:12). The scene on one half of the lid represents a bearded Joseph seated on a throne in his rôle as vizier to Pharaoh, receiving his brothers incognito (Gen., 42:6–8). In the scene below is shown the confrontation of Joseph with his youngest brother Benjamin (Gen., 45:4–15), in the background, we see Pharaoh gazing from a window at the family reunion.

On a small sheet of paper, Rembrandt (1606–69), with restrained perfection and with a minimum of strokes, captures the story of the healing of Tobit (plate 195). It is the first Rembrandt drawing in the Museum's collection and has been dated to the years between 1642–4. This tiny masterpiece shows the tonal, painterly approach characteristic of the middle period of Rembrandt's creative life and is a beautiful product of his most lyrical phase. This work of art again achieves that ideal aim mentioned above.

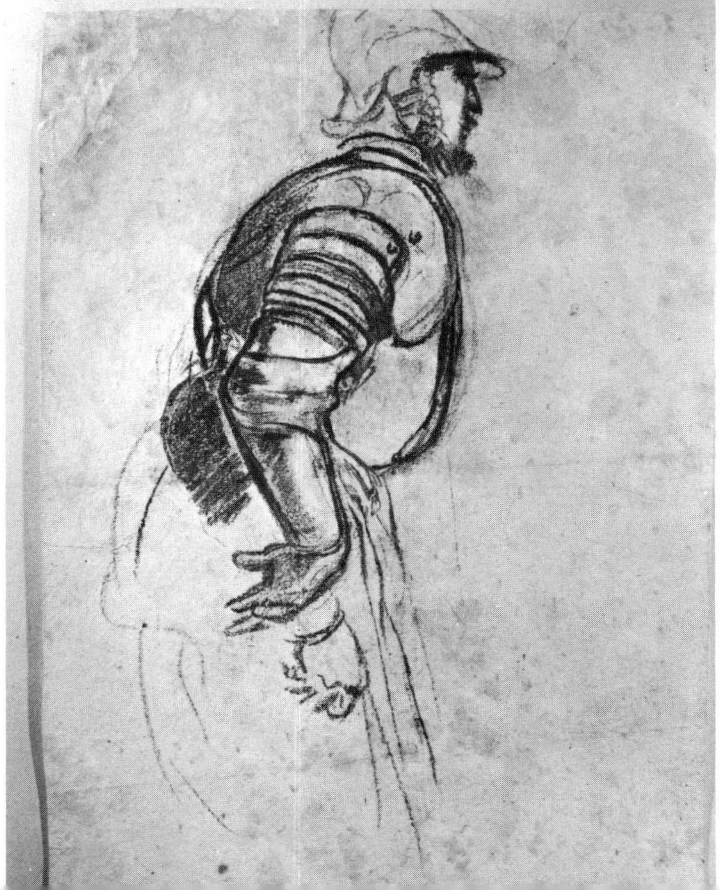

196 (*above*)

ALBERT CUYP
Return from the Hunt

Dutch, 1641, oil on canvas

(Gift of Mr and Mrs Joseph R. Nash, Paris)

Executed by the artist when he was 21 years old, this fine work represents a family of landowners with the age of each member noted below the representation.

197 (*left*)

BASSANO (JACOPO DA PONTE)
Man in Armour

Italian, black chalk
A fluid sketch catching a moment of sudden movement, probably intended for use in a more complex composition.

198 (*right*)

ALBRECHT DURER
St Jerome in Penitence

German, engraving B. 61 – Watermark: Towers connected through wall

(Gift of Mr F. M. Mayer, New York)

A brilliant example of the young Durer's superb craftsmanship.

A nearly contemporary painting by Emanuel de Witte (1607–92) (plate 199) almost satisfies the same criteria. He was a well-known Dutch painter of church interiors who, apparently, created a number of synagogue views as well. During the seventeenth century, the Portuguese Jewish community, descendants of the Jews who had fled from Iberia in the late fifteenth century, had attained an important position in Amsterdam and were affluent enough to dedicate this grand synagogue in 1675. Shortly afterwards de Witte was commissioned to depict the interior. He did so, but placed two dogs in the picture, reflecting either his own cynicism and general anti-religious feeling, or the traditional Dutch mannerism of placing animals in the foreground. This magnificent synagogue still stands, almost exactly as it is in this nearly three hundred year old painting. It is an important monument in Jewish architecture. As in Sephardic synagogues, the bimah, the platform on which the service is conducted and the Pentateuch read, stands well toward the rear. On the wall facing Jerusalem, above the Ark, apparently for the first time in synagogal architecture, the Decalogue appears in the form of two tablets. This synagogue, which seated close to seventeen hundred worshippers, soon became a landmark in the city of Amsterdam and has been one ever since. To the seventeenth-century Jewish community in Amsterdam, their new synagogue bore a definite relationship to the Temple in Jerusalem, and in fact there were architectural analogies relating the new synagogue to a Jesuit's reconstruction of the Temple, printed some thirty years before.

199
EMANUEL DE WITTE
Portuguese Synagague in Amsterdam

Oil on canvas
Dutch, c. 1680

(*Donated by a group of Friends in Paris through Mr Maurice Fischer*)

A rare example by a major Dutch artist of a synagogue interior. The building and this interior can be seen to the present day.

200
IZAAK LUTTICHUYS
Jacob Ben Aaron Sasportas
Oil on canvas
Dutch, 1671
(*Gift of Friends in Holland through M. Bernard Houthakker, Amsterdam*)
A portrait of the rabbi of the Portuguese synagogues of Amsterdam and London.

Izaak Luttichuys (1616–73) painted a portrait of the Rabbi Jacob ben Aaron Sasportas (plate 200), who was later to become the rabbi of the Portuguese synagogue in Amsterdam, from 1693 to 1698. This scholar, born in Oran, was an outspoken critic of the false messiah, Shabbetai Zvi. As well as being the rabbi in Amsterdam, he also officiated at the Portuguese synagogue in London. Luttichuys' portrait shows the sage at the age of sixty-one with an open Hebrew book, the object most indicative of the man.

An inventory of the fine old paintings in the Israel Museum proves that the majority are seventeenth-century Dutch. The *River Scene*

201
JAN VAN GOYEN
River Scene

Oil on wood
Dutch, 1647
(Bequest of Mr Eduard Vis, Lausanne)

A mature painting in Van Goyen's monochrome style which nevertheless gives the colourful atmosphere of a typical canal scene.

by Jan van Goyen (1596–1656) (plate 201) bears the date 1647, a period during which the artist's work became increasingly monochromatic. Delicately balanced shades of brown and yellow blend into an harmonious golden tone, giving this painting its particular charm.

As the quality and quantity of the Museum's Old Master paintings improve, a larger area will be allocated for the regular showing of these works of art. The lack of balance between old and new painting is corrected by regularly mounting exhibitions of loaned paintings, drawings and graphics which fill gaps in the permanent collection of the Museum.

202 and 203 (*left and right*)

COFANETTO

Enamel, mounted in gilded copper
France, Limoges, sixteenth century

(*Mr and Mrs Sidney J. Lamon, New York*)

In the miniaturist's manner, the Limoges artist depicts the dramatic narrative of Joseph's life.

204 (*overleaf left*)

PAUL CÉZANNE
Country House by the Riverside

Oil on canvas
French, c. 1882

(*Gift of the 'Hanadiv' Rothschild Foundation*)

Possibly Emile Zola's house as seen by the master artist who tried to give substance and solid form to fleeting images.

205 (*overleaf right*)

VINCENT VAN GOGH
Harvest in Provence

Oil on canvas
Dutch, 1888

(*Gift of the 'Hanadiv' Rothschild Foundation*)

The harvest scene was painted in Arles in a lyric period, two years before the artist's tragic death.

The graphic cabinet, more than any other area of the Museum's collection, shows how the Museum has actually developed over the last sixty years. By 1921, the first Museum's inventory of paintings and drawings numbered forty-two sheets. Most of the works were by living Jewish painters and printmakers who showed a personal interest in the then 'new centre of the arts' in Jerusalem. They were gifts of the artists to the Museum's founder and director, Professor Boris Schatz. Today, the Graphic Department houses close to forty thousand prints and drawings, ranging from the great printmakers and draughtsmen of the late fifteenth century to contemporary works of art. Through constant effort, we are slowly closing the gaps and raising standards. In the 1930s, influenced by Narkis and following the influx of Jewish refugees from Germany, the Graphic Department underwent accelerated expansion. At that time in Germany, and subsequently in Austria and Czechoslovakia, it became increasingly difficult to remove valuable paintings and sculpture from Nazi Europe, but for several years it remained comparatively easy to take out less bulky items such as graphic art. As a result of the sudden availability of good and even precious material, prints started to enter the Museum's collection in numbers, through gifts, bequests and purchases.

The stately *Portrait of a Nobleman* (plate 207) can be dated to the very beginning of the sixteenth century on the basis of costume detail. Scholars suggest differing regions for it, such as northern Italy, southern Germany, Burgundy or Naples. In the absence of paintings of that period in the Museum's collection, a work such as this one and its pendant, the *Portrait of a Scholar*, is a welcome example.

Important graphic works of art by the great early masters of woodcutting, engraving and etching, such as Durer (plate 198), Rembrandt, Piranesi and many others, have been coming to the Museum regularly through the generosity of fine collectors sensitive to the Museum's needs.

Side by side with European masters, both ancient and modern, the Graphic Department assiduously collects Israeli prints and drawings, an area where local artists such as Krakauer, Louise Schatz, Aschaim Pins, Moreh Rubin and others have attained international success. Obviously, the Israel Museum must strive for an incomparable collection of the finest works of art by Israelis.

The fine artist Anna Ticho has been a resident of Jerusalem for half a century and has a profound feeling for this city in the hills of Judea. Her *Old City Wall of Jerusalem* (plate 208) is an early drawing, done in the 1930s. It not only shows her excellent draughtsmanship, but reflects that deep love for the Jerusalem landscape which forms the spiritual centre of her work. Her most recent wash, charcoal and brush drawings show a brilliant development toward greater freedom

206
CHAIM SOUTINE
Boy in Blue
Oil on canvas
Lithuanian
(*Mr and Mrs Harry Fischbach, New York*)
Unseated and unsettled, the poignant portrait reveals a tormented youth.

207

ANONYMOUS PORTRAIT OF A NOBLEMAN

Pen, ink and watercolour
Italian, early sixteenth century

The drawing of a noble, who has not as yet been identified, is the work of an artist whose identity is also unknown.

208

ANNA TICHO
Old City Wall of Jerusalem

Pencil
Israeli, c. 1930
(*Gift of the artist*)

Jerusalem's parchment-toned stones, ancient hills and gnarled trees, have been immortalised by this fine artist.

and expression, and the totality of her work makes a remarkable history of a city and an artist.

Tuvia Be'eri (b. 1929) studied in Paris with Johnny Friedländer. His delicate etchings, and aquatints show the masterly craftsmanship of this young artist and his use of semi-abstract shapes floating in undefined space, create a dream-like, highly poetic atmosphere (plate 222). He is but one of a number of fine young graphic artists, working in Israel and abroad, whose works are regularly collected and exhibited in groups or in one-man shows by the Museum.

The pomegranate is one of Israel's indigenous fruits. In Franz Bernheimer's (b. 1911) impressive black wash drawing (plate 209) its shape is used 'for a variation on a theme'. His art combines expressionistic violence with the art nouveau love of ornamental design, in a very personal style

The Museum's Graphic Study Room is immediately accessible from the graphic exhibition gallery. The large holdings of works of art of every period in drawings, watercolours and prints are available to the interested public. Students of art history at the Hebrew University, whose campus is contiguous with the Museum complex, make regular use of this invaluable service which, among other things, gives them an opportunity to see works of art and stylistic examples of all periods by masters whose paintings are not yet available in the Museum.

By the time the Museum was three years old (in May 1968), over a million and a half people had visited its scores of exhibitions. On its first birthday, the new Youth Wing was opened. To help celebrate the occasion the Museum was given a gift of five Post-Impressionist canvases. They were presented by the 'Hanadiv' foundation, which perpetuates the memory of that distinguished philanthropist who did so much towards the establishment of a Jewish state, Baron Edmond de Rothschild (1845–1934). All five works were painted between the years 1882 and 1899, rich, creative years in the history of art. The Cézanne (1839–1906) was painted about 1882 (plate 204). Before this revolutionary master had gained recognition, and while his works were still being rejected by the Salon, he abandoned Impressionism to turn his paintings into 'something solid and enduring'. Substituting reason and intellect for emotion and transient beauty, he pursued his goal of interpreting nature, making classic paintings in the manner of Poussin. Emile Zola, a friend during Cezanne's youth, had bought a house in Médan near Paris, and the painter stayed there frequently. Occasionally he would take a boat on the Seine near Zola's house and paint. In the autumn of 1882 Cézanne spent some weeks at Médan and it is probable that this fine painting was done there. The weight of each colour and form in the painting has been carefully considered.

Van Gogh (1853–90) and Gauguin were friends who had a strange hold on each other. The landscape by the Dutch genius (plate 205) was

209

FRANZ BERNHEIMER
Pomegranates

Brush and ink
Israeli, 1962

Luminous effects are achieved, without the use of colour, to create counterpoints in black and white.

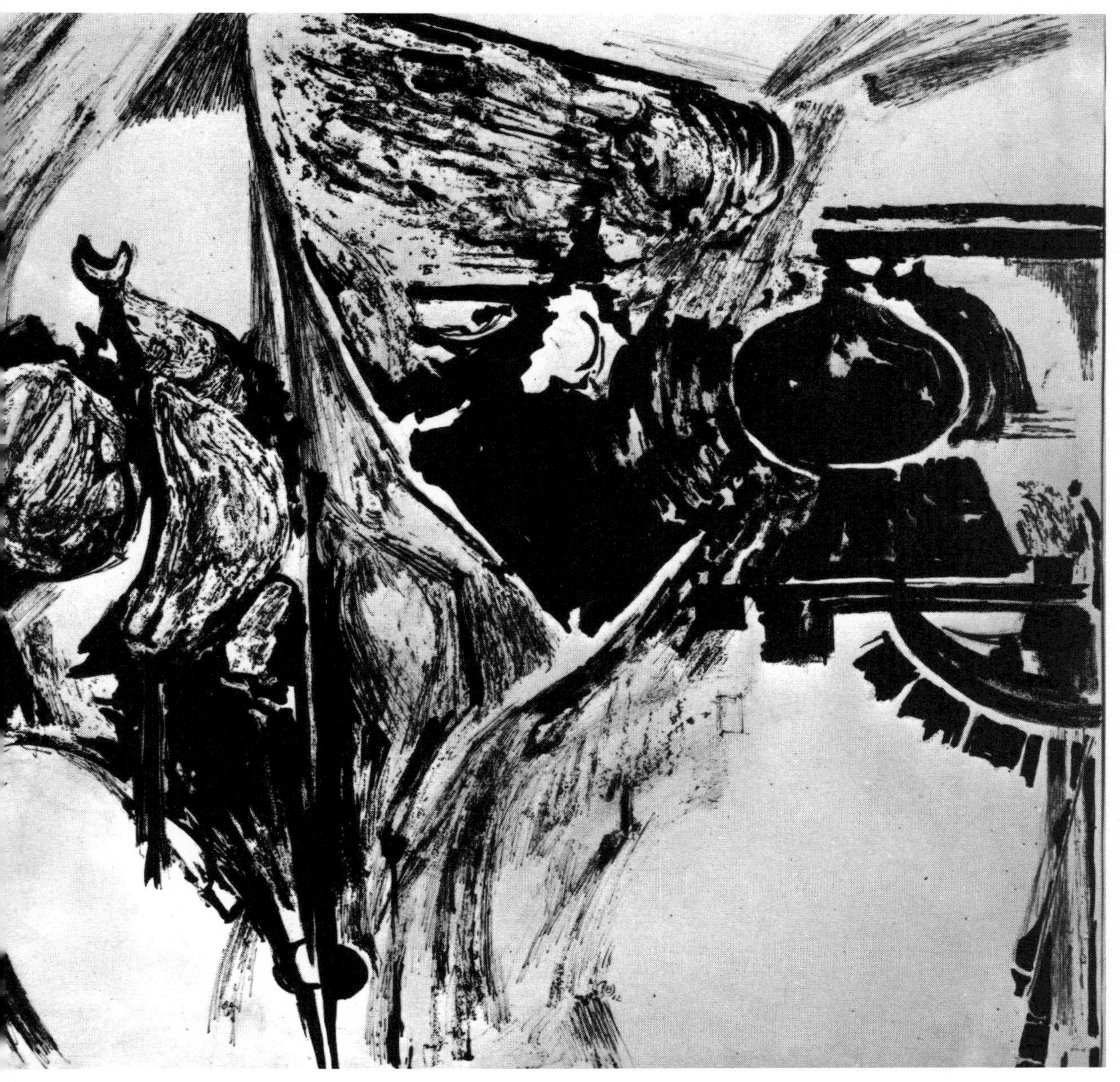

painted in Arles during 1888, two years before his tragic death. The scenery around this small village in the southern part of France could not have been more luxuriant and flamboyant even for the master who immortalised colours. Growth, fertility, the fullness of the land, the heat of the sun on the rich fields, were what Van Gogh needed. This painting and another the Museum received evince a perfect control over the medium, and express an optimism which was later to be shattered.

His friend Gauguin (1848–1903) made two trips to the South Seas; in 1891, he arrived in Tahiti but left two years later, returning in 1895. He lived his last years on that island and on the remote Dominiha, where he died eight years later. Included in the 'Hanadiv' gift were two paintings of the Tahitian period. The first (plate 211), dated 1891, shows the artist's initial reaction to the strange, exotic world which he had sought, when he was first captivated by its colours, mystery and drama. In this painting, called either *The Fire Dance* or *The Devil Speaks*, the artist, abandoning his more symbolic and stylised manner, accurately renders a scene which he actually witnessed. After a short and unhappy visit to France, the lure of the South Seas once more overwhelmed him and he returned. But life even there had become less attractive to him. Morbid and introspective paintings

210
PAUL GAUGUIN
Still Life
Oil on canvas
French, 1899
(*Gift of the 'Hanadiv' Rothschild Foundation*)
Painted shortly before his death, the painting is a summation of the diverse influences Gauguin assimilated throughout his life, from Impressionism to the theories of Cézanne.

211

PAUL GAUGUIN
The Fire Dance

Oil on canvas
French, 1891

(*Gift of the 'Hanadiv' Rothschild Foundation*)

A rare painting of a Tahitian scene made during Gauguin's first trip to the South Seas when the French artist was overwhelmed by those exotic surroundings.

ODILON REDON

213 (*above*)
HONORÉ DAUMIER
Members of the French Legislative Assembly
Bronze
French, c. 1830–2
(*The Billy Rose Collection*)
In order to understand the subjects he caricatured, Daumier first made these models, and then drew them.

212 (*left*)
ODILON REDON
Flower Still Life
Pastel on paper
French
(*Bequest of Miss Loula Lasker, New York*)
A rendering of a colourful arrangement of flowers in a vase which has overtones of a surreal atmosphere.

epitomise his work of this period. One of the last works he produced in Tahiti before he left for Dominiha was the other painting of his in our 'Hanadiv' gift, a still life of 1899 (plate 210). It is listed in the last inventory of canvases he sent to his dealer, Vollard.

It is paintings like these, or fine examples by Renoir and Monet or the still life by Odilon Redon (1840–1916) which now enable the Museum to display an orderly history of nineteenth century painting. *Flower Still Life* (plate 212) has that unreal quality which distinguishes so much of surrealist Redon's work. A strangeness can be felt in this simple, unassuming flower piece, painted with pastel chalks during the later years of his life. The colours achieve such an unusual and unnatural quality of saturated sweetness that one can almost sense the perfume coming from them. Flat areas of pure, luminous colours in rhythmic arrangements appear in a bright light which has no obvious source. The vase rests in an undefined space, making no attempt to give the illusion of reality.

During 1832–3 Honoré Daumier published a series of lithographic caricatures of well-known politicians, deputies of the French General Assembly. As studies towards the lithographs, Daumier modelled the heads in clay and later, in a limited edition, these heads were cast in bronze (plate 213). The sculptures are small but of monumental effect, and full of tension and harsh insight. Daumier (1810–79) was only in his early twenties when he created these perceptive representations of human weakness. They are a pivotal point for the great sculpture collection which the Museum is rapidly acquiring. The chief aim of the Sculpture Section is to assemble a representative collection of the very finest sculpture from Daumier, Bourdelle and Rodin to the works of the present day. Through a keen collecting awareness, it will try to keep creatively involved with the most exciting movements of our day. The impetus for this special emphasis on nineteenth- and twentieth-century sculpture comes from the existence at the Israel Museum of the Billy Rose Art Garden, a fascinating example of landscape architecture, lending an incomparable setting for sculpture by artists such as Malliol, Lipchitz, Zadkine, Archipenko and Vasarely. Small works like these Daumiers are housed in one of the two pavilions in the garden, built specially for the exhibition of small woods, plasters, fragile marbles and small bronzes.

The *Marble Doves* (plate 214) by Jacob Epstein (1880–1959) is an all too rare example of the artist's carving ability. It was done *c.* 1914–5 and belongs to what is called Epstein's Vorticist Period. It is unlike his highly expressive bronze sculpture, bearing a classical simplicity and beauty which clearly he was always capable of doing, but which he had rejected in preference to the more emotional malleability of modelled clay. The Museum owns a rich collection of Epstein's work in the original plasters. Many of his most famous portraits, such as the busts of Albert Einstein and Bertrand Russell, are at the Israel Museum, gifts of the artist through his widow.

Carving, modelling, and even the method of building up forms by appliqué has been gradually abandoned by many contemporary sculptors. Henry Moore (b. 1898) uses voids to give greater emphasis to form. His *Reclining Woman* (plate 5) is a fluid bronze surface, punctuated by holes which define shape and connote volume. The artist moulds three-dimensional space with both the positive and negative areas of form. The incorporation of space into and within the sculpture draws the viewer, who exists in that same space, into the work of art. This idea is one of the significant contributions to contemporary sculpture.

The monumental Picasso (b. 1881) (plate 3) takes this concept a step further. He opens up Henry Moore's space from concentrated areas and extends them almost endlessly. By creating a larger form which is penetrated by distant vistas, and sharp juxtapositions of angles, the artist makes the incorporated distant view as important as the immediate environment in which it exists. He also compels the viewer to circumambulate the piece in order to see it completely, since it has no frontality but many facets.

214
JACOB EPSTEIN
Third Marble Doves
Marble
British, 1914–5
(The Billy Rose Collection)
The finest of this series is this serene masterpiece of Epstein's Vorticist Period, clean and clear-cut.

Calder (b. 1898) adds a new dimension, chance – chance through movement. The unpredictable movement comes about simply because of the natural air flow. This puts Calder's *Mobile-Stabile* (plate 215) even more firmly into the three-dimensional space which we humans occupy. It stands in space, casting ever-changing shadows as it moves gently, elegantly, sometimes violently and abruptly. The rhythms of the breezes and winds, which at the same time cool or buffet us, move it also. The simple shapes derived from natural forms make this sculpture-in-movement a constant fascination.

215
ALEXANDER CALDER
Mobile-Stabile
Painted steel
American, 1966
(Gift of Mr and Mrs Samuel Perlman, New York)
Stylized forms respond to nature's changing course in elegant movements of colour and shape.

Israeli sculptors like Shemi, Danziger and Haber, have an important place in the Art Garden. There is a vital community of talented artists whose work is now reaching maturity. The Art Garden, with its dramatic open spaces, serves as a superb setting for Menashe Kadishman's (b. 1932) work (plate 4) which was commissioned by the Museum in 1966. It is a fine example of the new direction sculpture is taking. This bright yellow landmark in the Garden is a firm statement of simplified forms and tension. The artist does not attempt to suggest anything in nature: he simply uses the planes of three-dimensional geometrical shapes and combines them in delicately balanced relationships. This work is a valuable addition to the Museum's constantly growing collection of contemporary sculpture. In a sense, Kadishman's work represents an achievement of one aspect of the Zionist ideal, the 'normalisation' of the Jew. Kadishman's work cannot be identified as Israeli because it is part of the entire 'international scene' in art, and because in this sense it is unrecognisable and not 'Jewish', it is, in this way, Israeli.

In Europe in the nineteenth century a few Jewish painters attained success – Pissarro, Lieberman, Israëls. Unconcerned with religious tradition, they were artists in the secular world. They were romantic academics working in the style fashionable in the centres where they lived, the first Jewish artists to become liberated from the ghetto environment.

Further into the twentieth century the binding force of Expressionism took hold of a number of Jewish artists, and this common factor united them. Chagall's (b. 1887) *Rabbi* (plate 216) was painted on a linen shirt in 1912. The face of the learned layman reading his prayer book, seen with a Torah and a star of David in the background, is almost similar to the distortions we saw of Jews in the Birds' Head Haggadah (see plate 153). Fantastic, mystic, painted in glaring colours, this Expressionist work of art, like those of his contemporary co-religionists in painting and in sculpture, evinces that anti-intellectual and subjective approach which they all shared.

Soutine's (1894–1943) *Boy in Blue* seated on a stool (plate 206) appeals to the lonely, troubled, unintegrated and anguished. The subject is disturbing, self-conscious and sadly oppressive. Writers, like

216 (*left*)
MARC CHAGALL
Rabbi
Oil on linen
Russian, c. 1912
(*I.R.S.O.*)
A synthesis of an Expressionist point of view carried out in a Cubist manner.

Kafka, Max Brod and Sholom Aleichem are literary parallels to such paintings by Chagall and Soutine.

Expressionism was not limited to Jews, nor even to a country or a period. Certainly this painting by Francis Bacon (b. 1910) (plate 217), completed in 1964, brings in the added element of a self-conscious psychological approach to the same vision of the human condition and can be seen to be in direct continuity with the creative approaches of Chagall and Soutine. Bacon has placed his figure in a carefully contrived and yet emotionless area, inviting the adventurous viewer to penetrate it. The electric lightbulb does not illuminate, the subject is eyeless and unseeing. It does not come as a surprise to learn that this is a portrait of Lucien Freud, a grandson of Sigmund.

217 (*right*)
FRANCIS BACON
Study for the Portrait of Lucien Freud
Oil on canvas
British, 1964
(*Gift of the Marlborough Gallery, London*)
The subject is a figure in space, struggling with self, striving not to see and not to be seen.

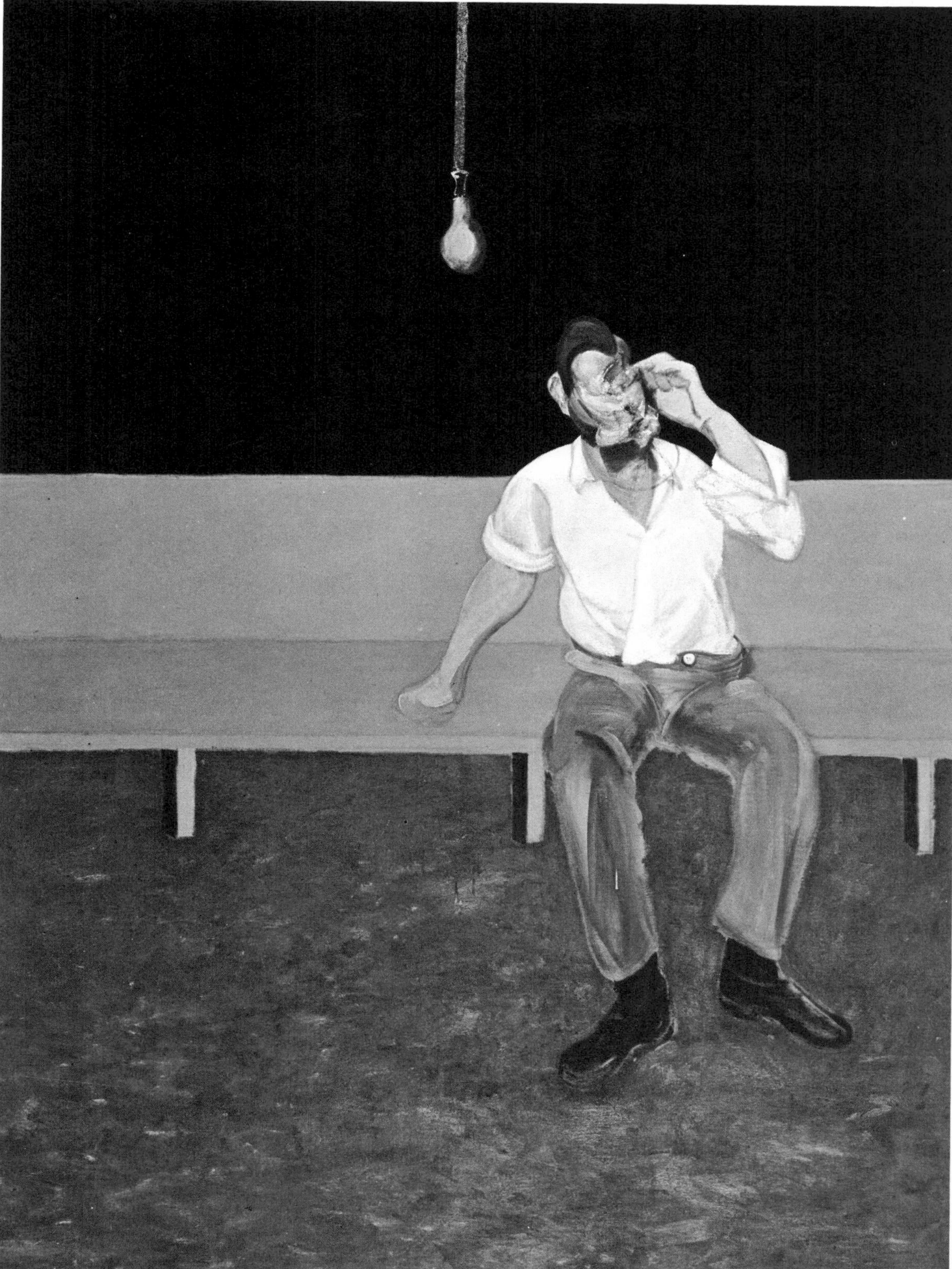

Of course portraits not only make it possible to understand the sitter; through them one can gain an understanding of the painter or sculptor. No portraits can escape this dualism. Jules Pascin's (1885–1930) early *Portrait of William Howard* (plate 219) of 1909 tells us a great deal about both subject and painter. The sitter, William Howard, was a German artist and somewhat of a dandy. It is one of the rare male portraits Pascin painted, and even here he introduces a female figure. Somewhat smug and self-satisfied, Howard projects a rather distant, disdainful look. Pascin, by that date, had rejected his Bulgarian birth and his original name, Pincas, which we find on an early drawing in the Museum's collection of over one hundred works by this artist. 'Pascin' is an anagram of that name. He was living in Paris when he painted this portrait and had already made a name for himself as an illustrator for the 'Simplicissimus' in Munich. He later emigrated from there to the United States, where he came to his tragic end.

Egon Schiele (1890–1918), who died at the terribly early age of twenty-eight, is represented by one of his large townscapes (plate 218),

219 (*right*)
JULES PASCIN
Portrait of William Howard
Oil on cardboard
Bulgarian, 1909
(*Gift of Mr Joseph Pincas, Paris*)
A facile, insightful portrait of the painter Howard, by Pascin, done when he was only 24 years old.

218 (*below*)
EGON SCHIELE
Cityscape
Oil on canvas
Austrian, 1915
(*I.R.S.O.*)
The colourful laundry, the twisted roofs, the jumbled houses makes the cityscape a modern artist's vehicle.

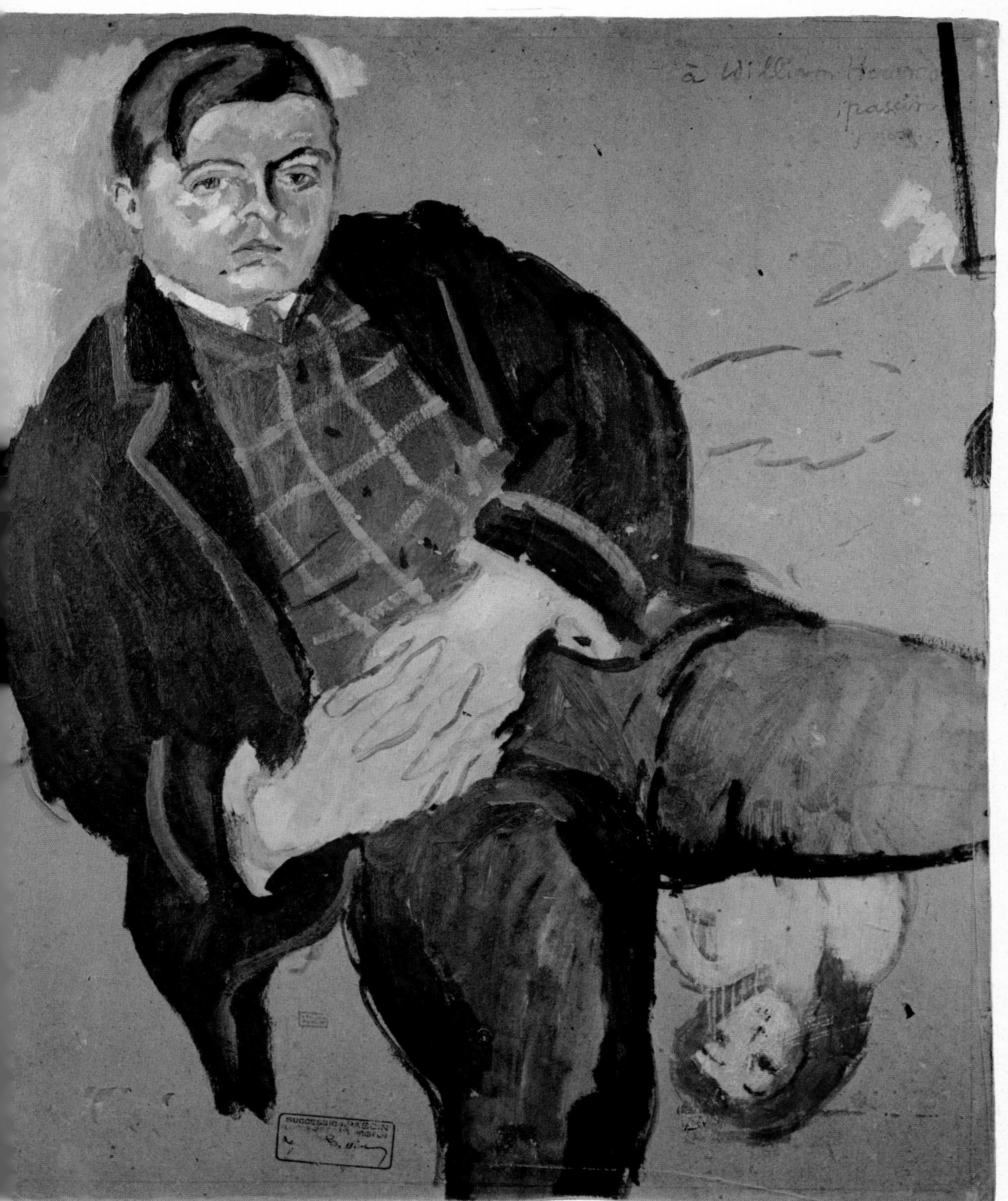
pascin
SUCCESSION PASCIN

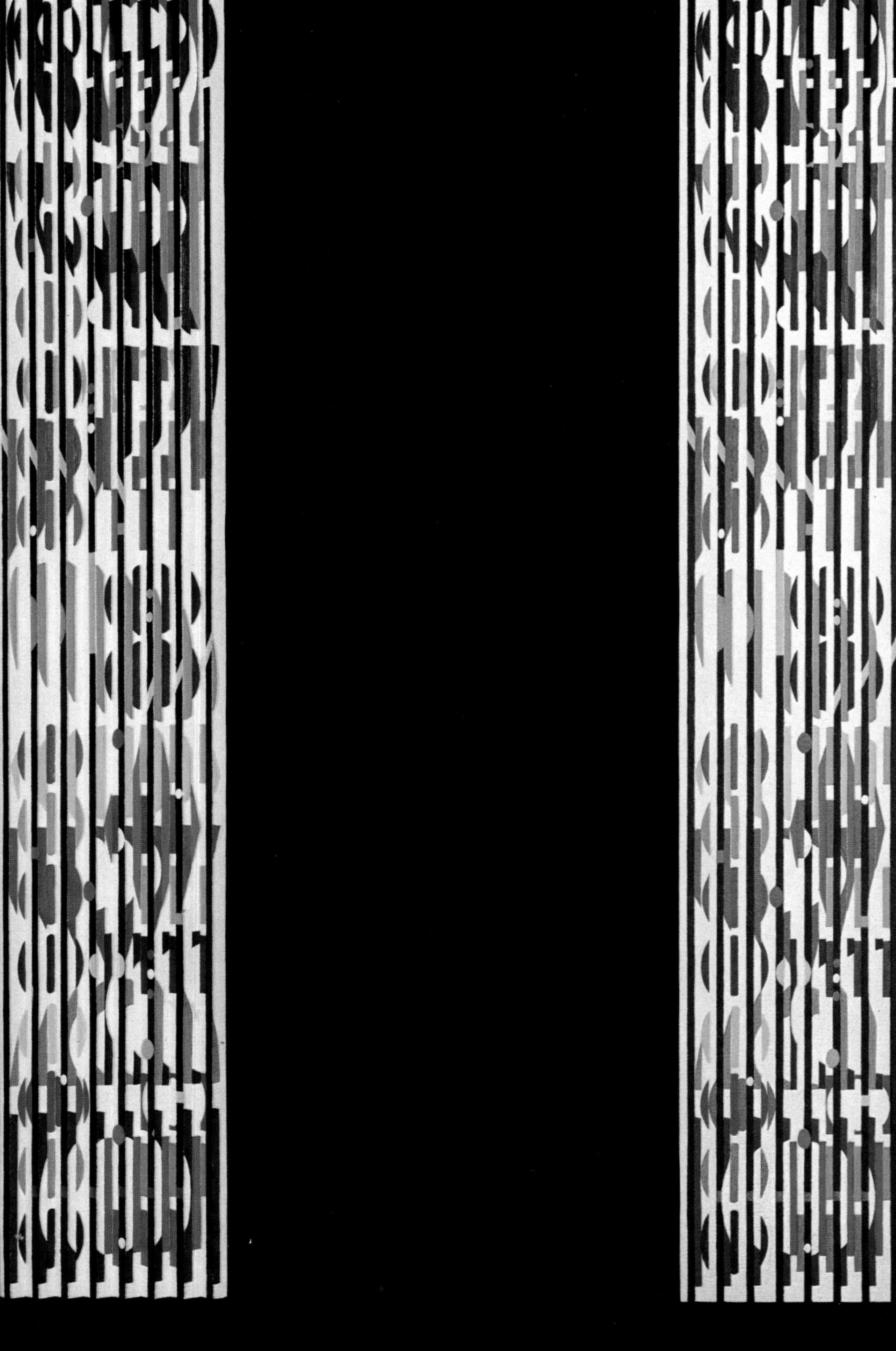

dated 1915. With its expressive play of rhythmical lines and its mood of intense sadness and sophisticated decay, the painting shows the artist's roots in art nouveau and urban romanticism.

There is a common denominator in the paintings of Schiele and Picasso (plate 221). Both paintings were created during periods of great upheaval, Schiele's during the First World War in Vienna, Picasso's in Paris during the Nazi Occupation. Picasso's colours are subdued, reflecting the gloomy atmosphere of the enemy-occupied capital. It is not a painting of protest nor is it a painting which rejects realities. It is a statement of the status quo – limited and joyless. The painting is based on old Cubist formulas but it is not analytic. The geometric shapes in which Picasso organises the whole space are imposed on to the surface in a way which suggests Cubism but without the intellectual implications.

In painting as in sculpture, we see somewhat the same evolution, the same progress towards the pure, non-figurative. Ya'akov Agam (b. 1928), an Israeli whose father is an orthodox rabbi, arrived at certain theoretical conclusions as a result of his background which are the foundations of his optic-joggling, kinetic works of art. He evolved concepts based on abstract, unseen and unceasing changes, (plate 220). Agam is now broadening his creative efforts and is at present working on a new dictionary, trying to create words which have simultaneities so that they achieve greater subtleties in language as well as visually; a theatre which is a total environment and surrounds the audience; and works of art which respond to the sound of the beholder.

In just twenty years of national history, the State of Israel, founded in 1948, can be proud of its artistic achievements. A score of years is not a long time in the history of states and artistic traditions, and yet during this short span, a number of painters and sculptors have been accorded recognition through major exhibitions and commissions, and are represented in important public and private collections. In the mid-thirties it would have been difficult to say that there was a progressive, forward-looking art movement in Palestine, but with the troubled times in Europe, then at the brink of a great tragedy, many artists came to British Mandatory Palestine, people who had been exposed to the most advanced ideas of the time. They came to what was certainly a relative wilderness in the field of contemporary art and had significant effects on the art of Palestine and now Israel.

Joseph Zaritzky (b. 1891) left the Kiev Academy of Art in Russia nearly forty-five years ago to settle in Jerusalem. He spent four years in Palestine (1922–6) before returning to Europe to paint in Paris. Fortunately, he exposed himself to the most exciting artistic stimuli in Europe and came back to Israel to become the leader of the abstract movement. It was he who was the primary force in the founding of the group called 'New Horizons'. His paintings of abstracted forms are

220
YA'AKOV AGAM
Diptych
Oil on wood
Israeli, 1964
(*Gift of Mr George Jaffin, New York*)
The viewer changes the static painting of forms and colours into a work of art in flux.

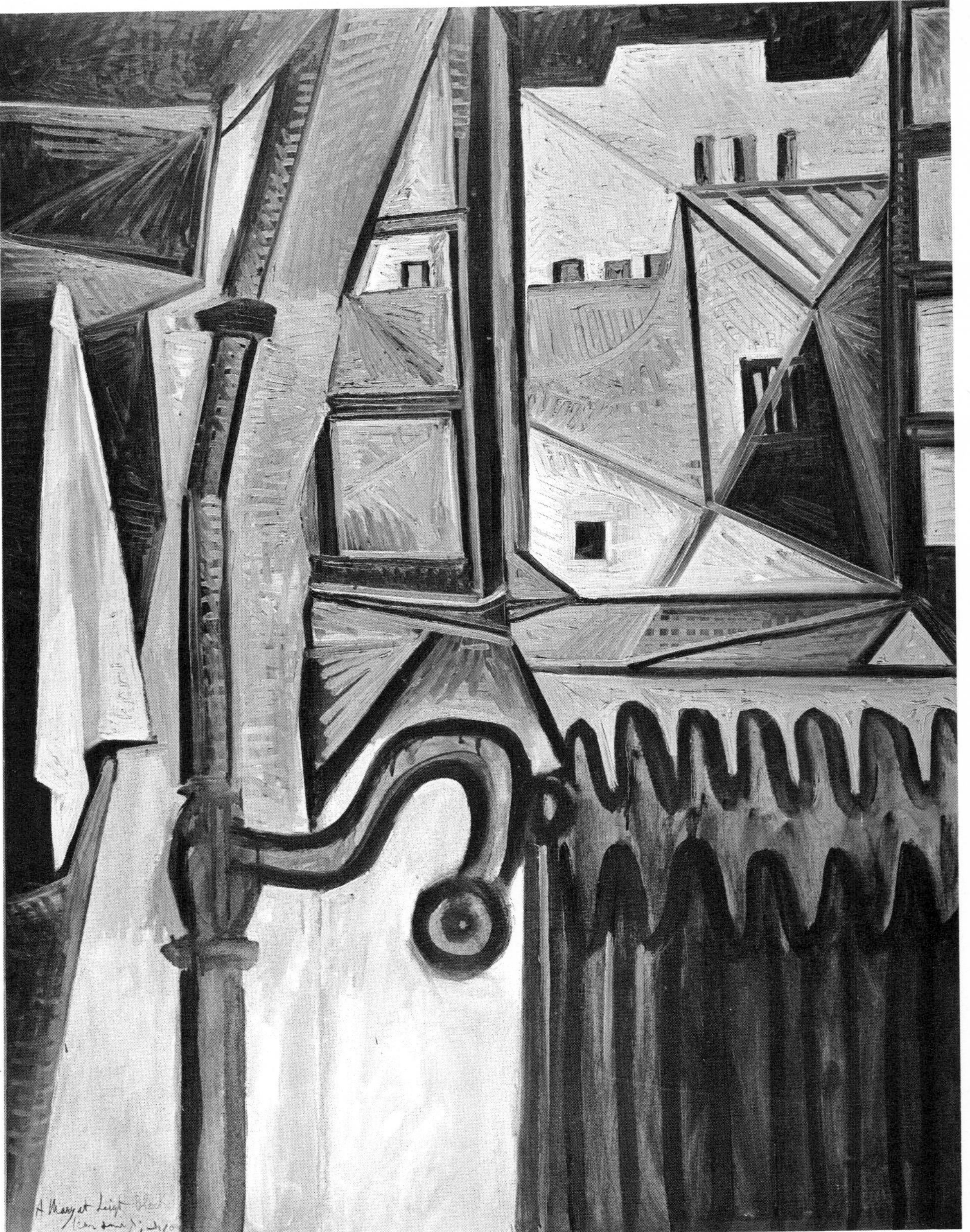

222 (*below*)
TUVIA BE'ERI
Moon Landscape
Etching and aquatint
Israeli, c. 1964
Although this is only a small print, it nevertheless conveys the feeling of endless space.

221 (*left*)
PABLO PICASSO
The Studio Window
Oil on canvas
Spanish, 1943
(*Gift of Mr and Mrs Leigh Block, Chicago*)
By reorganizing, emphasizing and distorting, the painter changes a prosaic view into a private vision.

223
JOSEPH ZARITZKY
Homage à Braque
Oil on canvas
Israeli, c. 1945
A pioneer in abstract art, Zaritzky has had an enormous influence on contemporary art in Israel.

fresh, lyrical and highly original. He extracts a light out of all his colours, using white in a very painterly, colourful way (plate 223). Today, this warm-hearted seventy-seven year old Russian-Jewish abstractionist is still one of the liveliest and most stimulating figures in Israeli art.

Avigdor Arikha (b. 1929) came to Israel from Rumania in 1944. This thirty-nine year old, who studied under Ardon at the Bezalel School, first became prominent as a virtuoso draughtsman. Though he has never abandoned drawing, he has ventured more and more into the world of colour and free form, constantly alluding, suggesting and implying form in sensitive, translucent colours (see plate 226).

After the Six Day War, Igael Tumarkin (b. 1933) received permission from the Israel Defence Forces to collect some war debris from the Sinai Desert. The mangled, tangled, steel pieces of the destroyed war machine – the burnt, singed, black objects – became, as he assembled and created powerful juxtapositions, part of a collection of sculptures which cried out for an end to the chaos and exposed the grotesque and ludicrous side of war (see plate 224). Tumarkin's paintings and assemblages evoke strange worlds, in which destruction is a significant factor and hope or beauty are absent.

For nearly thirty-five years a quiet, elderly man in Jerusalem has been evolving a language of his own, a rich, profound, colourful form of communication which makes intellectual demands on the viewer at one level and overwhelms him with a spectrum of visual impressions at another. The symbols which Mordechai Ardon (b. 1896) paints with such technical brilliance and in such well-ordered compositions, in miraculous colours which he grinds himself, hint of his Bauhaus studies in Weimar with Klee, Kandinsky, Feininger and Itten. The sources for his iconography are Psalms, Cabbala, Zohar and the legends and mysticism that permeate the rich culture of east European Jewry. They are, however, integrally connected with this land, which for him is a timeless place where historic events have shaped man, a place which has witnessed crucial history.

The triptych *At the Gates of Jerusalem* (plate 227) was painted in 1967 after the Six Day War. It was conceived before the war and has an almost prophetic quality about it. The three parts are 'Sign', 'Ladders', and 'Rock'. By using the traditional format of a central panel with two wings, Ardon succeeds in creating an epic within the format of a religious painting. The wing on the left (reproduced in part on the front of the jacket of this book) utilises elements from the mystical book of the Cabbalists, the Zohar (which first appeared in thirteenth-century Spain). On a parchment-toned background, Ardon places the first letter of the Hebrew alphabet, alef, in an imposing position, using the form of the letter as it appeared in pre-printing Hebrew manuscripts. Below, the fortieth chapter from

224
IGAEL TUMARKIN
Rex
Wood and metal on canvas
Israeli, 1964
(*Gift of the artist*)
An aesthetic of violence, the artist harasses the canvas and his material and torments the viewer.

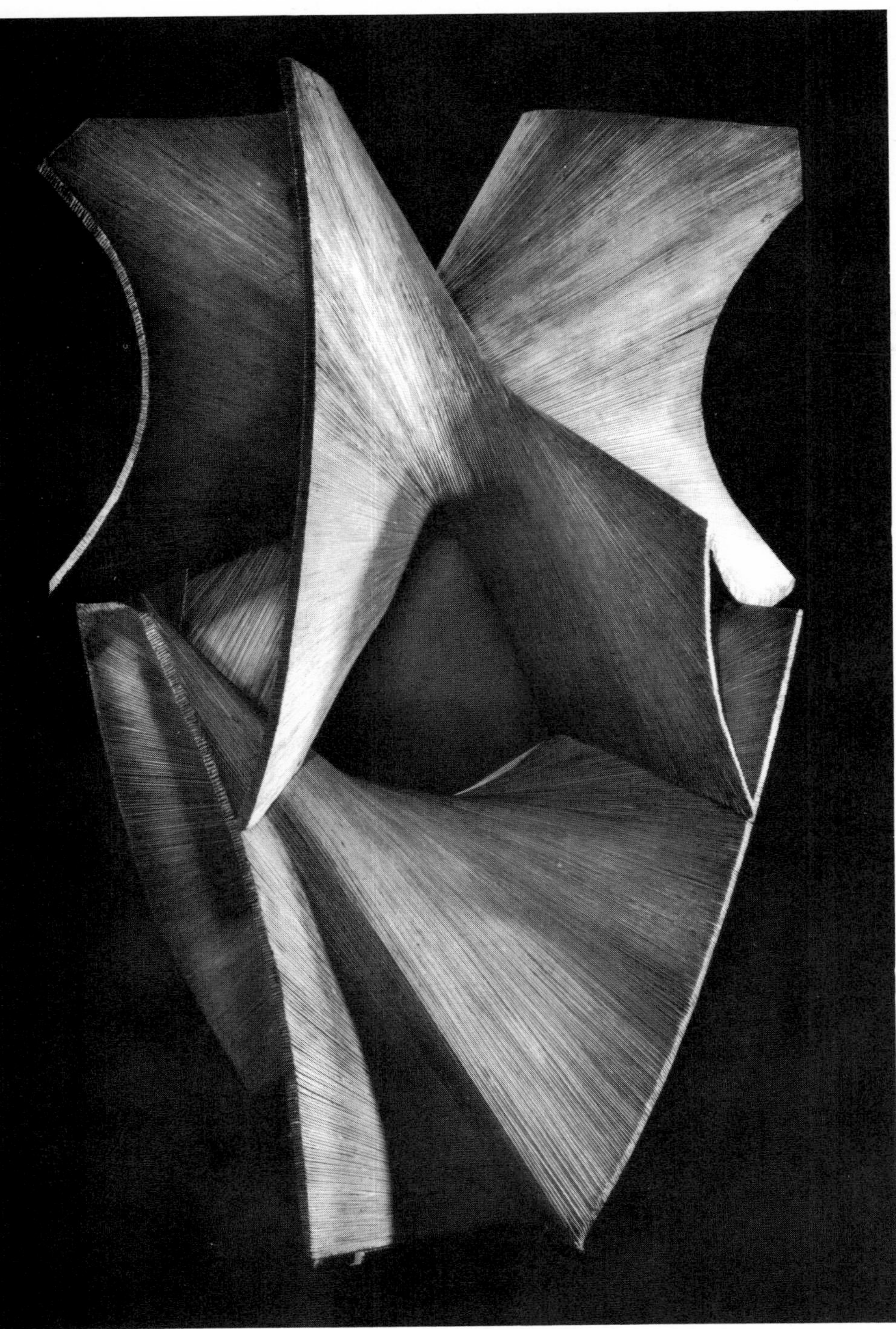

225 (*left*)

ANTOINE PEVSNER
Construction in Space in the Third and Fourth Dimensions

Bronze
Russian, 1961
(*Gift of Mr and Mrs Alex L. Hillman, New York, in memory of their son Richard*)

Spatial geometry of non-objective forms combine to create the impression of flight.

226 (*right*)

AVIGDOR ARIKHA
Forms II

Casein on paper mounted on canvas
Israeli, 1965

Illusive forms, created by translucent colours merging and suggesting shapes.

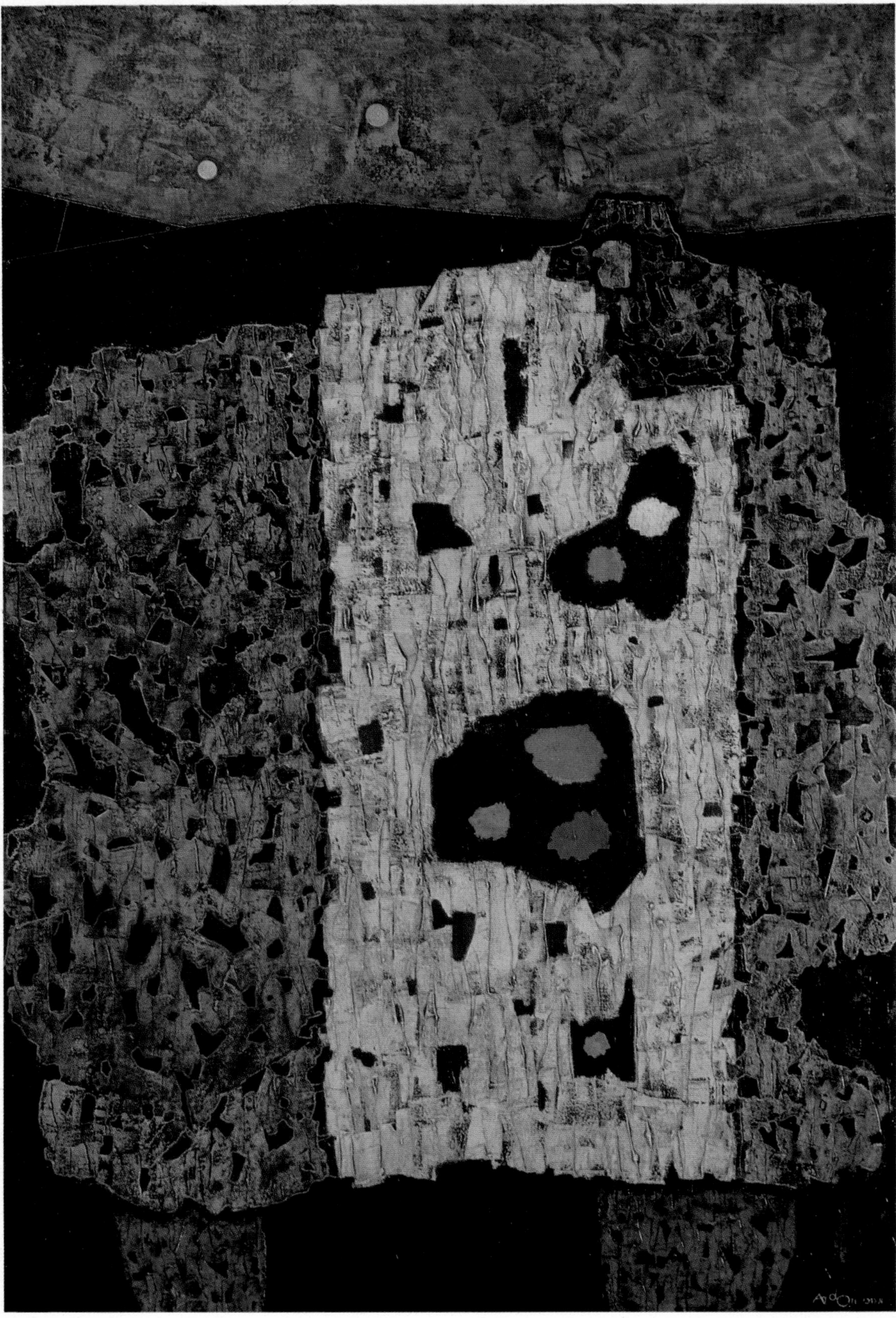

227
MORDECHAI ARDON
At the Gates of Jerusalem
Oil on canvas
Israeli, 1967
(*Gift of the artist*)
The artist's vision of Jerusalem, and the eternal aspiration, its mystique, and its fleeting beauty revealed.

Isaiah barely emerges from the scroll-coloured background in which the prophet says:

> Comfort ye, comfort ye my people, saith your God. Speak ye comfortably to Jerusalem, and cry unto her, that her warfare is accomplished, that her iniquity is pardoned: for she hath received of the Lord's hand double for all her sins.

These elements, together with the cabbalistic symbols, are an attempt to convey Jerusalem's profound and historic meaning.

The central panel is a series of inter-related ladders. The ladder, frequent in Ardon's painting, signifies both aspiration and frustration. According to tradition, there are two Jerusalems, the second being a heavenly one above the earthbound city; it is the hope of everyone to reach this celestial Jerusalem. In Ardon's painting, the ladder is used as a symbol for man's effort to penetrate the unknown, to rise to that city beyond. From the smoke rising heavenward from the altar on which the ram was sacrificed instead of Isaac, to the ladder in Jacob's dream and the ascensions of Christ and Muhammed, people have attempted to reach this hidden place called Heaven and the profusion of ladders in the picture is symbolic of these and other quests.

The Zohar notes that God hurled a great stone from Heaven when he created the world. One rock projected from that stone, to become the centre of the world, and the world grew around it. That 'rock', it is said, is in the centre of Jerusalem. Ardon's stone is a cross-section of a fantasy excavation through the centre of Jerusalem, a city whose whole history may one day be revealed, but whose mystery will always remain unfathomable.

Catalogue and List of Plates

1

The Israel Museum, general view.

2

The Billy Rose Art Garden, general view.

3

PABLO PICASSO – Profile

Sand blasted concrete – c. 5·50 m.

Spanish, 1967

Gift of the artist and Friends of the Israel Museum in Antwerp

I.M. no. 591.67/107

4

MENASHE KADISHMAN – Suspense

Painted and welded iron – 3 × 2 × 0·40 m.

Israeli, 1966

(Gift of the artist, with the help of Audrey Sacher)

I.M. no. 1702.66/41

5

HENRY MOORE – Reclining Woman

Bronze – 7 × 2 × 6 m.

British, c. 1953–4

Permanent loan from Mr and Mrs Joel Starrels, Chicago

I.M. no. 65.32

6

AUGUSTE RODIN – Adam

Bronze

(The Billy Rose Collection)

7

The Shrine of the Book, exterior view

8

The Shrine of the Book, interior

9, 10

Interior views of the Museum

11

The Bezalel National Art Museum in 1906

12–19

General views of the Museum

20

PEBBLE-TOOLS

Chopper – *ht: 8·5 cm.*

Spheroid

Both: Lower Palaeolithic, Ubeidiya excavations

21

POINTS AND MICROLITHS

Four points – *ht: (top left) 12·8 cm.*

All: Lower Palaeolithic, Abu Zif

Microliths – *ht. (top right) 2·5 cm.*

All: Upper Palaeolithic, Kefar Vitkin

22

HAND-AXES

Stone, *Ubeidiya excavations*

Flint, *Holon*

Basalt, *Gesher Benot Ya'aqov*

Flint – *ht. 19 cm., Ma'ayan Barukh*

All: Lower Palaeolithic

23

'CAVE OF THE TREASURE' – 'CROWN'

Copper

Chalcolithic Period, from a cave near the Dead Sea

24

MORTARS AND PESTLE

Mortar and Pestle

Upper Palaeolithic, En Gev

Mortar

Basalt – ht. 59 cm., diam. 4 cm.

Late Mesolithic (Natufian Culture), Eynan excavations

25

SCHEMATIC HUMAN FIGURE

Basalt – length of big horizontal pestle: 18 cm.

Mesolithic (Natufian Culture), Eynan excavations

26

SCHEMATIC FACES

Stone – ht. (top) 7·2 cm.

Mesolithic (Natufian Culture), Eynan excavations

27

AGRICULTURAL IMPLEMENTS WITH RECONSTRUCTED HANDLES

Axe

Stone – length of reconstruction: 52·5 cm.

Neolithic Period, pre-Ceramic Phase

Adze

Stone

Neolithic Period, pre-Ceramic Phase

Sickle

Stone

Late Mesolithic (Natufian Culture)

Sickle

Stone

Neolithic Period

28

DOMESTIC POTTERY

Two Jars and two Bowls

Big Bowl – ht. 24 cm., diam. 25 cm.

All: Neolithic Period, Ceramic Phase, Shaar Hagolan excavations

29

ANIMAL FIGURINES

Pottery

(Second from left) Possibly a boar – length: 6 cm.

All: Neolithic Period, pre-Ceramic Phase except for boar, Neolithic Period, Ceramic Phase

Boar: *Horvat Minha excavations*

Others: *Nahal Oren*

30

HUMAN FIGURINES

Pottery – ht. (far right) 4·5 cm.

Neolithic Period, pre-Ceramic Phase, Horvat Minha excavations

31

MOTHER GODDESS

Pottery – ht. 14 cm.

Neolithic Period, Ceramic Phase, Horvat Minha excavations

32

BEERSHEBA IVORY

Female Figurine – *ht. 11 cm.*

Chalcolithic Period, Beersheba excavations

33
BEERSHEBA IVORY *(detail)*
Male Figure
Chalcolithic Period, Beersheba excavations

34
AZOR OSSUARIES
Clay – ht. (left front) 59 cm., l. 1·40 cm. w. 31 cm.
Chalcolithic Period, Azor excavations

35
'CAVE OF THE TREASURE' – 'SCEPTRES'
Copper – ht. (on far left) 26·5 cm.
Chalcolithic Period, from a cave near the Dead Sea

36
'CAVE OF THE TREASURE' – MACE-HEADS
Copper – Average ht. 3–3·5 cm.
Chalcolithic Period, from a cave near the Dead Sea

37
EN GEDI SANCTUARY *(Plaster model)*

38
'CAVE OF THE TREASURE' – 'SCEPTRE'
Copper – ht. 26 cm.
Chalcolithic Period, from a cave near the Dead Sea

39
HOUSE MODELS
Tower-shaped incense stand – *ht. 37 cm.*
Early Canaanite Period, Ai excavations
Red-painted Broad-House
Early Canaanite Period, Arad excavations

40
MOTHER AND CHILD FIGURINE
Pottery – ht. 6·5 cm.
Early Canaanite Period, Bet Yerah excavations

41
CULT MASK
Pottery – ht. 13·5 cm.
Late Canaanite, Hazor excavations

42
IMPORTED POTTERY
Two painted Mycenaean vases – *Hazor excavations*
Syrian elongated flask – *ht. 33 cm.*
Cypriot juglet and bowl – *diam. of bowl: 18 cm.*
All: Late Canaanite Period

43
'BET YERAH WARE'
Two hour-glass shaped stands – *ht. (of larger) 47 cm., diam. 42 cm.*
Large bowl
Dish
Early Bronze Period

44
COPPER TOOLS AND WEAPON
Saw – *l. 70 cm.*
Curved knife
Spearhead – *wt.: 2·05 kg.*
Early Canaanite Period, Kefar Monash

45
DOMESTIC POTTERY
'Teapot'
Jar
Beaker
Beginning of the Middle Canaanite Period

46
CANAANITE POTTERY OF THE PATRIARCHAL AGE
'Yahudiyeh' juglet from Afula
Egg-shell-thin walled goblet from Barqai
Dish from Gibeon – *diam. 25 cm.*
Quatrefoil bowl from Hazor
All: Latter part of Middle Canaanite Period

47
SCARABS
Mostly steatite
Average length: 1·8 cm.
Middle Canaanite Period, from a tomb of Tel Nagila

48
CYLINDER SEALS
1 Haematite
Old Babylonian Period, 1830–1600 BC
2 Haematite
Old Babylonian Period, 1830–1600 BC
3 Agate
Kassite Period, fifteenth century BC
4 Steatite
Second Syrian Group, 1600–1350 BC
5 Haematite
Mitannian Period, 1500–1400 BC
(Gift of the Hahn-Voss family to the Department of Antiquities)

49
OFFERINGS FROM A CANAANITE HIGH PLACE
Seven-cup offering vessel
Bird figurine
Miniature juglet
Juglet with neck in shape of a monkey – *ht. 13 cm.*
Miniature bowl
Pottery
Middle Canaanite Period, Nahariya excavations

50
OFFERINGS FROM A CANAANITE HIGH PLACE
Figurines, silver
Middle Canaanite Period, Nahariya excavations

51
STONE MOULD FOR CASTING FIGURINE OF HORNED GODDESS *(with modern bronze cast)*
Ht. 20·8 cm.
Middle Canaanite Period, Nahariya excavations

52
LION ORTHOSTAT
Basalt – 1·8 × 1·2 m.
Late Canaanite Period, Hazor excavations

53
'SHRINE OF THE STELAE'
Statuette of seated man – *ht. 38 cm.*
Stele incised with raised hands – *ht. 46 cm.*
Lion orthostat – *33 × 45·5 cm.*
All: Basalt
Late Canaanite Period, Hazor excavations

54
POTTER'S WHEEL
Basalt
Ht. of lower part: 8 cm., diam., 16·2 cm.
Late Canaanite Period, Hazor excavations

55
GILGAMESH EPIC FRAGMENT
Clay tablet, cuneiform – ht. 10 cm.
Late Canaanite Period, Megiddo
LIVER MODEL FOR TEMPLE DIVINERS
Clay, two fragments
Late Canaanite Period, Hazor excavations

56
'ASTARTE' FIGURINES
Pottery – ht. (central figurine): 14·5 cm.
Late Canaanite Period
(Central figurine from the Reifenberg Collection, Jerusalem)

57
PHILISTINE POTTERY
Jug – *ht. 25 cm.*
Azor excavations
Krater
Tel Zippor excavations
Both: Beginning of the Israelite Period

58
HIGH-STEMMED BOWL AND INCENSE STAND
Pottery, painted and burnished – ht. (on left) 36 cm.
Israelite Period (eleventh-tenth centuries BC), Tel Zafit excavations
Israelite Period (tenth-ninth centuries BC), Tel Amal excavations

59
PHOENICIAN POTTERY
Painted mask – *ht. 14 cm.*
Red-burnished jugs
Ht. of biggest: 29 cm.
Late Israelite Period, Akhziv excavations

60
PHOENICIAN FAN HANDLE
Ivory – 19 × 8·5 cm.
Phoenician, c. 800 BC
(Permanent loan from E. Borowski, Basel)
Obverse: Man with attendant in front of priest. Phoenician inscription: 'belonging to Abdubaal'.

61
FACE FROM ANTHROPOID SARCOPHAGUS
Clay – ht. 15·5 cm.
Beginning of the Israelite Period, Tel Rehov

62
PHILISTINE ANTHROPOID SARCOPHAGUS
Diagrammatic reconstruction

63
ISRAELITE POTTERY
Jar
Jug with spout – *ht. 27 cm.*
'Pilgrim bottle'
Tel Amal excavations
Oil lamp – *l. 12 cm.*
En Gev excavations
All: Israelite Period

64
'HORNED ALTAR'
Limestone – 64 × 31 cm.
Tenth-ninth centuries BC, Megiddo excavations

65
'ASTARTE' OR DEA NUTRIX FIGURINES
Pillar-shaped – *ht. 17 cm.*
(*right*) with human head
(*left*) 'bird-headed'
Pottery
Judaean types, seventh century BC
(Reifenberg Collection, Jerusalem)

66
ARSLAN TASH IVORY
Cow suckling calf – *5 × 8 cm.*
Phoenician workmanship, second half of the ninth century BC
(Collection E. Borowski, Basel)

67
ARSLAN TASH IVORY
King or Priest (*detail*) – *ht. (of detail) 8 cm.*
Phoenician workmanship, second half of the ninth century BC
(Collection E. Borowski, Basel)

68
ARSLAN TASH IVORY
Lion's Head – *ht. 7 × 6·5 cm.*
Phoenician workmanship, second half of the ninth century BC
(Collection E. Borowski, Basel)

69
ARSLAN TASH IVORY
'Woman at the window' – *ht. 8 cm.*
Phoenician workmanship, second half of the ninth century BC
(Collection E. Borowski, Basel)

70
STONE BALUSTRADE
36 × 120 cm.
Phoenician style, seventh century BC, Ramat Rahel excavations

71
HEBREW OSTRACON
Clay, c. 700 BC, Arad excavations

72
HEBREW OSTRACA
Clay, c. 700 BC, Arad excavations

73
PHOENICIAN MINOR ARTS
Glass amphoriskos – *ht. 9 cm.*
Glass eye-beads
Cosmetic palette and bone spatula
Seals
Amulets
Weaving implements
All: Israelite Period, eighth-sixth centuries BC

74
PROTO-IONIC CAPITAL
Stone – 46 × 100 cm.
Seventh century BC, Ramat Rahel excavations

75
'HOLY OF HOLIES' – *From the Temple at Arad*
Dimensions of the entire structure: 2·2 × 1·6 m.
Two Stone Altars
Ht. of larger – 50 × 28 cm.

Ht. of smaller – 37 × 21 cm.
Ninth century BC, Arad excavations

76
HEBREW GRAFFITI FROM TOMB-CAVE NEAR AMAZIA
c. 700 BC

77
STAMPED ROYAL JAR HANDLE
Pottery
Seventh century BC, Ramat Rahel excavations

78
SILVER INGOTS AND POT
Ht. of pot – 10·5 cm.
End of Judaean Monarchy, c. 600 BC, En Gedi excavations

79
'YEHUD' COIN
Silver – diam. 0·85 cm.
Persian Period, sixth-fourth centuries BC
(From the collection of Hyman Bessin, Ottawa (Canada))

80
FIGURINE OF PREGNANT WOMAN
Terracotta – ht. 22·5 cm.
Syrian-Phoenician type, fifth-fourth centuries BC,
Akhziv excavations

81
ATTIC BLACK-FIGURE LEKYTHOS
Battle scene (*rolled-out*) from a pottery oil bottle
Ht. of painted scene: 6·5 cm.
Early fifth century BC, Bat Yam

82
OIL LAMPS AND LAMP-FILLER
Various local types of pottery
Lamp-filler – l. 12 cm.
Persian-Hellenistic Periods, from various sites

83
HOARD OF ALEXANDER TETRADRACHMS
Silver
Juglet in which hoard was found – ht. 15 cm.
Hellenistic Period, c. 310 BC, Tel Zippor excavations

84
STAMPED RHODIAN JAR AND SMALL IMITATION
Pottery
Ht. of big jar: 67 cm.
Hellenistic Period
Rhodian jar from Tel Mor excavations, and imitation from Deir el-Asad

85
GREEK STAMPS ON RHODIAN JAR
Pottery
Hellenistic Period, Tel Mor excavations

86
STATUE OF YOUNG SATYR
Marble – ht. 1·35 m.
Roman copy of Hellenistic original, Caesarea Maritima excavations

87
COIN OF MATTATHIAS ANTIGONUS
Bronze – 40–37 BC
Reverse: 'of the King' (in Greek) and menorah
(Collection of the Archaeological Institute, the Hebrew University, Jerusalem)

88
FOUR OIL LAMPS
Pottery and (top left) bronze
Bronze lamp: 10·5 × 5·5 cm.
Hellenistic and Roman Periods, Avdat excavations

89
GOLD EARRING
In shape of ram's head – 2 × 1·5 cm.
Achaemenian workmanship, sixth-fourth centuries BC, Ashdod excavations

90
GLASS VESSELS OF THE ROMAN PERIOD
All blown, except for the mould-pressed bowl to the right
Two free-blown unguentaria
Ht. of the left one: 12 cm.
Mould-blown juglet of Sidonian style
Ribbed bowl
All: Early Roman Imperial Period

91
GLASS VESSELS OF THE BYZANTINE PERIOD
Ht. of glass bottle to the right: 22 cm.

92
FIGURINE OF DEFIANT PANTHER
Bronze – 4·5 × 5·5 cm.
Hellenistic-Nabataean style, first century AD, Avdat excavations

93
OSSUARIES
Limestone
Jerusalem area, 50 BC – AD 70

94
DEDICATORY INSCRIPTION OF PONTIUS PILATE
Limestone – 80 × 65 cm.
AD 26–36, Caesarea Maritima excavations

95
COINS OF THE JEWISH WARS, AND 'JUDAEA CAPTA' COIN
(*top*) Silver shekel of the First Jewish War (AD 66–73)
Obverse: Stem with three pomegranates; 'Jerusalem the Holy'
Reverse: Chalice; 'Year Three – Shekel Israel'
(*centre*) Bronze coin
Reverse: 'Judaea Capta' – S(enatus) C(onsulto)
Obverse: (not reproduced) Bust of Titus
(*bottom*) Silver tetradrachm of the Second Jewish War (AD 132–5)
Observe: Temple façade; 'Simon'
Reverse: lulav; 'For the Freedom of Jerusalem'
(All from the Reifenberg Collection, Jerusalem)

96
ARTICLES FOUND AT MASADA

97
THREE STAMPED TILES OF THE TENTH LEGION
Pottery
(top) fragment, stamped with a boar, emblem of the Legion,
first century AD, Jerusalem
(bottom) fragment, stamped

'Antoniniana,' name of the Legion, early third century AD, Jerusalem
(left) complete (18 × 18 cm.), stamped 'Leg(io) X Fr(etensis)', third century AD, Ramat Rahel excavations

98
WINGED GRIFFON OF NEMESIS, WITH 'WHEEL OF FATE'
Marble – ht. 48 cm., l. 50 cm.
Trajanic style (AD 98–117), found at Erez

99
ARTEMIS EPHESIA
Marble – ht. 1·60 m.
Graeco-Roman style, second century AD, Caesarea Maritima excavations

100
MOSAIC WITH REPRESENTATION OF FISH
Fragment of mosaic floor – *44 × 130 cm.*
Fourth century AD, Bet Shean excavations

101
FRESCO FROM A BYZANTINE MAUSOLEUM
Portrait medallion of a young man – *66 × 90 cm.*
c. fifth century AD, from a mausoleum at Or-Haner
(Gift of Mr and Mrs K. Sobel, Hamilton (Canada), in memory of Timothy Fenston)

102
SYNAGOGUE MOSAIC PAVEMENT
4·20 × 3 m.
Byzantine Period, sixth century AD, Synagogue at Bet Shean, Bet Shean excavations

103
TWO JEWISH GOLD GLASSES
Top: diam. 9 cm.
Byzantine Period, fourth century AD, probably from Jewish catacombs in Rome
(Both are the gift of Mr Jakob Michael New York, in memory of his wife, Erna Michael)

104
THREE LEAD SARCOPHAGI
Pagan sarcophagus – *30 × 30 cm.*
First half of the third century AD, Jerusalem
Christian sarcophagus – *60 × 25 cm.*
Fifth century AD, Jerusalem
Jewish sarcophagus – *22 × 35 cm.*
Fourth century AD, Bet Shearim excavations

105
CHRISTIAN CHANCEL SCREEN AND POST
Marble
Ht. of post: 1·15 m.
Byzantine Period, fifth-sixth centuries AD
Post: from a church at Horvat Hadat
Screen: from a church at Massuot Yizhaq

106
CHRISTIAN OBJECTS
Bronze lamp with cross-shaped handle on bronze stand
Ht: 28 cm.
Bronze lamp with cross-shaped handle and bull's head on lid
Both: Bet Shean excavations
Pottery ampulla, decorated in relief with representation of Annunciation and Greek inscription
Provenance unknown
Clay plaque in shape of fish, inlaid with 'mirror' against the evil eye
L.: 16 cm.
Horvat Zikrin excavations
All: Byzantine Period, fourth-seventh centuries AD

107
JEWISH 'EVIL EYE PLAQUE'
Stone – 31 × 27 cm.
Byzantine Period, c. fifth century AD

108
THREE OIL LAMPS WITH MENORAH DESIGN
LAMP – *l. 9 cm.*
(Reifenberg Collection, Jerusalem)
LAMP
(Collection of the Archaeological Institute, the Hebrew University)
LAMP
(Reifenberg Collection, Jerusalem)
Pottery
All: third-fourth centuries AD

109
MENORAH LAMP
Bronze – 16 × 11 cm.
c. fourth century AD
(From the collection of Mrs Mizyam Shaar Schloessinger, New York. Loaned to the Museum in memory of the late Mr A. Reifenburg)

110
DIADEM
Gold band set with glass, stone and mother-of-pearl – l. 30 cm.
Third century AD, from a tomb at Kefar Giladi

111
ARAB GOLD JEWEL HOARD
Found in glazed pot – ht. 12 cm.
The hoard includes:
Six large gold beads *with granulation*
Six filigree gold beads, *globular and biconical, large and small*
Beads, *carnelian and glass*
Bronze amulet *with a Koranic verse*
All: Caesarea-Maritima

112
BYZANTINE POTTERY
Two jugs
One mug
Potter's wheel of stone
All: Byzantine Period, Bet Shean excavations

113
SHOWCASE: A JEWISH FARMER'S TOMB
Pottery
Ht. of jar: 70 cm.
Lamp
Agricultural implements of iron
A selection of glass vessels
Jewelry and coins
Byzantine Period, fourth century AD

114
CRUSADER CAPITAL *(Detail)*
Stone – 30 × 28 cm. (detail)

Eleventh century AD, from excavations at the Church of the Annunciation, Nazareth

115
View from the Khirbet Qumran caves

116
Two jars from Khirbet Qumran which contained scrolls

117, 118
The Shrine of the Book, interior views

119
The Habakkuk Commentary

120
Textile fragment

121
Articles dating from the Bar-Kochba revolt

122
The Nachal Hever caves

123
The Thanksgiving Scroll

124
The Zealots' Synagogue

125
Fragment of the Ben Sira Scroll

126
Land-lease dating from the Bar-Kochba revolt

127
View of the Khirbet Qumran caves

128
REGENSBURG PENTATEUCH
Parchment – 246 leaves, 24·5 × 18·5 cm.
Germany, Bavaria (Regensburg), c. 1300
I.M. no. 180/52

129
VITTORIO VENETO SYNAGOGUE
Wood, gilt, brass and silver – 7 × 13 × 7 m.
Italy, Vittorio Veneto, 1701
(Gift of Mr Jakob Michael, New York, in memory of his wife Erna Michael)

130
THE YAHUDA HAGGADAH
Parchment – 40 leaves, 23·5 × 17 cm.
Southern Germany, mid-fifteenth century
(Gift of Mrs Rachel Ethel Yahuda, Conn.)
I.M. no. 180/50

131
BET ALPHA SYNAGOGUE FLOOR
Diagrammatic reconstruction
Mosaic
Israel, sixth century

132
SYNAGOGUE DOORS
Carved wood panels – Each door, 240 × 90 cm; each panel, 45 × 20 cm.
Egypt, Fustat, twelfth century
(Acquired with the aid of Baroness Alix de Rothschild, Paris and donated by Mr Astorre Mayer, Milan, in memory of his father Sally Mayer)
I.M. no. 194/4

LINTEL
Carved wood – 211 × 20 cm.
Egypt, Fustat, thirteenth century
(Gift of Mr Jakob Michael, New York, in memory of his wife Erna Michael)
I.M. no. 194/5

133
TORAH ARK DOORS
Painted lead on wood – Each door, 146 × 34 cm.
Poland, Krakow, early seventeenth century
(Gift of H. Jacobowitz in memory of Mr and Mrs Mathatias and Havah Rivka Jacobowitz)
I.M. no. 195/5

134
THE YAHUDA HAGGADAH
Parchment – 40 leaves, 23·5 × 17 cm.
Southern Germany, mid-fifteenth century
(Gift of Mrs Rachel Ethel Yahuda, Conn.)
I.M. no. 180/50

135
GERMAN TORAH GROUP
MANTLE
Velvet with silver thread embroidery – 91 × 45 cm.
Germany, 1749
I.M. no. 151/16

RIMMONIM
Silver, partly gilt – 31 × 8 cm.
Germany, early nineteenth century
(I.R.S.O.)
I.M. no. 147/75

POINTER
Silver gilt – l. 30 cm.
Germany, Nuremburg, early seventeenth century
(Gift of Mrs Joseph Hirsch, Jerusalem, in memory of her husband)
I.M. no. 149/60

TASS
Silver, partly gilt – 27 × 26 cm.
Germany, early eighteenth century
I.M. no. 148/100

ARK CURTAIN
Brocade, silver lace, silver thread embroidery on damask – 166 × 116 cm.
Silesia, Glogau, 1795
I.M. no. 152/53

136
ITALIAN TORAH GROUP
MANTLE
Silk with gold thread embroidery – 252 × 85 cm.
Italy, seventeenth century
(Gift of Mr Jakob Michael, New York)
I.M. no. 151/77

TASS
Silver – 13 × 24 cm.
Italy, 1776
I.M. no. 148/109

CROWN
Silver, partly gilt – diam. 38 cm., ht. 22·5 cm.
Italy, 1742
I.M. no. 146/26

FINIALS
Silver – 40 × 11 cm.
Italy, Padua, eighteenth century
(Gift of the Paduan Jewish Community)
I.M. no. 147/69

ARK CURTAIN
Italian silk, with silver and silk thread

embroidery – 166 × 144 cm.
Turkey, eighteenth century
I.M. no. 152/57

137
NORTH AFRICAN TORAH GROUP:
MANTLE
Velvet, with gold and silver thread embroidery, leather-backed – diam. 30 cm., ht. 63 cm.
Morocco, nineteenth century
I.M. no. 151/90
FINIALS
Silver, partly gilt and enamel – 37 × 75 cm.
North Africa, nineteenth century
I.M. no. 147/33

138
DURA EUROPOS
Fresco
Syria, AD 245

139
DURA EUROPOS
Fresco
Syria, AD 245

140
TORAH SCROLL CASES
Silver, partly gilt – ht. 116 cm., diam. 29 cm.
India, nineteenth century
(Gift of the Beth-El Synagogue, Calcutta)
I.M. no. 145/11
Velvet-covered with silver and partly gilt decorations – ht. 160 cm., diam. 28 cm.
Iran, 1799
I.M. no. 145/12

141
SPICE BOXES
(left) BIRD'S WING SPICE BOX
Silver – 29·5 × 5·5 cm.
Poland, late eighteenth century
I.M. no. 124/364
BELL-TOWER SPICE BOX
Silver – 37·5 × 8 cm.
Germany, early nineteenth century
I.M. no. 124/270
ROSEWATER SPRINKLER SPICE BOX
Silver – 27 × 10 cm.
Germany (?), eighteenth century
(Gift of Mr A. Burstein, Lugano)
I.M. no. 124/236
CASTLE SPICE BOX
Silver, partly gilt – 31 × 9·2 cm.
Germany, seventeenth century
(I.R.S.O.)
I.M. no. 124/365

142
MENORAH
Limestone – 51·5 × 58 cm.
Israel, Tiberias, second to third centuries

143
HAVDALAH GROUP
CANDLE HOLDER
Silver – ht. 33 cm.
Germany, Frankfurt, first half eighteenth century
(Acquisition by Mordechai Narkiss Fund)
I.M. no. 124/396
KIDDUSH GOBLET
Gold – ht. 15·2 cm., diam. 9·5 cm.
Germany, early seventeenth century
(I.R.S.O.)
I.M. no. 133/120
SPICE BOX
Silver, and partly gilt – 29·3 × 6 cm.
Austria, 1817
I.M. no. 124/363

144
THE YAHUDA HAGGADAH
Parchment – 40 leaves, 23·5 × 17 cm.
Southern Germany, mid-fifteenth century
(Gift of Mrs Rachel Ethel Yahuda, Conn.)
I.M. no. 180/50

145
SABBATH LAMP
Silver repoussé – ht. 80 cm.
Italy, eighteenth century
I.M. no. 117/136

146
CHANNUKIOT
(left) Bronze – 15·3 × 18·5 cm.
France, fourteenth century
I.M. no. 118/351
(right) Bronze – 17·7 × 26·5 cm.
Italy, sixteenth century
(Gift of Mr Nafi, Rome)
I.M. no. 118/349

147
ROTHSCHILD MANUSCRIPT 24
Thin vellum – 473 leaves, 21 × 11·6 cm.
Italy, Ferrara (?), c. 1470
(Presented to the Museum anonymously)
I.M. no. 180/51

148
CHANNUKIOT
(left) Brass – 35 × 24 cm.
Poland, eighteenth century
(Gift of the Burstein Collection, Lugano)
I.M. no. 118/249
(right) Copper and brass – 28 × 32 cm.
Algeria, late nineteenth century
(Gift of Mr Z. Schulmann, Paris)
I.M. no. 118/446

149
ORIENTAL CHANUKKAH LAMPS
(left) Brass – 26 × 32 cm.
Morocco, Tetouan, nineteenth century
(Gift of Mr Z. Schulmann, Paris)
I.M. no. 118/394
(centre) Brass, glass oil containers – 48 × 22 cm.
Iraq, Baghdad, eighteenth century
(Loan from the Ticho Collection)
I.M. no. 118/511
(right) Brass – 32 × 44 cm.
Morocco, Fez, nineteenth century
(Gift of Mr Z. Schulmann, Paris)
I.M. no. 118/402

150
ROTHSCHILD MANUSCRIPT 24
Thin vellum – 473 leaves, 21 × 11·6 cm.
Italy, Ferrara (?), c. 1470
(Presented to the Museum anonymously)
I.M. no. 180/51

151
THE YAHUDA HAGGADAH
Parchment – 40 leaves, 23·5 × 17 cm.
Southern Germany, mid-fifteenth century

(Gift of Mrs Rachel Ethel Yahuda, Conn.)

I.M. no. 180/50

152

REGENSBURG PENTATEUCH

Parchment – 246 leaves, 24·5 × 18·5 cm.

Germany, Bavaria (Regensburg), c. 1300

I.M. no. 180/52

153

THE BIRDS' HEAD HAGGADAH

Vellum – 47 leaves, 27 × 18·5 cm.

Germany, upper Rhine, c. 1300

(Gift of Mr H.Cohen with aid of Mr Fred Monosson, in memory of Dr Ludwig Marum, Karlsruhe, Germany)

I.M. no. 180/57

154

CHANNUKIAH

Bronze – 23 × 34·3 cm.

Germany or Holland, 1574

I.M. no. 118/350

155

CHANNUKIAH

Silver, partly gilt, mark $R^3$731 (CP) – 30 × 29 cm.

Germany, Augsburg, early eighteenth century

(Gift of Mr Ignazio Bauer, Madrid)

I.M. no. 118/80

156

CHANNUKIAH

Silver – mark: BD – 56 × 46 cm.

Germany, Augsburg, 1759

(Gift of Mr Jakob Michael, New York, in memory of his wife, Erna Michael)

I.M. no. 118/569

157

SUKKAH

Painted wood – 2·90 × 2·90 m. sq., ht. 210 cm.

Germany, Fischach, first-half nineteenth century

(Formerly owned by Mr Abraham Deller of Fischach and acquired by the late Dr H.Feuchtwanger)

158

ROTHSCHILD MANUSCRIPT 24

Thin vellum – 473 leaves, 21 × 11·6 cm.

Italy, Ferrara (?), c. 1470

(Presented to the Museum anonymously)

I.M. no. 180/51

159

ERNA MICHAEL HAGGADAH

Parchment – 77 leaves, 35 × 25·5 cm.

Germany, middle Rhine, c. 1400

(Gift of Mr Jakob Michael, New York, in memory of his wife, Erna Michael)

I.M. no. 180/58

160

SEDER PLATE

Majolica – diam. 56·5 cm.

Spain, c. 1450

(Gift of Mr Jakob Michael, New York, in memory of his wife Erna Michael)

I.M. no. 134/57

161

SIDDUR OF THE RABBI OF RIZIN

Parchment – 365 leaves (+5 leaves partly cut and not foliated), 18·5 × 14·5 cm.

Southern or eastern Germany, c. 1460

(Formerly in the possession of the nineteenth century Hassidic Rabbi Israel Friedman of Rižin)

I.M. no. 180/53

162

SEDER PLATE

Pewter – diam. 33 cm.

Germany, early nineteenth century

(Gift of Mrs Marianna Baer, in memory of her mother)

I.M. no. 134/3

163

DEBRY PSALTER

Vellum, velvet binding with silver, niello decorations applied – 10 × 6·5 cm.

Spain, late fifteenth century

(Gift of Mr Jakob Michael, New York, in memory of his wife, Erna Michael)

164

WINEBOTTLE

Polished glass, silver and gilt handle, lid, and base – 18·5 × 9·2 cm.

Austria, Eisenstadt, 1740

(Formerly owned by the Austerlitz family and donated by Dr Moshe Atlas, Jerusalem)

I.M. no. 138/4

SEDER CUP

Silver, partly gilt – diam. 9·5 cm., ht. 16·5 cm.

Germany, late seventeenth century

(Permanent loan from Mr and Mrs Victor Carter, Los Angeles, ex-Sholom Asch Collection)

I.M. no. 133/141

165

ROTHSCHILD MANUSCRIPT 24

Thin vellum – 473 leaves, 21 × 11·6 cm.

Italy, Ferrara (?), c. 1470

(Presented to the Museum anonymously)

I.M. no. 180/51

166

SIDDUR OF THE RABBI OF RIŻIN

Parchment – 365 leaves (+5 leaves partly cut and not foliated), 18·5 × 14·5 cm.

Southern or eastern Germany, c. 1460

(Formerly in the possession of the nineteenth century Hassidic Rabbi Israel Friedman of Rižin)

I.M. no. 180/53

167

ERNA MICHAEL HAGGADAH

Parchment – 77 leaves, 35 × 25·5 cm.

Germany, middle Rhine, c. 1400

(Gift of Mr Jakob Michael, New York, in memory of his wife, Erna Michael)

I.M. no. 180/58

168

SHOFARS

(from the top, left to right)

(a) *Ram's horn – l. 60 cm.*

Yemen, nineteenth century

I.M. no. 189/1

(b) *Horn – l. 50 cm.*

Central Europe, early nineteenth century

I.M. no. 189/6

(c) *Horn – l. 24 cm.*

Tripoli, early nineteenth century

I.M. no. 189/11

(d) *Horn – l. 32 cm.*

Morocco, Fez, c. nineteenth century

(Gift of Mr Z. Schulmann, Paris)

I.M. no. 189/17

(e) *Horn – l. 36 cm.*

Algeria, nineteenth century

(Gift of Mr Z. Schulmann, Paris)

I.M. no. 189/15

(f) *Horn – l. 43 cm.*

Germany, eighteenth century
(Burstein Collection, Lugano)

I.M. no. 189/8

(g) *Horn – l. 55 cm.*

Hungary, early nineteenth century
I.M. no. 189/5

(h) *Horn – l. 78 cm.*

Yemen, eighteenth century
(On loan from Hechal Shlomo Museum, Jerusalem)

169

BOOKBINDINGS

Silver, gilt and filigree – 14 × 9 cm.
Italy, 1771
(Gift of Mr A. Burstein, Lugano)
I.M. no. 142/15

Silver, 22 × 13·5 cm.
Galicia, early nineteenth century
I.M. no. 142/40

Silver – 29·5 × 17 cm.
Italy, 1753
(Gift of the Jewish Community, Rome)
I.M. no. 142/41

170

ROTHSCHILD MANUSCRIPT 24

Thin vellum – 473 leaves, 21 × 11·6 cm.

Italy, Ferrara (?), c. 1470

(Presented to the Museum anonymously)

I.M. no. 180/51

171

MEZUZOT

Porcelain – 20·5 × 3 cm.
Germany, eighteenth century
I.M. no. 107/29

Silver, mark: 84, HK, AD *– 25·5 × 5 cm.*
Russia, 1873
(Gift of Joseph Wilenski, Petah Tikva)
I.M. no. 107/40

172

MOHEL MANUSCRIPT

Parchment – 14 × 10 cm.
Germany, Hamburg-Altona, 1729
(Gift of Mr Joel Snoman, Tel-Aviv)
I.M. no. 183/11

CIRCUMCISION FLASK

Silver – 7 × 4 cm.
France, nineteenth century
I.M. no. 112/20B

CIRCUMCISION KNIFE

Steel and porcelain – l. 17 cm.
Bohemia, 1813
(Gift of Mr Jacob Tedesco, Paris, in memory of his father)
I.M. no. 112/4

CIRCUMCISION CLAMP

Silver with lacquer paint – 6 × 4 cm.
Morocco, nineteenth century
(Gift of Mr Z. Schulmann, Paris)
I.M. no. 112/65

CIRCUMCISION KNIFE

Steel, silver and amber – l. 19·5 cm.
Near East, 1819
I.M. no. 112/59

173

COFANETTO

Silver, partly gilt, niello – 12 × 7 cm.

Italy, Ferrara, second-half fifteenth century

(Gift of Mr Astorre Mayer, Milan)

I.M. no. 131/30

174

KETUBAH

Parchment – 48 × 39 cm.

Holland, Rotterdam, 1648

(Gift of Mr H. Gans, Amsterdam)

I.M. no. 179/6

175

AMULETS

(upper left) Silver – 14·5 × 9 cm.
Italy, nineteenth century
(Collection Mr A. Burstein, Lugano)
I.M. no. 103/136

(upper right) Silver, semiprecious stones – 31 × 13 cm.
Kurdistan, eighteenth century
I.M. no. 103/108

(centre left) Silver – 10 × 5·7 cm.
Iran, eighteenth century
I.M. no. 103/74

(bottom right) Silver, carnelian stones – 8 × 10·5 cm.
Yemen, eighteenth century
I.M. no. 103/338

(bottom left) Gold – diam. 8 cm.

Holland, Amsterdam 1665

(Gift of Mr Moshe Oved, London)

I.M. no. 104/3

176

ESTHER SCROLL CASES

Silver filigree – l. 31 cm.
Turkey, nineteenth century
I.M. no. 140/54

Silver – l. 29·5 cm.
Russia, nineteenth century
I.M. no. 140/48

Silver – l. 16 cm.
Salonica, nineteenth century
(Gift of Mr Sistero, Rome)
I.M. no. 140/8

Silver gilt, with polished coral – l. 17 cm.
I.M. no. 140/21
Italy, c. nineteenth century
(Gift of Henry M. Rein, New York)
I.M. No. 140/21

Silver, partly gilt – l. 25 cm.
Italy, late seventeenth century
I.M. no. 140/41

ESTHER SCROLL

Parchment – ht. 24·5 cm.
Germany, Alsace, eighteenth century
I.M. no. 182/81

177

KETUBAH

Paper – 93 × 68 cm.

Iran, Isfahan, 1860

(Gift of Mr Eliezer Ben Dov, Teheran)

I.M. no. 179/89

178

KETUBAH

Parchment – 93 × 63 cm.
Italy, Rome, 1857
I.M. no. 179/11

179

KETUBAH

Parchment – 42 × 26 cm.

Yemen, San'a, 1794

I.M. no. 179/8

180

ENGRAVING BY PUSCHNER

From a book by Paul Christian Kirchner, Jüdisches Ceremoniel, Nürnberg c. 1730
I.M. no. 184/28

181

MARRIAGE STONE

Red sandstone – 46 × 62 cm.

Germany, Bingen, c. 1700

(Gift of the Jewish Community, Cologne)

I.M. no. 199/22

182

BURIAL AND CHARITY BOXES

CHARITY BOX

Bronze – diam. 11 cm., ht. 17·4 cm.

Italy, Reggio, end of seventeenth century

(Gift of Mr and Mrs Siegfried Kramarsky, New York)

I.M. no. 130/38

'HOLY BURIAL SOCIETY OF PRAGUE' GLASS

Glass with enamel painting – ht. 24·5 cm., diam. top 14·5 cm., base 15·7 cm.

Bohemia-Moravia, 1713

I.M. no. 133/113

183

'HOLY BURIAL SOCIETY OF PRAGUE' GLASS

See plate 182

184

YEMENITE BRIDE

Brocade, silver and gilt beads, white pearls, corals, bead embroidery

Yemen, San'a – modern reconstruction of traditional costume

185

NORTH AFRICAN GROUP

Black costume

Velvet, embroidered with ribbon, lace and golden thread, silver filigree buttons, large Muslim sleeves, golden thread woven girdle

Morocco, Tetouan, late nineteenth – early twentieth centuries

(Gift of Mr Z. Schulman, Paris)

186

HUNTING SCENE PLATE

Silver with gilt, repoussé – diam. 223 cm
Persia c. fourth-fifth centuries, Sassanian
(Anonymous collection, permanent loan)

187

BOKHARAN JEWELRY

Gold and semiprecious stones

'Pirkhona' ornament for the forehead, and earrings for a Jewish woman of Bokhara

188

IBEX HANDLE

Gold – ht. 27·7 cm.

Persia, Achaemenian, c. fifth century BC
(Anonymous collection, permanent loan)

I.M. no. 65·1

189

RHYTON

Gold – ht. 22·5 cm.

Persia, Achaemenian, c. fifth century BC

(Gift of Mr A. Rabenou, Paris)

I.M. no. 4278-12-64

190

BOWL

Terracotta, champlevé ware, green glaze – diam. 21·5 cm.

Persia, Yasukand, c. eleventh-twelfth centuries

**(Gift of Mr and Mrs Edward M. M. Warburg, New York)*

I.M. no. 544-6-59

CUP

Terracotta, overglaze painted – ht. 11·5 cm. diam.: top: 9·0 cm., base: 6·0 cm.

Persia, Rayy, c. thirteenth century

**(Gift of Mr and Mrs Edward M. M. Warburg, New York)*

I.M. no. 542-6-59

191

PLATE WITH EAGLE

Silver repoussé – diam. 26·5 cm.

Persia, Sassanian, fourth-fifth centuries

(Anonymous collection, permanent loan)

I.M. no. 65·2

192

SALON (*Detail*)

Wood, painted and gilt, gobelins and paintings

France, Paris, eighteenth century

(Gift of Baron Edmond de Rothschild, Paris)

193

PRAYER NICHE

Glazed ceramic mosaic tiles – ht. 304 cm., w. 245 cm.

Persia, Isfahan, seventeenth century

(Gift of Mr A. Rabenou, Paris, in memory of Khalil Rabenou)

I.M. no. 4279-12-64

194

PETER PAUL RUBENS – Destruction of Pharaoh's Host in the Red Sea

Oil on canvas – 87·5 × 100 cm.

Flemish, c. 1604–5

(Mr and Mrs Philip J. Goldberg, London)

195

REMBRANDT VAN RIJN
The Healing of Tobit

Pen, bistre and wash drawing – 9·8 × 13·8 cm. – Benesch 544

Dutch, c. 1642–4

(Gift of the Schocken family)

I.M. no. 1103-7-66

196

ALBERT CUYP – Return from the Hunt

Dutch, 1641

Oil on canvas – 155 × 245 cm.

(Gift of Mr and Mrs Joseph R. Nash, Paris)

I.M. no. 504/18

197

BASSANO (JACOPO DA PONTE)
Man in Armour

Italian

Black chalk – 37 × 15·5 cm.

(Acquisition)

I.M. no. 529-3-66

198

ALBRECHT DURER – St Jerome in Penitence

German

Engraving, B. 61 – 31·6 × 22·2 cm.
Watermark: Towers connected through wall

**(Gift of Mr F. M. Mayer, New York)*

I.M. no. 621-5-66

199

EMANUEL DE WITTE – Portuguese Synagogue in Amsterdam

Oil on canvas – 108 × 123 cm.

Dutch, c. 1680

(Donated by a group of Friends in

Paris through Mr Maurice Fischer)
I.M. no. 504/49

200
IZAAK LUTTICHUYS – Jacob Ben Aaron Sasportas
Oil on canvas – 88 × 78 cm.
Dutch, 1671
(Gift of Friends in Holland through M. Bernard Houthakker, Amsterdam)
I.M. no. 504/22

201
JAN VAN GOYEN – River Scene
Oil on wood – 45·5 × 76·5 cm.
Dutch, 1647
(Bequest of Mr Eduard Vis, Lausanne)
I.M. no. 504/14

202 and 203
COFANETTO
Enamel, mounted in gilded copper – 25·5 × 12·7 cm.
France, Limoges, sixteenth century
(Mr and Mrs Sidney J. Lamon, New York)

204
PAUL CÉZANNE – Country House by the Riverside
Oil on canvas – 81 × 65 cm.
French, c. 1882
(Gift of the 'Hanadiv' Rothschild Foundation)
I.M. no. 505/170

205
VINCENT VAN GOGH – Harvest in Provence
Oil on canvas – 51 × 60 cm.
Dutch, 1888
(Gift of the 'Hanadiv' Rothschild Foundation)
I.M. no. 504/135

206
CHAIM SOUTINE – Boy in Blue
Oil on canvas – 91·3 × 72·5 cm.
Lithuanian
(Mr and Mrs Harry Fischbach, New York)

207
ANONYMOUS PORTRAIT OF A NOBLEMAN
Pen, ink and watercolour – 31 × 27 cm.
Italian, early sixteenth century
I.M. no. 698-8-58

208
ANNA TICHO – Old City Wall of Jerusalem
Pencil – 41·5 × 47·5 cm.
Israeli, c. 1930
(Gift of the artist)
I.M. no. P1049-6-590s

209
FRANZ BERNHEIMER
Pomegranates
Brush and ink – 62·5 × 88 cm.
Israeli, 1962
I.M. no. 2323-10-63

210
PAUL GAUGUIN – Still Life
French, 1899
Oil on canvas – 44 × 60 cm.
(Gift of the 'Hanadiv' Rothschild Foundation)
I.M. no. 505/172

211
PAUL GAUGUIN – The Fire Dance
Oil on Canvas – 73 × 92 cm.
French, 1891
(Gift of the 'Hanadiv' Rothschild Foundation)
I.M. no. 505/171

212
ODILON REDON – Flower still life
Pastel on paper – 43 × 34 cm.
French
* *(Bequest of Miss Loula Lasker, New York)*
I.M. no. 505/103

213
HONORÉ DAUMIER – Members of the French Legislative Assembly
Bronze – c. 13–19 cm.
French, c. 1830–2
* *(The Billy Rose Collection)*

214
JACOB EPSTEIN – Third Marble Doves
Marble – 48·1 × 72·5 cm.
British, 1914–5
* *(The Billy Rose Collection)*
I.M. no. 1655·66/30

215
ALEXANDER CALDER
Mobile-Stabile
Painted steel – c. 2·80 cm.
American, 1966
* *(Gift of Mr and Mrs Samuel Perlman, New York)*
I.M. no. 593·67/150

216
MARC CHAGALL – Rabbi
Oil on linen – 40 × 31 cm.
Russian, c. 1912
(I.R.S.O.)
I.M. no. 505A/10

217
FRANCIS BACON – Study for the Portrait of Lucien Freud
Oil on canvas – 196 × 146 cm.
British, 1964
(Gift of the Marlborough Gallery, London)
I.M. no. 507/47

218
EGON SCHIELE – Cityscape
Oil on canvas – 109·7 × 140 cm.
Austrian, 1915
(I.R.S.O.)
I.M. no. 506/68

219
JULES PASCIN – Portrait of William Howard
Oil on cardboard – 55 × 46 cm.
Bulgarian, 1909
(Gift of Mr Joseph Pincas, Paris)
I.M. no. 505A/27

220
YA'AKOV AGAM – Diptych
Oil on wood – 49 × 16 cm. Israeli, 1964
* *(Gift of Mr George Jaffin, New York)*
I.M. no. 509/256

221
PABLO PICASSO – The Studio Window
Oil on canvas – 130 × 96·5 cm.

Spanish, 1943
* (*Gift of Mr and Mrs Leigh Block, Chicago*)
I.M. no. 501/117

222
TUVIA BE'ERI – Moon Landscape
Israeli, c. 1964
Etching and aquatint – 12·5 × 24 cm.
I.M. no. 3423-11-63

223
JOSEPH ZARITZKY – Homage à Braque
Oil on canvas – 73 × 100 cm.
Israeli, c. 1945
I.M. no. 509/68

224
IGAEL TUMARKIN – Rex
Wood, metal on canvas – 116 × 89 cm.
Israeli, 1964
(*Gift of the artist*)
I.M. no. 509/240

225
ANTOINE PEVSNER – Construction in Space in the Third and Fourth Dimensions
Russian, 1961
Bronze – 101·25 × 76·25 cm.
(*Gift of Mr and Mrs Alex L. Hillman, New York, in memory of their son Richard*)

226
AVIGDOR ARIKHA – Forms II
Casein on paper mounted on canvas – 109 × 150 cm.
Israeli, 1965
I.M. no. 509/245

227
MORDECHAI ARDON – At the Gates of Jerusalem
Oil on canvas – side panels 194 × 130 cm., central panel 265 × 194 cm.
Israeli, 1967
(*Gift of the artist*)
I.M. no. 509/265

I.R.S.O.: Jewish Restitution Succession Organisation

* All items marked with an asterisk are on permanent loan from the Collection of the America-Israel Cultural Foundation, New York.

Acknowledgements

The authors would particularly like to thank the following individuals for their help in the preparation of this book, for reading the manuscript and making important suggestions: Mrs E. Cohen, Mrs H. Feuchtwanger, Mr I. Haley-Levin, Dr Stephen Kayser, Miss Elaine Kushner, Dr Bezalel Narkiss, Professor Cecil Roth, Dr William Sandberg and Dr I. Shachar.

The authors also wish to thank Prof. N. Avigad, Dr Hava Baer, Dr A. Biran, Miriam Black, Alice Bronson, Mr Yona Fisher, Mrs A. Gordon, Mr P. Kanelsky, Aviva Lancet-Muller, Louisa Latham, Irene Lewitt, Meyer Meir, Jean Sulzberger and Shoshana Yisraeli.

David Harris, to whom the authors and publishers extend especial thanks, took the photographs for this book.

For the photographs of a few items not in the Museum the authors and publishers wish to thank the following: H. Bieberkraut for plates 116 and 126; Dura-Europos Publications for plates 138 and 139: Y. Lehmann for plate 206; Hans Lehmann for plates 163, 202 and 203; H. Samuel for plate 192; Derrick Witty for plate 194 and A. Volk for plate 124.